BATTLEGROUND ATLANTIC

BATTLEGROUND ATLANTIC

···

HOW THE SINKING OF A SINGLE JAPANESE SUBMARINE
ASSURED THE OUTCOME OF WORLD WAR II

RICHARD N. BILLINGS

NAL
CALIBER

NAL Caliber
Published by New American Library, a division of
Penguin Group (USA) Inc., 375 Hudson Street,
New York, New York 10014, USA
Penguin Group (Canada), 90 Eglinton Avenue East, Suite 700, Toronto,
Ontario M4P 2Y3, Canada (a division of Pearson Penguin Canada Inc.)
Penguin Books Ltd., 80 Strand, London WC2R 0RL, England
Penguin Ireland, 25 St. Stephen's Green, Dublin 2,
Ireland (a division of Penguin Books Ltd.)
Penguin Group (Australia), 250 Camberwell Road, Camberwell, Victoria 3124,
Australia (a division of Pearson Australia Group Pty. Ltd.)
Penguin Books India Pvt. Ltd., 11 Community Centre, Panchsheel Park,
New Delhi - 110 017, India
Penguin Group (NZ), cnr Airborne and Rosedale Roads, Albany,
Auckland 1310, New Zealand (a division of Pearson New Zealand Ltd.)
Penguin Books (South Africa) (Pty.) Ltd., 24 Sturdee Avenue,
Rosebank, Johannesburg 2196, South Africa

Penguin Books Ltd., Registered Offices:
80 Strand, London WC2R 0RL, England

First published by NAL Caliber, an imprint of New American Library,
a division of Penguin Group (USA) Inc.

First Printing, April 2006
10   9   8   7   6   5   4   3   2   1

LIBRARY OF CONGRESS CATALOGING-IN-PUBLICATION DATA:

Billings, Richard N.
   Battleground Atlantic: how the sinking of a single Japanese submarine assured the
outcome of World War II/Richard N. Billings.
      p.   cm.
   Includes bibliographical references and index.
   ISBN 0-451-21766-7
   1. I-52 (Submarine)   2. World War, 1939–1945—Naval operations—Submarine.
3. World War, 1939–1945—Naval operations, Japanese.   4. World War, 1939–1945—
Aerial operations, American.   5. World War, 1939–1945—Naval operations, American.
6. Submarines (Ships)—Salvaging—Atlantic Ocean.   7. Tidwell, Paul.   I. Title.
   D783.7.B56 2006
   940.54'293—dc22   2005028562

Set in Minion
Designed by Daniel Lagin

Printed in the United States of America

To Sandy Greenwood, whose presence I cherish

CONTENTS

1. A DREAMER WHO DARED

After resting in silence these many years the *I-52* was missing no longer. Evidence of her presence had spilled upon the ocean floor as she neared the end of her spiral plunge, so the path to her watery grave was clearly marked. Twisted shards of steel ripped from the hull lay alongside intricate pieces of plumbing and other mechanical parts. Without warning, a death scene was revealed: kitchen utensils and bunks from the crew quarters, shoes never in pairs, a sweater whose wearer had long since vanished.

Approaching from the southwest, the visitors ran abreast of the starboard bow and noticed how the World War II Japanese submarine was listing to port, yet her conning tower appeared to be unscathed. On the bridge, where the captain had stood, there were windows with watch standers' binoculars still in place. On the afterdeck, trained on an avenue of anticipated attack, a 25-millimeter machine gun looked loaded and ready to fire.

Paul Tidwell motioned for a closer look and his Russian pilot cautiously obeyed, knowing that a bump at the wrong time and place could cause the wreck to topple and entomb them. The markings on the boat were faded but readable—a symbol resembling the letter *I* and the number *52*. The *I-52* was last heard from in June 1944.

Tidwell is a professional salvager of sunken ships—for twenty-five years he has been in business, in part for the profits that finance his expeditions and may someday make him wealthy. There is, however, more to Tidwell and his work than monetary concerns. He is an oceanic explorer, influenced by the creative design of Jules Verne and the inventive engineering of Jacques Cousteau. He is determined to reach the last frontier, as the ocean floor has been called, and retrieve a little of what man has lost while making his way in a dark and distant world.

And sometimes he betrays an artistic bent, as when he founded his first company and named it Raven Enterprises, with Edgar Allan Poe in mind:

> *Deep into that darkness peering,*
> *Long I stood there, wondering, fearing,*
> *Doubting, dreaming dreams*
> *No mortal ever dared to dream before.*

Tidwell has ambitious plans for exploring a region that only recently was opened to private enterprise. Shortly after World War II, governments began to develop the technology that would enable them to reach a depth of twenty thousand feet, and then the Big Two, the United States and the Soviet Union, kept their discoveries to themselves as they engaged in secret antisubmarine warfare (ASW). The Cold War ended with the collapse of the USSR in 1991, and the wherewithal of deep-ocean activity, scientific and commercial, was part of the peace dividend. Literally hundreds of sunken warships and merchant vessels with precious cargoes were suddenly within a salvage company's range.

Tidwell discovered the wreck of the *I-52* in May 1995. Two months later William Broad of the *New York Times* broke the *I-52* story, and he had more to say in a book published in 1997, *The Universe Below*. "I asked Tidwell what the future might hold for deep recovery. To me, he seemed like the logical person to ask. After all, he knew not only his own projects but, by virtue of having worked as a maritime researcher, knew of many other projects around the world, an unusual thing in so secretive a business." Tidwell predicted that in fifty years most of the big gold shipments will be recovered from the sea, causing Broad to comment: "If Paul Tidwell . . . is correct in his assessments, the exploratory wave in the next century will shake up thousands of deep wrecks. For better or worse, we are at a turning point in the history of history."

A LIFE OF ADVENTURE

Tidwell spent his childhood in central Florida watching space-bound rockets lift off from Cape Canaveral. His family moved to Louisiana when he was eleven, and over the next ten years he attended high school, met his future wife, and served two tours in Vietnam as a U.S. Army infantryman. He came home in 1969 a decorated hero (two Bronze Stars, two Purple Hearts), and completed his education, earning a bachelor's in sociology at Southeastern Louisiana College. He did not pursue an advanced degree, but he was a self-taught engineer versed in computer technology when he embarked on a career of maritime research and ship salvage. Early on, he experienced both success and frustration searching for the *Luckenback,* a freighter sunk by a mine during World War II off the Florida coast, and the *Merida,* which was bound for New York from Mexico with eleven tons of silver when it went down off Virginia in 1911. These wrecks were in coastal waters—not the sort of deep-ocean operations that would soon entice Tidwell—but the *Luckenback* yielded a profitable amount of mineral ore. As for the *Merida,* she was turned upside down, and her cargo was out of reach.

In the 1980s he did a stint with Mel Fisher, who had become rich and famous hunting ancient Spanish galleons off Florida, but digging in the sand for disintegrating hulls was of little interest to Tidwell. What did get his attention were the hundreds of warships lost in battle during two world wars, many of them sunk at depths so great they had been officially lost for decades. One that he found especially intriguing was the *John Barry,* an American Liberty Ship sunk in 1944 by a German submarine, the *U-859,* in the Arabian Sea. His interest in the *Barry* was stimulated as much by the mysterious circumstances of her mission and her fate as by her cargo of 3 million Saudi Arabian riyals. It seems that King Ibn Saud of Saudi Arabia had been persuaded to award a lease to American oil interests, excluding the British, and the riyals, freshly minted in Philadelphia, were for use in forming Aramco, the Arabian American Oil Company. It was alleged that a resentful British government actually directed its intelligence service to prescribe a course for the *Barry* that put her in the crosshairs of the *U-859*'s periscope.

Given these circumstances, Tidwell found it ironic that a British company, Blue Water Recoveries Ltd., reached the *John Barry* at eighty-five hundred feet in 1994 and recovered $1.5 million in coins. His interest was not totally academic, for Tidwell was retained as a consultant by Blue Water, and he became convinced that here was a fiction thriller waiting to be written and produced as a motion picture—to the extent that he sought out a survivor, the ship's purser, and purchased the rights to his story. When Tidwell became interested in the *I-52*, however, he abandoned the *John Barry* project.

THE *I-52* AND HER GOLD

Tidwell began searching for the *I-52* in Washington with no preconceived notions other than a long-held belief that whenever a ship goes down with a cargo of gold, it must be accounted for by someone. Starting at the Library of Congress, he dug into a 1917 volume of *Foreign Relations of the United States,* perusing papers with titles that caught his eye: "Attacks on Unarmed Enemy Merchant Vessels"; "Management of Shipments of Precious Metals." Before long his strategy of working from the general to the specific guided him to the National Archives, Military Intelligence Division, where he became engrossed in a hefty tome, *Boundaries Around Japan—1917–1941.* By this time Tidwell had come to know John Taylor, a human encyclopedia with Record Group 457, the repository for National Security Agency (NSA) files. Taylor seemed taken by Tidwell's persistence and offered a helpful tip: World War II documents, including intercepted German and Japanese messages—sent by radio in codes that had been broken by the Allies—had recently been declassified.

With hundreds of thousands of pages of NSA intercepts to scan, Tidwell paid close attention to those that mentioned ship movements. It was a difficult task, but he knew he was on the right track when he read a listing under U.S. Navy records related to code breaking. It was titled "COMINCH File: Intelligence Summaries, January 1943–May 1945," and when he opened it, he noted the letterhead of each report: "United States Fleet, Headquarters of the Commander in Chief, Navy Department, Washington, D.C." He soon learned the system that was followed in preparing reports and knew to take account of references to "blockade running," especially when the subhead was "Jap Subs." As a student of World War II, Tidwell knew of Japanese efforts to ship gold by submarine to Europe for deposit in a German bank. He also knew of Allied efforts to intercept those shipments by means of a blockade across the Bay of Biscay.

Tidwell learned too that in May 1944 the movement of two Japanese submarines was being monitored: the *I-29*, headed for Japan from a port in occupied France, and the *I-52*, which was "inbound," having reached the Atlantic Ocean off the coast of Africa in early May. Tidwell recorded the dates, and his notes indicate that the COMINCH files occurred at random—May 11, May 31, and so on. When he came to June 22 and scanned the pages for the *I-52*, he felt his heart starting to pound and he was shaking, but he continued to read.

> *I-52*, 2500-ton Jap sub en route to Lorient, will [rendezvous] the outbound German *U-530* . . . 22 June about 900 miles west of the Cape Verde Islands (15N 40W). A German liaison officer, and latest German search gear, with operators, will be transferred. *I-52* will then cruise west of the Azores to France. . . .

Tidwell's brain was bursting; he was excited, but he was also certain he was being watched. Paranoia maybe, but word of what he was up to had gotten around. From his work on the *John Barry*,

Tidwell was known in the salvage business, which is tightly knit and very competitive. Well founded or not in this particular instance, his fears were justified.

Tidwell had learned it was a practice of U.S. Fleet Radio Intelligence to insert parenthetical advisories based on intercepted enemy messages, and one of these was an eye-opener:

> (Note: Besides a number of Jap technical experts *I-52* is carrying 2 tons of gold; 228 tons of tin, molybdenum, and tungsten; 54 tons of rubber, 3 tons of quinine and opium. . . .)

He covered up the page he was reading—quickly, but he hoped not noticeably—stood up, and walked around the reading room, collecting his thoughts. This was beyond his greatest expectations: a Japanese submarine carrying two tons of gold was to meet a German U-boat on June 22, 1944, and the U.S. Navy knew the rendezvous point. The obvious question was what had happened to the *I-52*, and Tidwell found the answer when he turned to a COMINCH file dated July 20 and read an entry labeled "Jap U/Boats." It was just a fragment but it was all he needed for now:

> Loss of the *I-52* (Momi) considered sunk 24 June west of the Cape Verde Islands by planes from U.S.S. *Bogue*. . . .

As he leafed through intercepted radio messages, Tidwell turned up one dated June 12, 1944, from the Bureau of Military Affairs in Tokyo to the Japanese naval attaché in Berlin. It contained a list of crew members and technical experts aboard submarine

I-52 and an account of her cargo, including the gold bullion: "146 bars weighing two tons packed in forty-nine metal boxes."

Tidwell methodically built a file on the *I-52*, code name Momi: she was on her maiden voyage when she went down, having been launched on December 18, 1943, at Kure, the center of Japanese naval activity. She was bound for Lorient, on the Atlantic coast of France, with raw materials for German industry in addition to the gold. She was to return with up-to-date arms and data on such new and deadly weapons as the V-2 rocket. He discovered that top secret "Ultra" intelligence—information obtained from broken enemy codes—had enabled the Allies to track down and destroy blockade runners. He also gathered data on Task Group 22.2, the *Bogue* group, and naval air squadron VC-69, which would mark June 23–24 as the night the unit sank its only submarine of the war.

Tidwell tackled the project knowing it would lead him into territory where no one had dared to tread without government authority. He knew too that Cold War activities at great depths and the associated technology had been closely guarded official secrets. But with the end of the superpower standoff, exotic equipment appeared on the open market—laser cameras, sonar scanners, submersible vehicles both manned and remote. Navigation satellites were available to entrepreneurs, as were such communications innovations as fiber-optic cable. Meanwhile, a digital revolution proceeded apace, and a generation of whiz kids—many trained by the military in secret operations—was ready to be recruited.

Tidwell developed a modus operandi based on an A-team concept. He preferred working with contractors rather than employees, drawing from a vast pool of talent—sonar technicians, marine biologists, artifact conservators. Consequently, his company—he

named it Cape Verde Explorations, Ltd., after locating the *I-52*—
consisted of just himself and his wife, and he ran it from his Virginia home.

Without needlessly looking for trouble, Tidwell believed it was
prudent to anticipate opposition, and he worried in particular
about the government of Japan. Under U.S. law the rights to a
wrecked vessel in international waters belong to a salvager, although a nation may lay claim to a sunken warship. He hoped to
avoid a confrontation and would meet with Japanese officials in
Washington and Tokyo—he later did—to discuss the delicate matter of human remains and personal effects of the *I-52* crew. He was
also prepared to play hardball and would warn the Japanese that
by raising the rights issue, they might call attention to the origin of
the gold, an absorbing story if not a pretty one. In its conquest of
Asia in the 1930s, the Japanese army swept southward from China
and Burma to Malaya and Singapore, looting government and cor-
porate treasuries, temples, and banks. The plunder amounted to
billions of dollars, most of it in gold—six thousand tons of bullion
from banks and businesses, and much more from illicit sources.
Tidwell knew from his research at the National Archives that the *I-52*
loaded her shipment of gold in Singapore, which would be consistent with a presumption that it was part of the "loot." And he knew
that if and when he recovered the gold, he would most likely be
able to determine its origin.

BETTING THE RANCH ON MOMI

Tidwell inhabited a topsy-turvy world as he prepared in the early
months of 1995 to go to sea in search of the *I-52* and her cargo of

gold. First of all, he had secured financing in the form of a $750,000 investment by a venture capitalist from Arkansas, and he had signed up a pair of specialized contractors to provide the expertise required for the mission he had in mind. One was a remotely operated vehicle (ROV) manufacturer in Seattle, Sound Ocean Systems, whose president, Ted Brockett, was an old friend of Tidwell's. In turn, Brockett recommended Meridian Sciences of Columbia, Maryland, whose sensitive work for the U.S. Navy entailed refining the navigation data of nuclear submarine missions. Meridian's president, Dave Jourdan—Jourdan was a Naval Academy graduate who had served as a submarine officer—had designed a computer program, called RENAV, to do the analysis for the navy, and he had coined the term "renavigation" to describe his secret system. When Tidwell asked if RENAV could be applied to World War II navigation data (from the logs of the *Bogue*, the carrier whose aircraft sank the *I-52* in 1944, and the *U-530*, a German submarine at the scene), Jourdan replied that it could. So Tidwell made him an offer—the standard fee plus permission to use photographs of the *I-52* to promote his company if the submarine search was successful. Jourdan accepted and promised to load RENAV onto his laptop computer in order to devote time to the project during spare moments on business trips.

Still depending on Brockett for advice, Tidwell chartered the research vessel *Yuzhmorgeologiya* from the Shirshov Institute in Moscow, though he might have thought better of the deal had he known he was the subject of a federal espionage investigation. The contract for the "Yuz" had just been signed when two U.S. Navy intelligence agents questioned a Tidwell associate in New Orleans. They were acting on an allegation by a disgruntled bureaucrat that Tidwell had improperly sought data from the Office of Oceanography in Mississippi, and it appears their suspicion was also aroused by his having chartered what was once a Soviet spy ship. Tidwell was willing to grant that a navy investigation was justified by his dealings with the Russians, and harassment of the "Yuz" by navy ships and planes during sea trials off California was also warranted. These actions were within the limits of fair play as he defines them. But Tidwell would not say the same for what occurred after his expedition left Bridgetown, Barbados, on April 12, 1995, for a five-day run to where he hoped to find the wreck of the *I-52*. On the third day out, both of the ship's diesel engines repeatedly broke down, and the Russian captain determined the cause to be tainted fuel. He had refueled in Panama, taking on about half of the ship's 1,446-ton capacity. Fortunately, it was possible to isolate the bad fuel in a storage bunker, leaving a usable amount of 700 tons, which would limit the submarine search but not cripple it. Taking the captain at his word, and therefore believing the fuel had been tampered with in an outright act of sabotage, Tidwell was left to wonder who might be trying so hard to prevent him from finding the *I-52*, and why.

Tidwell knew he had a formidable rival in the search for the *I-52*, though he doubted the British salvage company in question— Orca Ltd., named for a species of killer whale—was capable of sabotage. By the time he put to sea that April, Orca had been in search of the *I-52* for nearly three months aboard the *Mstislav Keldysh*, the lead vessel of the Russian research fleet. Just months earlier, when he learned of Orca's $3.6 million budget, Tidwell had made a bid to become a minority partner in the *I-52* search, but his offer was rejected. It was then that he decided to resort to deception, letting it be known that he had given up on the *I-52* and would search instead for the *West Lashaway*, an American freighter sunk during

World War II in the same vicinity of the mid-Atlantic. Tidwell had an informant aboard the *Keldysh*, an American playing both sides, and when this individual revealed Orca's coordinates for the location of the submarine, Tidwell did his best to sound encouraging. "Right on the money," he fibbed, secure in the belief that the killer whales were not even close.

There was one man on the Orca team who may not have been fooled by Tidwell's trickery, having learned from experience not to accept the word of a rival. He was Anatoly Sagalevitch, the head Russian aboard the *Keldysh*—shrewd and experienced and a hard man to fool. Sagalevitch was an Orca shareholder and stood to benefit financially from a successful search. For thirty-odd years with the Academy of Sciences in Moscow, Sagalevitch had been dedicated to the science of ocean exploration. He considered himself a disciple of William Beebe and Auguste Piccard, and for his pioneering work at record depths with the Mirs, a pair of submersibles whose mother ship was the *Keldysh*, he deserved to be regarded as such. Sagalevitch also had been a loyal soldier of the Soviet regime, and while ideology may have been just a means to an end, the collapse of Communism in August 1991 did not work to his advantage. All of a sudden the Shirshov Institute had to think commercially and seek big-dollar contracts for the *Keldysh* and the Mirs, which would explain how Sagalevitch, whether it suited him or not, cast his lot with the treasure hunters. Soon enough they would include Paul Tidwell.

It was taking Jourdan longer than expected to refine the data, so Tidwell began searching where the sinking occurred according to 1944 U.S. Navy navigation records. It was an agonizing process, as an acoustical tracking device on a twenty-thousand-foot cable was towed at 1.5 knots over a series of parallel lines—twelve hours to complete a line, another eight to turn around and head back. The equipment was a MAK-1 sidescan sonar, whose designer-operator, Midkat Ibreav, had been a KGB oceanographer before defecting from the Soviet Union and becoming a resident of Canada. (Ibreav died mysteriously later in 1995 on an airline flight to Moscow.) The MAK-1 could cover a thousand meters to the left and right on each line, but the size of the search area was greater than a thousand square kilometers. So with time running short due to the limited fuel supply, it was coming up on crunch time.

On April 26 there was a message from Jourdan over the Internet via satellite and in code, a precaution Tidwell insisted on since he assumed the Russians aboard his own ship, the "Yuz," were routinely monitoring his communications. The *I-52* position he had arrived at, using RENAV, was ten miles southwest of where old navy data had placed the submarine, and Tidwell was so impressed with the analysis that he favored going directly there. But Tom Dettweiler, a Meridian Sciences engineer whom Tidwell had named project manager, preferred a gradual approach that would mean searching the entire southwest quadrant of the thousand-square-kilometer area. Dettweiler spoke from experience, having been with Robert Ballard on two major discoveries, the *Titanic* and the German battleship *Bismarck*. Even though Dettweiler's method would require four or five days, Tidwell said okay.

DOWN TO THE LAST LINE

On the morning of May 2, 1995, Tidwell was forced to make an announcement on the public address system of the "Yuz": "This is the last line, guys." There was just enough fuel for two more days and the trip back to Barbados, and Tidwell would need time for photographic documentation should they get lucky and find the submarine. Breakfast was glum that morning, but everything changed when Ibreav reported a target at 17,400 feet on his acquisition monitor. And he was getting a strong return of digitally reprocessed images from Meridian Sciences' ORION software. Tidwell could make out a cigar-shaped object, pointed at each end, and he asked for a density check. A computer technician fixed the sonar crosshairs on the target, pressed a switch, and reported a reading of 100 percent. That was when Tidwell knew for certain that they were looking at a metallic object, not a rock.

Dettweiler hoped for better definition on a second pass by increasing the frequency from 30 to 100 kilohertz and reducing the range from 1,000 to 250 meters. But the MAK-1, a hundred feet from the bottom, passed directly over the target, blocking it from view. On a third pass, at three thirty on the morning of May 3, a distinct image appeared—cylindrical hull, conning tower, scattered debris torn loose and strewn about.

The rest of this mission, Tidwell realized, would be anticlimactic.

2. A MAIDEN VOYAGE, TO BE HER LAST

. . . .

From the day of her launching—December 18, 1943—at the naval station in Kure, Japan, the submarine *I-52* was on a secret deployment of vital importance in the war. And while her fate was not foreordained, she was cursed by a dreadful Imperial Navy statistic, a 50 percent mortality rate, which Japanese submariners had learned to live with. The *I-52*'s captain, Commander Kameo Uno, and his hundred-man crew had come to terms with the inevitable risk of warfare. But at this very moment of the war there were dangerous conditions they could not address, as they were unaware of their existence. In what amounted to an intelligence catastrophe, Japanese and German radio codes had been compromised, and the movements of the *I-52* were being monitored by the enemy. In early March 1944 the U.S. Fleet Radio Unit at Pearl Harbor intercepted a message from the Bureau of Military Affairs in Tokyo to the naval attaché at the Japanese embassy in Berlin, announcing that the *I-52* would sail from Kure in the middle of March. She arrived in Singapore on March 21 and loaded 270 tons of strategic materials before departing for Europe on April 23. On May 11, 1944, she was identified by U.S. Navy Intelligence as Momi, her code name, as she passed south of Madagascar.

One can imagine that Commander Kameo Uno was a worried man as he guided the *I-52* through the Singapore Strait on the long voyage to occupied France. The war was not going well, to say the least. Germany was fighting for survival, as Russian armies drove from the east, through Hungary and Poland, and British and American forces were poised for an invasion of the European continent. And Japan had been reeling since the naval disaster at Midway in June 1942 and the loss of Guadalcanal in a prolonged siege and another American victory at sea. Recent reports from the Marshall Islands were deeply disappointing: Kwajalein had fallen, and eight thousand Japanese fighting men had died; then Eniwetok, with the loss of twenty-seven hundred defenders. Meanwhile, a surprise attack by U.S. carrier forces at the island of Truk, the headquarters of the Japanese Combined Fleet, had destroyed 200,000 tons of Japanese shipping and forced the resignation of Admiral Osami Nagano as chief of the Naval General Staff. From Truk a month later had come news that was very disturbing for Uno personally: navy headquarters had dispatched submarines to bolster the defense of New Guinea, and four of them—including Uno's old ship, the *I-175*—were sunk by U.S. destroyers.

But now Uno was in command of a new fleet *kaidai*, a submarine of leviathan proportions, and as he watched from atop the forty-foot conning tower, he could put aside his concerns momentarily and enjoy a tinge of pride. He also must have sensed an awesome responsibility from having read his orders, sealed until departure, and learned that the success of this mission could actually affect the outcome of the war.

The *I-52*'s code name, Momi, meaning fir tree, had belonged to the *I-34*, which was sunk by a British submarine off the Strait of Malacca on November 13, 1943, two days after sailing for Europe from Singapore. Taking the name of a doomed sister ship was done on purpose, as if the *I-52* had joined the battle in relief of the *I-34*. Uno, of course, was well aware that a similar fate might await the *I-52*—the 50 percent factor—but it was not something he dwelled on as a submarine officer in wartime.

His first command had been the *I-75* (it was renamed *I-175* in 1942), one of thirty *kaidai* engaged in the Pearl Harbor attack on December 7, 1941. It was determined in a postmortem of that attack that submarines were of little significance (the only ones lost were the *I-70* and five midget subs sent into the harbor during the air attack). Accordingly, submarines were ordered by Admiral Isoroku Yamamoto, the commander in chief of the Combined Fleet, to direct their attention to enemy merchant vessels rather than warships. Uno's *I-75* remained in the area, and on December 18, 1941, in response to Admiral Yamamoto's order, she sank an American freighter.

MIDWAY AS THE WORLD TURNED

In the immediate aftermath of Pearl Harbor, Japan enjoyed a tremendous advantage in terms of sea power, so Yamamoto decided to finish off the battered U.S. Navy Pacific Fleet with a decisive

eastward thrust. The objective was Midway, a U.S. island outpost
strategically situated, as the name implies, in the mid-Pacific
twelve hundred miles northwest of Hawaii. It was a go-for-broke
maneuver, and Yamamoto amassed the full resources of the Combined Fleet, including submarines, thereby contradicting his order
confining their attack targets to merchantmen. The *I-175* was one
of a squadron, SubRon 3, which formed a picket line south of
French Frigate Shoal, in the Hawaiian chain; its mission was to
support seaplane reconnaissance operations and to intercept enemy forces approaching from Pearl Harbor. The U.S. Pacific Fleet
commander, Admiral Chester W. Nimitz, had been alerted to an
attack on Midway, however, and he seized the initiative. Yamamoto
would blame his submarines for being late to arrive on station, but
the Japanese disaster could be attributed primarily to an American
intelligence advantage. Having broken the Japanese naval code,
U.S. Navy analysts had figured from radio messages that Midway
had been targeted for the attack, enabling Nimitz to assemble his
three aircraft carriers in a classic ambush deployment. Japanese
losses were monumental in the two-day battle: four aircraft carriers and a heavy cruiser, with two thousand sailors aboard, plus
three hundred aircraft and their pilots, while the American toll
amounted to one carrier and one destroyer.

Uno was no doubt painfully aware of an abrupt change in
Japanese naval strategy as of mid-1942, from offense to defense.
This of course had not escaped the attention of Admiral Nimitz,
and an American assault on Guadalcanal, beginning in August,
was in response to an assessment of Japanese carrier-based airpower, which had been decimated at Midway. By February 1943,
when Guadalcanal finally fell, the American strategy was taking
shape. It stipulated bypassing islands where defenses were strong,

such as New Britain, letting them "wither on the vine," and attacking those where the defenses were weak. A prerequisite of this "leapfrog" scheme was the sealing of air and sea routes; so in order to deliver supplies to isolated outposts and evacuate the wounded, the Japanese resorted to submarines. I-boat captains, Uno for one, while mindful of the need in a desperate situation, vocally opposed the use of their boats and crews for what were disparagingly referred to as "*mogura* [mole] missions." Stripped of deck guns and torpedoes to make room for food and supplies, submarines on mole missions had but one defense, their ability to remain undetected, which would explain the loss of twenty-seven of them in 1943. Another statistic indicated that the Japanese submarine force in the Pacific far from matched the record of German U-boats prowling the Atlantic that year. While German U-boats sank 489 merchant ships in 1943, the Japanese kill in the Pacific amounted to 26 ships.

COMMANDER UNO'S COVERT OP

As an I-boat captain, Uno was an honored member of an elite service. A graduate of Etajima, the Japanese naval academy, he had trained for years in undersea warfare before being selected for schooling as a commander, finally reaching the top of the conning tower, figuratively speaking. Having succeeded in the long and often strenuous climb, Uno could be forgiven for an inflated ego and for taking offense when he felt his ship and his men had been demeaned or degraded, as was the case—or so Uno believed—with the *mogura* missions. A similar resentment applied to the voyage to Europe, for it demanded of the *I-52* a steer-clear approach to combat and emphasized her role as a freight hauler. Uno had bowed to necessity and allowed his ship's firepower to be diminished: a 5.5-inch deck gun had been replaced by a 4-centimeter weapon, and a half dozen manned torpedoes, called *kaitens*, had been left behind to make room for 54 tons of rubber. The cargo hold also contained industrial metals for German factories (228 tons of tin, tungsten, and molybdenum) and medicinal drugs (3 tons of quinine and 2.88 tons of opium). And the ship was overloaded with personnel—11 officers, 84 enlisted crewmen, 6 navy passengers, 7 civilian engineers, and a German language translator, for a total complement of 109.

The *I-52* was also a mail carrier, a function magnified by the fact that submarines had become the single means of secure communication—in the form of military and diplomatic messages as well as personal letters—between Asia and Europe in 1944. But this mail boat aspect of the mission reminded Uno that among the many pounds of paper on board, there were sensitive and highly classified documents to be delivered to Berlin. These would have included the orders for the return voyage of the *I-52*, a sealed copy of which had been received by Commander Uno. If he needed convincing, these orders did the trick. As he had suspected all along, this was to be an intelligence mission involving secret weapons systems that had been developed by the Germans. This would explain the gold bullion: 146 bars in forty-nine metal boxes weighing two tons. By order of the Ministry of Finance in Tokyo to the financial commissioner in the Japanese embassy in Berlin, the gold was to replenish a special account in the Reichsbank in Berlin. (This would be the second such gold shipment sent to Berlin by submarine in 1944, the first having been delivered by the *I-29* when she arrived in Europe in March.) The *I-52* had loaded the gold in Singapore, and Uno knew more about its origin than he was willing to admit. He also knew that a problem had arisen in efforts to deposit the plundered gold and exchange it for currency, so there was an abundance on hand for the purchase of weapons. Uno knew, however, that if the enemy learned he was transporting gold, the *I-52* would be a high-priority target when she reached the North Atlantic.

Uno would have realized that the odds on reaching the German naval base at the French port of Lorient were no better than fifty-fifty. The twenty-five-hundred-ton *I-52* was an enticing target—357 feet in length and able to cruise on the surface at no better than sixteen knots because her designers had traded horsepower for a twenty-one-thousand-mile cruising range. So with or without valuable cargo, the *I-52* was a likely target.

The payments in gold to the Germans would enable the Japanese to effect a technology transfer, the specifics of which would have been contained in Uno's secret orders. It would turn out the crucial phase of this mission was to occur on the return trip, as the *I-52* would be transporting to Japan up-to-date items of the German arms inventory—jet aircraft and rocket engines, which would explain the presence among the *I-52* passengers of engineers from Mitsubishi, the aircraft manufacturer. It would not have surprised Uno if the civilian passengers were in possession of secrets of their own, given their positions in the arms industry. There would be, however, one experimental weapon aboard that would not be a topic of idle conversation, since it was so significant and so highly classified. This weapon was called the *genzai bakudan*, the "bomb as of now."

THE LIAISON BOAT PROGRAM

Upon reading his orders and learning the delicate nature of the mission, Uno could take heart in knowing he was under the control of the naval attaché in Berlin. Since the beginning of the war a succession of officers serving in the position had been regarded as much more than diplomatic aides, and had in fact been the ranking Japanese naval officers in Europe. And it was not merely coincidental that the three of them—Naokuni Nomura, Katsuo Abe, and Hideo Kojima—had served in intelligence during much of their careers. Nomura had been captain of the cruiser *Haguro* and the aircraft carrier *Kaga,* as well as a submarine squadron commander, before being named chief of staff of the Combined Fleet in 1936. He then became chief of Joho Kyoku, the Bureau of Naval Intelligence, and with the signing of the Axis Pact in 1940 he was in charge of a Japanese naval mission in Berlin. Nomura was also the naval attaché until he returned to Tokyo in 1943 to take command of the naval station at Kure. He served briefly as navy minister in 1944—it was a period of political turmoil, as Japan was clearly losing the war at sea—and then was appointed commander in chief of the Grand Escort Command Headquarters (GEHQ). Nomura's successor as naval attaché in Berlin was Vice Admiral Katsuo Abe, who also had commanded a cruiser and a carrier before becoming chief of Joho Kyoku. Abe had been the naval attaché in Italy and then the Japanese member of the Tripartite Military Commission. When he was replaced as attaché by Rear Admiral Hideo Kojima, Abe remained the ranking Japanese naval officer in Europe and served secretly as chief of Japanese Naval Intelligence in Germany. Kojima, who arrived in Europe in March 1944 aboard the submarine *I-29,* was a career intelligence officer and a specialist in German military affairs. He had been the naval attaché in Germany in the 1930s, and then returned to Tokyo to become head of the German desk at Joho Kyoku.

The exchange by submarine of vital elements of warfare and

key personnel was called *Yamabuki,* in keeping with a curious Japanese custom of identifying warships and their activities by botanical names. *Yamabuki* (or *Kerria japonica,* a yellow-flowered shrub of the rose family) was a Navy Department operation coordinated by the attaché in Berlin with the immediate objective of succeeding where blockade runs by surface vessels, called *Yanagi,* had been thwarted by British and American naval forces. There had been a greater goal when *Yamabuki* was conceived, but like so many Japanese dreams of conquest, it was abandoned after the defeat at Midway. A victory there would have enabled the Combined Fleet to control the Pacific and deploy submarines into the Indian Ocean, where they could operate from the Malayan port of Penang. (The longer-range objective was to turn the Indian Ocean into an Axis lake by closing Suez Canal exits and blocking supply routes to Australia and India via the Cape of Good Hope.) The overall confidence of the Imperial Navy was such that an attack force of five long-range I-boats, three of them piggybacking two-man midget subs, was sent into the Indian Ocean in May 1942, a month before Midway. One of the midgets put a British battleship out of commission and sank an oil tanker. The midget sub was lost when it went aground on a coral reef, ending the Indian Ocean foray, but not before a Japanese presence had been established off the coast of Madagascar.

The *Yamabuki* program was officially inaugurated by the *I-30,* one of the Indian Ocean attackers. Having reached Madagascar, she had put a third of the trip behind her, so after refueling at sea she departed for France, arriving at Lorient in August. The commander in chief of the German navy, Erich Raeder, personally welcomed the first of the liaison boats (as intercontinental Japanese submarines were often called), but fate would have its way on the return voyage. Nearing Singapore in October 1942, the *I-30* struck a British mine and went down with thirteen crew members and a valuable cargo of weapons and radar equipment.

Next out was the *I-29,* code name Matsu (pine tree), though she went only as far as Madagascar, reaching there in April 1943 for a rendezvous with the *U-180* and an exchange of passengers and cargo. Aboard the German sub was Subhas Chandra Bose, an anti-British Indian nationalist en route to Japan, where he intended to raise an army of Indian conscripts to fight the British in Burma. Switching places with Bose was Commander Hideo Tomonaga, a technical officer who was bringing advanced Japanese weapons—three *kaiten* kamikaze torpedoes and a self-loading cannon—to demonstrate to the Germans. Tomonaga was also the custodian of several tons of gold to cover the cost of German technology, but he was not merely a courier. He was a naval architect who had invented a submarine depth control system, and as a student of nuclear physics he knew the basics of a so-called miracle weapon.

It must have occurred to Uno that Imperial Navy headquarters was acting carelessly in repeatedly issuing radio reports on the progress of his mission. Afraid the enemy might be listening, he would have been appalled to know the extent to which his fears were justified. The Japanese were apparently oblivious to the threat because they were blissfully unaware of the extent to which their codes had been broken. The intelligence disadvantage was a major factor throughout the war, accounting for enormous Japanese losses.

"The *I-52* will depart Kure the middle of March," read the coded message from Tokyo to Berlin that was intercepted by the U.S. Fleet Radio Unit, Pacific (FRUPAC). "While docked at Singapore, preparations will be made for her trip to Germany." Serving to make her all the more vulnerable, the *I-52* was referred to in a stream of messages overheard by British and American intelligence. The British first broke German U-boat codes in 1941, and the Americans had mastered both the Japanese naval codes and the equally important diplomatic code. As a matter of fact, Hiroshi Oshima, the ambassador to Germany, was a major American intelligence asset for the information he unwittingly provided in reports to Tokyo throughout the war. It was Oshima who alerted the British to the submarine attack at Madagascar in May 1942, and in January 1943 he revealed that Hitler intended to make a gift of two U-boats to the Japanese navy. This was the führer's not-so-subtle way of acting on the advice of naval experts, who had little use for clumsy twenty-five-hundred-ton I-boats. They reasoned that the experience of operating a late-model IX C U-boat would convince the Japanese of the advantage of a more streamlined design and reduced size. The length of the IX C was 105 feet less than boats of the *I-52*'s Type C2 class, and its displacement of 1,120 tons was less than half that of the *I-52*. Type IX C U-boats were only marginally faster, 18.3 knots to the *I-52*'s 17.7 knots submerged, but were more maneuverable, thus better able to elude hostile fire.

Uno had good reason to watch closely as the U-boat transfer played out over crucial months of combat. Admiral Karl Doenitz, the commander in chief of U-boats, opposed it, arguing that the Japanese, even if they adopted the German design, would not be able to act in time to alter the course of the war. But Hitler insisted, and the first of the two, the *U-511*, sailed from Kiel in April 1943 with Admiral Nomura and the German ambassador to Japanese-occupied China as passengers. On arrival in Kure the *U-511* became the *RO-500*, code name Satsuki I, but Doenitz's misgivings were justified: the Japanese never figured out the U-boat's complex design, and she spent the rest of the war as a training vessel confined to the Sea of Japan. The second of Hitler's gifts, the *U-1224*, became the *RO-501*, code name Satsuki II, when she was turned over to a Japanese crew in Danzig in late 1943. She departed from Kiel for Japan in March 1944, making it quite likely that she and the *I-52* would cross paths in the mid-Atlantic.

Uno had an immediate reason to ponder German-Japanese relations, as he soon would be dealing directly with the Kriegsmarine in a mid-Atlantic rendezvous with a U-boat. Its purpose was to bring aboard a German naval officer and two technicians to assist in guiding the *I-52* through the Bay of Biscay, evading elements of the Allied blockade. For the rest of the journey to France the three would be Uno's guests, and he was apprehensive, having been warned by Takaichi Kinashi, captain of the *I-29*, that Germans often complained about Japanese food.

In August 1943 the *U-178* reached the Japanese base at Penang and became the first of over fifty U-boats patrolling the Indian Ocean. German naval operations in the Far East were under the command of Admiral Paul Wenneker, the naval attaché in Tokyo, but submarines reported directly to Admiral Doenitz at U-boat headquarters in Paris. In early 1943, when Doenitz was promoted to commander in chief of the German navy, he moved to Berlin and took U-boat headquarters with him. A few months later the *I-8*, a Type 3 squadron flagship built in 1938, left Kure for France with forty-eight passengers, naval personnel who would become the crew of the *RO-501* (formerly the *U-1224*) and sail her back to Japan. The *I-8* rendezvoused with the *U-161* in the vicinity of the Azores in August and arrived in Brest in early September. Uno was especially interested in the movements of the *I-8*, whose commander, Shinji Uchino, was an esteemed colleague. He could even forgive Uchino for allowing his crew to be photographed frolicking at a French château (they looked foolish and belittled the Japanese navy, in the minds of some), for it was part of a deserved congratulation. In December 1943 the *I-8* docked at Kure, becoming the first Japanese submarine to complete a round-trip to Europe.

In March 1944, as the *I-52* was preparing to depart from Kure on her maiden voyage, there was a disturbing report of a grim atrocity having occurred on the *I-8*. Uchino was no longer in command, having been replaced by Tatsunoke Ariizumi, who allegedly ordered the drowning of the crew of a Dutch merchant vessel that had been sunk by the *I-8* in the Indian Ocean, south of Ceylon. It was a heinous act, for sure, but Uno knew full well that the murder of survivors of ship sinkings was an unwritten policy that had been articulated by Hitler himself early in the war. Merchant shipping would be sunk without warning, he proclaimed in a meeting with Ambassador Oshima, with the intention of killing as many of the crew as possible. "Once it is known that most seamen die when their ship is sunk," Hitler added, "the enemy will find it difficult to find new people to replace them."

ENDANGERED BY A TECHNOLOGY LAG

For the time being Uno would probably be spared decisions that hinged on the ethics of warfare at sea. His job, simply, was to proceed quietly, avoiding contact with a ubiquitous enemy, though he knew all about the odds that barely favored reaching his destination safely. He had a vast ocean in which to maneuver, and submarines were designed to capitalize on stealth. But Great Britain and the United States had been dealing with the German U-boat menace for some time, and they had developed protective strategies. More to the point—and of greater concern for someone in Uno's shoes—they had made significant strides in the technology of antisubmarine warfare. ASW was a laboratory science in England and America, and while the Germans had more or less managed to keep up, they had shared little of what they had learned—about radar, for instance—with the Japanese, who were far behind. (The reason was poor communications, which were limited to radio, broken codes and all, and the occasional blockade-running submarine.) The Japanese attitude was also at fault, whether based on arrogance or defeatism. "Japan failed in ASW largely because her Navy disregarded the importance of the problem," wrote an Imperial Navy staff officer, Captain Atsushi Oi, after the war had ended. A naval strategy based on historic victories—in the Sino-Japanese War of 1894–95 and Russo-Japanese War of 1904–5—stressed an offensive fleet to the virtual exclusion of a defensive option. Uno nevertheless was familiar with the navigation and detection devices the enemy employed, knowing them by their English-language acronyms: radar (radio detection and ranging) and sonar (sound navigation ranging). It is fair to assume that Uno was plagued by an expectation that he would eventually be denied refuge in the darkness of night or deepness of the sea.

Uno was a career officer and naval strategist whose view of a world at war had been framed by a submarine's periscope. He had celebrated early Japanese victories and agonized over recent defeats, in particular Midway, which was regarded as the turning point of the war, and it certainly was in terms of airpower. For sub-marines, though, the reversal was not so obvious, as it occurred far to the north in the western Aleutian Islands. I-boats had been sent there in the hope of diverting U.S. forces from the central Pacific. The stratagem failed, but several of the I-boats remained there as a reconnaissance force. On June 21, patrolling in a dense fog, the *I-5* was suddenly under attack. The captain ordered a crash dive, no doubt wondering after a narrow escape how his ship had been tar-geted when visibility was zero. The answer was that U.S. forces were utilizing radar systems to locate targets and conduct attacks. This was bad news for the Imperial Navy, and Uno must have known just how bad, for submarines especially.

Radar was invented by a British physicist in the 1930s, but credit for much of the groundwork was owed to a Japanese scien-tist, Hidetsugu Yagi, who was best known as the inventor of a tele-vision receiving antenna. Yagi and two of his students at Tohoku University had experimented with various types of magnetrons, as power sources for microwave communications, by the time a low-powered cavity magnetron was unveiled in England, in 1940. American scientists became involved and learned from the British how a magnetron could generate radar waves of less than fifty cen-timeters. Following two years of microwave research at the Massa-chusetts Institute of Technology, ten-centimeter radar sets were ready for delivery to Allied ASW forces. In Japan, meanwhile, mil-itary leaders were preoccupied with offensive strategies and failed to pay heed to discoveries resulting from magnetron experimenta-tion by Yagi. It was not until 1944 that Japanese scientists fashioned a high-powered transmitting tube whose centimeter microwaves could track targets; and the first operational radar was to be in-stalled on the *I-15*, scheduled to go on station in May.

These developments were of little benefit to Uno, who could only resort to an evasive strategy, cruising on the surface at night, using his diesel engines to charge batteries, and staying submerged during the day. And he had no choice but to accept a new reality—he was vulnerable to attack by an enemy who could see in the dark. Uno was aware that the Germans had designed a novel device—rather, they had stolen it from the defeated Dutch navy—that would enable a submarine to run its diesels and charge batteries while submerged. It was called a snorkel and consisted of a steel cylinder that inhaled air and exhausted carbon monoxide, yet was so small that it was not detectable by radar. The *I-52* was to have a snorkel installed while in Lorient, but reaching the French port would depend in large measure on Naxos, a search receiver designed by the Germans to detect radar in the eight-to-twelve-centimeter range. It was Naxos—known also as Fumb Type 7—that had guided the *I-29* through the Allied blockade in March, so Uno looked forward to the U-boat rendezvous and the arrival aboard of the Germans—two radar technicians who would install and operate Naxos, and a U-boat officer, who would pilot the *I-52* on the final leg of her journey to Lorient.

Sonar was the source of further concern for Uno, and on this point he had himself to blame. He knew that submarine strategists of the Imperial Navy, himself included, had paid scant attention to such esoteric details as sound promulgation in relation to temperature layers or water stratification. Japanese submariners, moreover, had largely ignored an ASW doctrine that could lead to careful maneuvering while submerged and thus reduce the risk of detection. Even though larger than the submarines of other navies, I-boats could move along at sixteen knots on the surface, but they were fat targets when submerged—difficult to maneuver and with a limited diving depth. Finally, the Japanese had failed to emphasize noise reduction in submarine design, which would prove to be a fatal flaw upon the development of efficient sonar. The *I-52* had a prominent pair of conical hydrophones mounted forward of the conning tower, and they were undoubtedly useful as a listening device—during rendezvous with a U-boat, for example. But as Uno may have known from intelligence reports, American scientists had invented effective weaponry utilizing the sonar principle: a device called a sonobuoy, which transmitted position data by radio, and an acoustic torpedo, which used such position data to locate and attack a target. (The Germans were developing a similar torpedo, the Zaunkoenig T-5.) So Japanese fleet submarines were at a disadvantage, and not just on paper, for it was this advanced U.S. technology—the sonobuoy and the acoustic torpedo—that would seal the fate of the *I-52*.

BRITISH ULTRA, AMERICAN MAGIC

As blockade runners, submarines and the surface vessels that preceded them were equally vulnerable. The problem was partly human, in that crews on lonely long voyages tended to regard the radio as a way of connecting with home. Then again it was institutional, as the amount of official radio traffic demonstrated—between Tokyo and Berlin and ships at sea with little discernible concern for who might be listening. (German U-boat commanders were under orders from Admiral Doenitz to post a daily position.) Then there was the ambassador in Berlin, Hiroshi Oshima, who announced in March 1943 that the Germans intended to "inaugurate a submarine transport service." They did so in June, dispatching eleven cargo-hauling U-boats from France to the Far East, and then wondered why five of them were sunk.

Often in wartime, significant events occur in odd places, far from the front, and for Great Britain in World War II such a place was Bletchley Park, fifty miles north of London, where the Government Code and Cipher School (G.C.C.S.) occupied a redbrick Victorian mansion. The "back-room boys at Bletchley Park," they called themselves—many were noted mathematicians from nearby Oxford and Cambridge—and they had worked for months adding up to years without success at cracking a complex array of German codes called Enigma. Then on May 9, 1941, a German submarine, the *U-110*, was captured off Greenland by a British destroyer, and there was time before she went down to retrieve her Enigma encryption machine. The U-boat captain was killed in the action, and the German crew was unaware that the Enigma was in British hands, so it was hoped by the British and later confirmed that B-Dienst (Beobachtungs-Dienst), the intelligence arm of the German naval staff, was none the wiser.

In August 1941 Stewart Menzies, the head of the Secret Intelligence Service, advised Prime Minister Churchill on the status of Ultra, a special intelligence program that remained Britain's most closely guarded secret of World War II. The German Enigma cipher—called Hydra by the British—that was used by German warships in the North and Baltic Seas and by U-boats everywhere had been broken. A year later, in August 1942, Ultra was accounting for forty thousand broken enemy signals a month, but a contest continued between the British S.I.S. and B-Dienst. The Germans could boast of several successes of their own, notably the breaking of British Naval Cipher No. 3, the convoy code, early in the war, and for quite a long time the British were baffled by a U-boat cipher called Triton, known as Shark at Bletchley Park. From February to October 1942, with the advantage of a secure code, the Germans more than tripled U-boat operations in the Atlantic— from thirty to a hundred boats at sea—while the sinking of Allied vessels by U-boats reached a record 500,000 tons a month. But the British got lucky again when on October 23, 1942, the *U-559* was sunk in shallow water off the coast of Egypt. Her Enigma machine was found by divers and shipped immediately to London. Shark was broken in a matter of weeks, and in July 1943 Churchill reported to President Roosevelt on the sinking of "canaries," as he whimsically called them—eighty-five U-boats over a period of ninety-one days. At the same time, in Berlin, Doenitz presented the grim statistics to Hitler: the enemy's location devices were responsible for the loss of over thirty U-boats a month.

By the spring of 1944 the German war machine had been completely compromised by British Ultra, and Japanese forces— including warships like the *I-52*—were affected, since they had been issued Enigma machines and communicated using penetrated German codes. On November 15, 1943, the naval attaché in Berlin, Admiral Abe, had advised Tokyo that questions had been raised about the security of Enigma, and machines currently in use—eight hundred of them had been ordered by the Japanese navy—were vulnerable and would be replaced by a new model. The attaché's message was sent—and routinely intercepted by Ultra—two days after the sinking of the *I-34*, whose position had been betrayed by a broken code. (For internal communications the Japanese navy had its own secret system, a complex machine cipher that the Americans had been trying to crack with some success.)

Historically, British code breakers had progressed in a logical manner from Room 40 of the Admiralty, where they read German naval codes and exposed the Zimmermann telegram, which helped draw the United States into World War I. In the 1920s they adopted the G.C.C.S. disguise, fooling no one, and occupied a corner of the S.I.S. office at 54 Broadway, off Parliament Square, a part of London later made famous by the fiction of Ian Fleming. By the time they moved to Bletchley Park in 1939, the men in charge had apprenticed at the Admiralty and remained on board for two decades of peace, preserving a tradition of tight-lipped secrecy that would serve Britain well in World War II.

The American counterpart of the "back-room boys" was Herbert Yardley, who began his government career in 1912 at the State Department as a $900-a-year clerk-telegrapher. Yardley learned cryptography by studying references at the Library of Congress and practicing on coded diplomatic messages. When he had an opportunity in 1916 to decipher an important message to President Wilson from Colonel Edward House on a meeting with the kaiser in Berlin, he did so in just two hours. Yardley had demonstrated his skill while showing that U.S. codes were easily solved, and he emphasized both points by drafting a detailed analysis of the vulnerability of American cryptography. In June 1917, shortly after the United States entered the war, Yardley was transferred to the War Department as an army second lieutenant and put in charge of MI-8, the division of military intelligence responsible for codes and ciphers.

MI-8 was reorganized in 1919, which meant essentially that

security was tightened because spying was no longer considered fair play. Yardley stayed on as director, answering to the Departments of War and State, which shared the $100,000 budget. Military funding was "off the books," and it was decided to move MI-8 out of Washington and give it a clandestine identity. Accordingly, in May 1919 Yardley set up shop in Manhattan as the American Black Chamber, modeled on secret agencies that monitored diplomatic mail in the capitals of eighteenth-century Europe. The Black Chamber was responsible for solving Japanese codes, and did so just in time for a naval disarmament conference in Washington, enabling Secretary of State Charles Evans Hughes to hold out for treaty terms more favorable to the United States and Britain. This notable feat was a result of Yardley's skill and determination, but his usefulness had come to an end, at least for the time being. As the nation enjoyed peace and prosperity, there was a diminished need for code breaking, and he was further burdened by the passage of federal legislation, such as the Radio Act of 1927. It was already a crime for employees of cable and telegraph companies to divulge the contents of messages, and the new law extended liability to those who received such communications. And due to a drastic decline in government intercepts to be decoded, traffic between the Black Chamber and its clients at the State and War Departments was near zero by 1925.

The Black Chamber by this time depended entirely on State Department funding, so when President Hoover was inaugurated in 1929, its fate was in the hands of Secretary of State Henry Stimson. Yardley was a poker player and knew not to tip his hand, so he waited until Stimson had been in office a few months before sending him Japanese diplomatic messages that he had deciphered. Stimson was a statesman of stature and puritanical integrity, and he reacted by withdrawing all support of the Black Chamber and issuing what was to become a famous statement: "Gentlemen do not read each other's mail."

At the onset of the Great Depression, Yardley was out of work and desperate. His financial plight was reason enough to sell his story in the form of a book, *The American Black Chamber,* and he convinced himself that it was his patriotic obligation to expose men like Stimson as obstinate and hypocritical. Touted by an advance serialization in the *Saturday Evening Post,* the book was a bestseller when it appeared in June 1931—eighteen thousand copies sold in the United States, ten thousand or so in Europe, and almost thirty-three thousand in Japan, where it caused a furor. The foreign office in Tokyo, while admitting to laxity for having failed to scramble ciphers, accused the State Department in Washington of acting dishonorably and did its best to destroy Yardley. He had come to them during the disarmament conference, offering to be bought off, the Japanese claimed. Whether or not he was guilty, Yardley was a pariah, and his only government job thereafter was with the World War II Office of Price Administration. His lasting legacy would be in the form of a federal law intended, in the words of Senator Tom Connally of Texas, "to make it a criminal offense for a scoundrel to betray his confidential relationship with the Government. . . ."

The Japanese responded to Yardley's account of their broken codes by demanding an immediate and complete revamping of their signals security system. Machine code technology did exist, as the Germans had discovered, but it remained to be seen if an insoluble cipher might be devised. While the theoretical principles of the Enigma were familiar to the Japanese—a typewriter keyboard sending impulses to a series of rotors via a complicated wiring arrangement—they were seeking to apply the concept to a unique design. The resulting product was introduced by the Imperial Navy in 1931: Type 91, so named for the Japanese calendar year, 2591; and a modified version adapted by the foreign office, Type 91-A, would be known in diplomatic circles as the Red Machine. These were primitive models soon proven insecure, so the Japanese navy's special signals unit took another six years to develop the Alphabetical Typewriter Type 97, called Purple by interested parties in the United States and Great Britain. It was comparable to Enigma as a top-quality enciphering system, far superior to the British Typex and American Sigaba, and it ranked with Enigma also for the confidence placed in its invulnerability to cryptanalytical intrusion.

With Yardley in exile and the intricate strategies of signal intelligence in the hands of the U.S. Army and Navy, a few uniquely talented individuals appeared in the picture. One was William F. Friedman, the War Department's chief cryptanalyst, who became the director of the army's Signal Intelligence Service when it was created in 1929 to handle codes and ciphers that had been the responsibility of the State Department. Friedman's immediate challenge at S.I.S. (not to be confused with the British Secret Intelligence Service) was the Japanese Purple enciphering system, and he realized there was little hope of obtaining a confiscated machine, as the British had with Enigma. Purple was for diplomatic codes: the machines were under lock and key in Tokyo and in certain embassies around the world, and the Japanese were not likely to risk deploying them at military bases or on warships. (Facing defeat in 1945, the Japanese destroyed the Purple machines. All were lost save one that was recovered in pieces from the

Japanese embassy in Berlin following the German surrender.) Nor could Friedman expect to come across clues from the machines in British hands, as there was no reason to believe that Purple was a direct derivative of Enigma. So Friedman was confronted with the daunting task of duplicating the functions of a complex device by constructing a copy without being able to examine the original. It was a demonstration of sheer intellectual resolve, accomplished by analyzing signals and aided immeasurably by a Japanese tendency to transmit the same signal on the Red and Purple ciphers. "Eventually the solution reached the point where the cryptanalysts had a pretty good pencil-and-paper analog of the Purple machine," wrote David Kahn in *The Codebreakers,* published in 1967. "S.I.S. then constructed a mechanism that would do automatically what the cryptanalysts could do manually."

Friedman became known as "the man who broke Purple," though he was not all by himself in the endeavor, as he explained to a congressional committee in 1946. "It was only by very closely coordinated teamwork that we were able to solve it . . ." he said. Three mathematicians who assisted Friedman—Solomon Kullback, Frank Rowlett, and Abraham Sinkoff—would become key figures in the communications field, and Friedman's navy counterpart, Laurence F. Safford, would become commander of the cryptically named Op-20-G (Section G, 20th Division, Office of the Chief of Naval Operations). Under the terms of a unique army-navy agreement, S.I.S. and Op-20-G pooled resources and shared responsibility for monitoring and deciphering Japanese diplomatic and naval systems. Along the way the commander of the Office of Naval Intelligence, Rear Admiral Walter Anderson, was alluding to the mysteries of signal intelligence, calling it American Magic, a name that would endure.

* * *

Within hours of the attack on Pearl Harbor, the Japanese fleet cryptographic system JN25 became the target of a sweeping assault by Op-20-G and theater units. Two of those units, however—in Corregidor and Singapore—soon had to be evacuated, leaving the Pacific Fleet Radio Unit in Hawaii with an enormous challenge. (To disguise its activities the unit was renamed the Combat Intelligence Unit, while it was commonly known by its intercept network designation, Station Hypo.) Lieutenant Commander Joseph Rochefort and his Hypo team seldom left their basement office at the Honolulu Navy Yard, working twelve-hour shifts for months on end. By early May 1942 the team had all but broken the current code, JN25b, having recovered enough to be able to read 90 percent of an everyday message. But JN25b, in use since December 1940, was about to be replaced by JN25c, meaning U.S. code breakers would be starting from scratch. But a delay in distributing code books to ships at sea and island installations prevented the Japanese from making the change on schedule. "Her failure to do so," concluded Kahn in *The Codebreakers,* "meant that she was masking her Midway preparation messages behind a cryptographic smoke screen that American cryptanalysts had almost entirely blown away."

On May 20 Yamamoto issued an operations order detailing his strategy: a diversion in the direction of the Aleutians to be followed by a main assault, and when ships of the U.S. Pacific Fleet responded they would be destroyed by a superior Imperial Navy. Within a week, thanks to Station Hypo, Admiral Nimitz knew all he needed about the attack except when and where it would occur. To determine when, two officers—a cryptanalyst and a Japanese language specialist—struggled for weeks with mixed-cipher alphabets and two different systems of Japanese syllabic writing until finally concluding the attack would occur on June 3. As for where, Rochefort knew that the Japanese code coordinates for Midway were AF, and he had noticed that the co-ordinates of the attack location in Yamamoto's order were AF as well. He assumed the attack would occur at Midway, but so much was riding on his being right that he was ordered by Washington to confirm his finding. So Rochefort resorted to a ruse. He requested a message from Midway—sent in the clear, to be sure the Japanese would read it—reporting the breakdown of a water distillation plant. When an intercepted Japanese dispatch then referred to a water problem at AF, Rochefort had the confirmation he needed.

Showing his appreciation, Nimitz wrote in his battle report: "Midway was essentially a victory of intelligence."

THE COST OF BLUNDERS

A negative aspect of American intelligence activity in the Pacific was revealed in a communication to Nimitz from the U.S. Fleet commander in chief, Admiral Ernest J. King, blaming a security failure for an account of the Midway battle that appeared in the *Chicago Tribune* on June 7, 1942. The writer had identified Japanese warships and implied that Nimitz's knowledge of the enemy order of battle was based on signal intelligence. It was an academic matter strategically, since the Japanese had converted to JN25c, removing the U.S. intelligence advantage for the time being. But Magic had been compromised, and on June 20 an angry Admiral King issued an order on the "control of dissemination and use of radio intelligence." In it he directed that such special intelligence "should be passed without reference to its secret source and should contain, somewhere near the beginning of the message, the word ULTRA. . . ." King was seeing to it that intelligence obtained from the breaking of Japanese naval and military codes would become Ultra intelligence, credited to Bletchley Park. As for Magic, the less said the better, though the name still applied to what was obtained by penetrating Japanese diplomatic ciphers.

Rochefort was relieved of his command in the fall of 1942 and exiled to a training center in California. A recommendation awarding him a Distinguished Service Medal—endorsed by Nimitz, among others—was twice denied, but finally approved nine years after his death. In issuing his angry order, King apparently was reacting to a British objection to the leaked account of Midway that appeared in the *Chicago Tribune,* but what is not clear is how he hoped to placate Churchill and his commanders by identifying U.S. signal intercepts as Ultra intelligence. The British were irate because lax U.S. security was causing the Japanese to change codes at a time of high anxiety in Britain over an expected invasion of India.

The crisis passed, but there was another a year later that convinced Stewart Menzies, the head of British S.I.S., that the Americans had, in the words of Menzies's biographer, Anthony Cave Brown, "demonstrated a predisposition . . . to use Magic for purely tactical or prestige purposes." It follows that in April 1943 U.S. signal intelligence was instrumental in the assassination of Yamamoto, as there was no other explanation of how Army Air Force P-38s managed to intercept the admiral's aircraft on a flight from Rabaul to Bougainville. The Japanese could again assume that their codes had been broken and change them accordingly.

Menzies, known as "C," may have worried about security lapses by U.S. intelligence, but he was everlastingly grateful to American Magic—and William Friedman in particular—for the breaking of Purple, which is widely considered the single most significant intelligence achievement of the war. Friedman deserved this sort of acclaim if only for how Purple recorded the words of the Japanese ambassador to Germany, Hiroshi Oshima, as he spoke volumes to his government in Tokyo. Oshima enjoyed the confidence of Hitler, and he reported studiously on meetings with the führer and Joachim von Ribbentrop, the foreign minister, never realizing that his audience extended to the Allied high command in London and Washington and to British and American field commanders, who studied intelligence decrypts drawn from the ambassador's reports. Oshima had come to Berlin in 1934 as an army colonel and the military attaché, and in just four years, having gained favor with the Nazis, he advanced to the rank of lieutenant general and was named ambassador. But in 1939 the government in Japan was having doubts about German expansionism, and Oshima was discredited for having idolized Hitler and identified with von Ribbentrop. He was recalled and spent a year in Japan promoting a militant pro-German policy, and his position was enhanced by the success of the German army as it swept across Europe. When a new government came to power in Tokyo in 1940, Japan signed the Tripartite Pact with Germany and Italy, and Oshima returned to Berlin as ambassador. He soon established his usefulness as an unwitting Allied informant by a thousand-word report to the foreign office in Tokyo on April 16, 1941. Based on a briefing by von

Ribbentrop, it revealed Hitler's grand-scale strategy: he was not planning to invade Britain but did intend to attack Russia, confident that Germany could wage war on two fronts.

WHAT DID ROOSEVELT KNOW?

A question lingered after World War II as to how much President Roosevelt and his advisers knew about Japanese intentions in advance of December 7, 1941. The answer finally reached was consistent with past denials—the plan to attack Pearl Harbor had been a well-kept secret. Instructions to Japanese envoys in Washington in a fourteen-part Purple-coded dispatch—immediately decoded and translated by S.I.S. and Op-20-G and forwarded to Army G-2—contained no hint of imminent action. Suspicions might have been justified by an order to the envoys to destroy one of their cipher machines, but that was nothing more than circumstantial evidence of an unspecific warlike intention. Upon a declaration of war in response to the attack, the army's responsibility was expanded to include all Japanese diplomatic intercepts, but the attention of S.I.S. cryptanalysts remained firmly fixed on the Berlin-Tokyo circuit. Their efforts were rewarded when, on December 8, they obtained a text of a supplemental Tripartite Pact, signed on December 11—the day Hitler declared war on the United States—by von Ribbentrop, Oshima, and Dino Alfieri, the Italian ambassador to Germany. (On December 14 Hitler personally bestowed the Order of Merit of the German Eagle on Oshima for his contribution to German-Japanese cooperation.)

Oshima's output multiplied in volume and value to the Allies—from one hundred messages in 1942 to six hundred in 1944. A four-hour meeting with von Ribbentrop in December 1942, to mark the anniversary of Japan's entering the war, served to illustrate the Allied intelligence advantage. Von Ribbentrop acknowledged the successful landing of U.S. forces in North Africa in October, followed by the British victory at El Alamein. "Bad news for us Germans," he allowed, referring to the retreat of forces commanded by Field Marshal Erwin Rommel. "It was the greatest fizzle we have seen in this war." The foreign minister also lamented the loss of supply ships sent to sustain Rommel, though he failed to understand why they had been systematically sunk. Von Ribbentrop noted that details of ship loadings in Italian ports, as well as departure times and course data, had been transmitted to Rommel using an Enigma code, although he did not know that the transmissions were being routinely monitored by British Ultra. Nor did either von Ribbentrop and Oshima realize that their conversation in Berlin two months hence was being overheard word for word by American Magic. In a classic bit of wartime irony, they were players on a world stage as Allied intelligence provided an audience.

Ambassador Oshima met with Hitler for the last time on May 29, 1944. The subject was submarines, and Hitler spoke optimistically though in vague generalities about a new undersea war that he hoped would be effectively under way in months to come. Oshima went on to say he was grateful for the führer's kind words. "He congratulated me deeply on the glorious victories of the Imperial Navy and went on to say that in this great war, in order to win the victory, the armies of both Japan and Germany must of extreme necessity always be provided with ultramodern materiel and that Germany would not keep anything whatsoever secret from Japan but would let her have any and everything. That was how honestly he spoke."

As Oshima's account of his conversation with Hitler was being transmitted to Tokyo, the *I-52* was rounding the southern coast of Africa and heading into the Atlantic, "straight into the meshes of the Allied signal intelligence net," as Ronald Lewin, an author versed in signal communications, viewed it. "Magic (with its command of the diplomatic signals and the Japanese-German naval attaché code)," Lewin writes, "and . . . the British ability to read the German Enigma cipher contributed intelligence about . . . operations which, cumulatively but decisively, aborted them."

3. A RENDEZVOUS RUDELY INTERRUPTED

The *I-29* and the *I-52*, while not exactly twins, were very similar in appearance—357 feet in length and a 2,500–2,600-ton displacement—but they differed notably in speed and range. The older Type B *I-29*, launched in February 1942, was powered by a pair of diesel engines with a total horsepower of 12,400, and could travel (surfaced) at twenty-three knots over a range of fourteen thousand miles. The Type C *I-52*, meanwhile, was equipped with two diesels, each rated at 4,700 shp (shaft horsepower), enabling her to reach a top speed on the surface of sixteen knots over a range of twenty-one thousand miles. (As Commander Uno intended to prove, the *I-52*'s greater range would make it possible to reach the destination in France without refueling.) In actual conditions and taking into account stormy weather and heavy seas, those cruising speeds would be reduced to less than ten knots, and the threat of enemy attack would require long periods of remaining submerged and running at just two knots.

The danger that accompanied Japanese warships on transoceanic voyages was addressed in a dispatch on November 18, 1943, from the Bureau of Military Affairs in Tokyo to the naval attaché Abe in Berlin, telling of the loss five days earlier of the *I-34* as she set sail for Europe and became the first blockade-running submarine to go down. In this account of the *I-34*'s sinking by a British submarine, the HMS *Taurus,* in the Strait of Malacca, south of Penang, Malaya, it was noted that the *I-29,* code name Matsu, "will operate as scheduled," meaning she would depart for Europe from Penang in December. The *I-29*'s progress would not escape the attention of American monitors, who would have in hand a Tokyo-to-Berlin dispatch, dated January 2, 1944, "the movement schedule of the Matsu," listing dates and position coordinates from January 11 to March 1. Then a GI comment: "A dispatch of 7 March stated that Matsu (*I-29*) was scheduled to arrive Lorient on 11 March. She was to depart Lorient on 18 April, apparently for Japan."

BAY OF BISCAY BREAKTHROUGH

The captain of the *I-29,* Commander Takaichi Kinashi, had earned the respect of a comrade, Zenji Orita, who wrote a book after the war in which he referred to Kinashi as "Japan's top sub skipper." Commanding the *I-19* on September 15, 1942, in the battle for the Solomon Islands, Orita wrote, Kinashi fired six torpedoes at U.S. warships and scored three deadly hits, sinking the aircraft carrier *Wasp* and disabling the battleship *North Carolina* and a destroyer, the *O'Brien.* Then came the publicized meeting of the *I-29* and *U-180* off Madagascar in April 1943, followed by an order to embark on his current mission, in which Kinashi would become only the third Japanese submarine commander to enter the treacherous Atlantic battleground.

From Berlin, four days after the *I-29* docked at Lorient, Kinashi filed a report on highlights of the voyage and his observations of a world at war. He mentioned that on December 30 and January 4 he received 187 tons of fuel from German supply ships, though he did not name them, nor did he reveal where the refueling occurred. Leave it to enemy GI monitors, who were able to comment upon the *I-29*'s arrival in France that she was refueled in January in the Indian Ocean by the German tanker *Bogota*. (Like so many Japanese submariners, Kinashi never would understand the full extent of the Allied advantage based on broken codes, and how it affected his vulnerability.) Kinashi continued with his report:

Crossed equator going north on 1 February. Rendezvoused with German submarine on the 14th and received from her a lieutenant (j.g.) liaison officer, two petty officers and a radar. We proceeded in general along the planned route breaking through the Bay of Biscay and getting an escort on 10 March, consisting of two German destroyers, two large German torpedo boats . . . and eight planes at the regular times during the day. On the morning of the 11th we came under the protection of numerous anti-torpedo and anti-aircraft vessels. . . .

It was a strenuous journey due to bad weather in the vicinity of South Africa and later off the Azores, making it necessary on each occasion to proceed submerged for four days. Also in connection with the timing of our rendezvous with the German submarine, we kept submerged during the day . . . (we were instructed by dispatch from the naval attaché in Germany to do so north of 25 degrees). East of longitude 22 degrees west we proceeded submerged except when charging our batteries at night. After rendezvousing with the German escort unit . . . we proceeded on the surface.

The most chilling moments were those spent in the presence of the enemy. "Once at dark in the Indian Ocean," Kinashi recalled, "we saw a single merchantman, and again in the Atlantic Ocean near our rendezvous point with the German submarine we saw an auxiliary aircraft carrier accompanied by an escort vessel. On both occasions we were too far away to attack." The German U-boat was close enough to attack the carrier and did so on the night of February 13, but then was under attack for three hours by four U.S. destroyers.

Continuing with Kinashi's account:

While we were running on the surface charging our batteries in position 42 degrees, 30 minutes north by 12 degrees west, we were suddenly strafed by enemy planes close to our stern. We made an emergency dive and thought we had no casualties, but gun pointer Issoo Kami disappeared, and his whereabouts is unknown. We were again attacked by aircraft after being met by the German escort unit on the morning of 10 March, but no damage was done to us. But a German plane was shot down in the ensuing air battle, and the group commander who was directing operations and his crew were killed. After this there were no more attacks.

As Kinashi implied, the German air and sea escort provided sufficient protection for the *I-29* to remain on the surface for the Bay of Biscay breakthrough. It is important to note as well that the radar search receiver had been installed, affording Matsu with an early-warning system. In a separate report on technical matters, dated April 1, Kinashi stressed the necessity of keeping pace with British and American scientific advances. "The radar equipment in enemy aircraft is being rapidly developed," he declared, "as is the radar search receiver. If the equipment is not of the very latest design, it cannot be effective. This was shown very clearly in the experience of the Matsu." He also listed a few items he deemed essential in future efforts by submarines to run the blockade, assuming they would be spending a lot of time submerged: periscope-elevating equipment, bilge pumps, and a cooling pump for a gyrocompass.

Rear Admiral Hideo Kojima, an *I-29* passenger headed for Germany as the new naval attaché, had elaborate praise for the German navy, "which is faced with a difficult situation on account of the unexpected development of enemy radar. . . ." (There was nothing unexpected about the British and American scientific advances, as Kojima, an intelligence officer for much of his career, certainly knew.) Referring to Matsu's breakthrough, Kojima said, "It appears necessary to put these operations into effect," and he offered some guidelines for submarines.

1. They should be equipped with the newest type radar devices and manned by experienced personnel who have had sufficient instruction.
2. They should be as new as possible, between two months and one year after commissioning, and should have had experience in difficult tactical operations.
3. Cruising on the surface for charging batteries is to be avoided as much as possible during the short nights of the summer, and the period of the new moon is to be chosen for breaking through the Bay of Biscay.
4. Because of changes in the warning system in European

waters and the constant advance of the radar instruments of both sides, even maintaining a #1 condition of alert, it is almost impossible to break through the Bay of Biscay if you do not meet a German submarine at a suitable opportunity en route and take aboard a capable German liaison officer, skilled operators, and the newest type German radar equipment.

5. Sufficient preparations should be completed for long periods of cruising submerged as well as for cruising submerged silently under enemy pressure.

. . . .

When Kojima paid an official call on Admiral Karl Doenitz, the commander in chief and Wilhelm Meisel, the chief of staff of the German navy, on March 17, it was a rare opportunity for a newly arrived Japanese officer to meet directly with German military leaders and bring important messages from officials in Japan without fear of the enemy listening in. Kojima reported at length on the meeting the following day. He had offered condolences to Doenitz on the death in action of a son, and he had expressed to Meisel Japanese approval of intensive German navy operations in the Indian Ocean, but these were not the essential matters discussed with these and other officers of the German high command. Kojima also talked about his three-month trip by submarine and running the Bay of Biscay blockade, but this wasn't topic A either. What was mainly on his mind—the urgent subject of briefings by his Imperial Navy superiors before Kojima left for Europe—was the miracle weapon, the *genzai bakudan*. Details were secret certainly, but the Germans were known to be working on a devastating weapon, as were the Japanese, not to mention the enemy. Kojima undoubtedly posed the question in one way or another: How was the work progressing? And he may well have been authorized to propose a cooperative effort in an attack on the American mainland.

On April 18 Kinashi notified the General Affairs Section in Tokyo (ATTN: Foreign Minister, CINC Combined Fleet, CINC Kure, SubRon 8) that he was bound for Japan: "Left Lorient on the 16th and am now headed for the vicinity of our southern base." There were of course the unintended recipients of the message, for U.S. Fleet Intelligence was alert as usual. "Matsu (*I-29*) arrived at Lorient 11 March, left Lorient 16 April for Singapore, where it arrived 14 July." The enemy's interest in Matsu was intensified by a Berlin-to-Tokyo dispatch on July 17 listing items of her cargo—radar apparatus, Enigma coding machines, rocket-type launchers, parts of a British Mosquito aircraft.

THE *BOGUE* TO RECKON WITH

Convicted of war crimes and awaiting execution in 1948, Hideki Tojo, Japan's prime minister from 1941 to 1944, confided to General MacArthur what he believed to be three main elements of the American victory in the Pacific. Submarine superiority and the island-hopping selective attack strategy topped Tojo's list, and then he cited the unique use of aircraft carriers on search-and-destroy missions. He was referring to an aggressive strategy conceived by the Allies early in the war as a defense against German U-boats preying on convoys in the North Atlantic. Out of this initiative came unlikely heroes of the war at sea: escort carriers, or CVEs in

U.S. Navy shorthand, which were deployed as CVE groups, consisting of a carrier with fighter and bomber aircraft aboard and destroyer escorts protecting the flanks.

A CVE hunter-killer program gained momentum in 1940 when President Roosevelt directed the Navy Department to determine the feasibility of stepping up aircraft carrier production by converting yet-to-be-built freighters. Navy Secretary Frank Knox responded in the positive, and three weeks after Pearl Harbor, he approved the conversion of twenty-four C-3 merchant hulls into escort carriers. The CVE class was named for the USS *Bogue* (as in Bogue Sound, North Carolina, and a family of eighteenth-century settlers). With her 440-foot topside runway, the *Bogue* looked like a parking lot afloat. She could do no better than eighteen knots, barely keeping pace with surfaced submarines, but her armament was impressive—a pair of five-inch guns and up to thirty-five 40-millimeter and 20-millimeter weapons. Commissioned at the Puget Sound Navy Yard in Tacoma, Washington, in September 1942, she headed for Norfolk, Virginia, arriving on January 1, 1943. The first U.S. carrier assigned to convoy support, she put to sea in February with a squadron of nine Grumman Wildcat fighters and twelve Grumman Avenger torpedo-bombers and a four-destroyer screen. At this time the German Triton cipher had been broken by the British, and U-boats were exposed. But the first three sorties were uneventful for the *Bogue*—two U-boats sighted, zero sinkings—and she was ordered to Great Britain in April for further training.

The *Bogue* (CVE 9) returned to convoy duty and the training soon paid off. On May 22, a sighting by high-frequency direction finder (HF/DF, or "huff-duff") turned out to be the *U-569*, just twenty miles away. A pair of Avengers attacked and did such damage to the sub that her captain immediately surrendered. He and twenty-four crewmen were rescued and sent to the United States as war prisoners. The *U-569* was the *Bogue* CVE group's only kill on this outing, but Convoy ON-184 reached its destination in Europe unscathed. In the opinion of esteemed World War II historian Samuel Eliot Morison, the value of the escort carrier and its aircraft—the Avenger, in particular—in the antisubmarine Atlantic campaign had been demonstrated. The *Bogue* at this point was affected by the formation of the Tenth Fleet to coordinate the antisubmarine war, a move of such importance that the U.S. Fleet commander in chief, Admiral King, was in command, though he left the details to his chief of staff, Rear Admiral Francis S. Low. The Tenth Fleet had no ships, and its single crucial function was intelligence support. When Admiral Low was drafting an order for the new command, he decided that escort carriers on ASW missions ought to report directly to Tenth Fleet headquarters. Admiral King thought better of the idea, and the escort carriers remained in the Atlantic Fleet.

Admiral Royal Ingersoll, commander in chief of the Atlantic Fleet (CINCLANT), had issued an order to CVE groups authorizing commanders to pursue enemy submarines when their presence was indicated by a huff-duff position fix. The order was welcomed by Captain Giles Short, commanding officer of the *Bogue,* as he sailed on May 30 from Argentia, Newfoundland, for the Azores to support convoys en route to North Africa. U-boat engagements were quick to occur. On June 5 two *Bogue* aircraft, a Wildcat and an Avenger, teamed up and sank the *U-217*. Three days later two Avengers subjected the surfaced *U-758* to an intense bombing, but the sub fought back with 20-millimeter antiaircraft guns and escaped, though with heavy damage. On June 12 the *Bogue* encountered the *U-118*, a "milch cow" supply ship, right after she had refueled the *U-758* and taken aboard her wounded from the bombing four days earlier. The sixteen-hundred-ton *U-118* was no match for the *Bogue*, and she went down after a sustained attack by eight aircraft dropping fourteen depth charges and firing thousands of machine gun rounds. (Seventeen survivors were rescued by the *Osmand Ingram,* a *Bogue* group destroyer escort.) On the return voyage to Norfolk in late June, the *Bogue* and her air squadron, VC-9, shared credit for two more U-boats sunk, but upon review an otherwise successful cruise had been marred by procedural deficiencies. For one, pilots had failed to make full use of radar, preferring to rely on eyesight in daylight action.

FIVE SINKINGS IN SIX WEEKS

When the *Bogue* departed once again from Norfolk, on November 14, 1943, there was sufficient confidence in the combat effectiveness of CVE groups that they were ordered to take the offensive and attack U-boats where they lurked. A more aggressive ASW tactic was also a defensive response to a new German homing torpedo, the T-5, but whatever the reason, it worked well for the *Bogue*: five U-boats sunk during the six-week sortie. There was a brief hiatus in early 1944, as the *Bogue* assisted in preparations for the Allied invasion of France, delivering army fighter planes to Scotland. She was back on patrol in May as the leader of Task Group 22.2, and she had a new captain, Aurelius B. Vosseller, a former commander of the Atlantic Fleet Antisubmarine Development Detachment. With that background, Vosseller could be expected to put the latest ASW technology to a rigorous test, made all the more necessary by a new German navy submarine strategy. U-boats were staying out of sight, using snorkels or surfacing at night to recharge batteries. Therefore, pilots of VC-69, the squadron now aboard the *Bogue,* flew more frequent nighttime patrols—893 hours, over a quarter of the total, during the cruise of May–June 1944—searching by radar and attacking with sonar-guided weapons.

U.S. Fleet Intelligence in Washington was busy stitching pieces of intelligence from British Ultra and American Magic into an illuminating tableau of Axis activities and intentions. American analysts were engaged in a game of guesswork and hunches, though the stakes were high, and lives were on the line. "An enemy aircraft carrier has appeared in the Central Atlantic," the Japanese naval attaché in Berlin warned in early May 1944. The message was intercepted by Ultra when it was radioed to the Navy Department in Tokyo for relay to the captains of Momi, Matsu, and Satsuki II. "It will be necessary to follow closely the sailing directions designated by the German Naval Operations Section." U.S. Navy analysts often inserted comments in longhand on the decoded and translated decrypts and customarily labeled them "GI" (government intelligence). In this case Matsu and Satsuki II were accurately identified as the *I-29*, which had sailed homeward from Lorient in April, and the *RO-501*, the converted German U-boat. There was some uncertainty about Momi, so an analyst wrote: "Identity not known." The question was answered on May 7 when Momi was identified as the *I-52*, and on May 10 the approximate positions of the three submarines were revealed: *I-29*—25-21 N, 40-09 W; *RO-501*—11-51 N, 37-27 W; *I-52*—20-39 S, 77-27 E. And when Fleet Headquarters of the Commander in Chief (COMINCH) issued a U/Boat Intelligence Summary on May 13, there was quite a bit to add about the *I-52*. She was identified as Momi and was estimated as of May 11 to be south of Madagascar at 37 S, 48 E. "She is believed to be carrying 150 tons of cargo including 80 tons of rubber. Any one of five east-bound U-boats might possibly cross her track in the Capetown area within the next two weeks." COMINCH took note of the warning by the Japanese naval attaché in Berlin about enemy action in the Central Atlantic, and identified the aircraft carrier as the *Croatan,* a *Bogue*-class CVE, which was conducting operations northwest of the Cape Verde Islands with five destroyer escorts.

The *Bogue* at this time was not far from the *Croatan* group, having set out on May 4 for an area west of the Cape Verdes. On May 13 one of the destroyers, the *Francis M. Robinson,* made sonar contact with a probable target. The *Robinson* attacked with depth charges and a device called a hedgehog, which propelled explosive shells in the direction the destroyer was headed, so they would hit the water before sonar contact was disturbed by engine noise. And while depth charges explode at a certain depth, hedgehog shells detonate on contact. The crew of the *Robinson* recorded a series of five explosions—three depth charges and two hedgehogs—and sonar contact was suddenly broken, a reliable indication of one or more crippling hits. Without a doubt, a submarine had gone down, but her identity was unconfirmed. In his operations report Vosseller recorded an enemy submarine kill, the first of the cruise and the first ever for the *Robinson.*

THE FATE OF SATSUKI II

A brief message from Satsuki II dated May 11 was forwarded by the Bureau of Military Affairs in Tokyo to the captains of Matsu and Momi. "On the 6th we passed through point 30 degrees north and 37 degrees west. . . . The vicinity was strictly patrolled, and although we received depth charges for three days, we suffered no damage." Satsuki II was not heard from again, though her status on May 11 was revealed in a relatively detailed comment by U.S. Fleet

Intelligence (GI-A). "Satsuki (#2) is the *RO-501*, an ex-German sub now en route to the Far East. The position given in the message . . . was an alternative refueling position, not definitely located but probably about 15N-33W . . . Matsu is the Japanese *I-29*, also en route to Far East, but behind *RO-501*. Momi is believed to be the *I-52*, outbound for Europe from Singapore, probably in the Indian Ocean."

Commander Uno on the *I-52* was hardly heard from in May and early June, but his ship and her mission were referred to often on Berlin-Tokyo radio, which caught the attention of Allied intelligence monitors. On June 1 the naval attaché in Berlin requested a list of personnel and cargo, and the Navy Department complied with the names of officers and civilian passengers and a breakdown of the cargo, including two tons of gold. In so doing, Japanese officials were forthcoming to a fault. "The gold being sent by Momi on her present voyage is for the replenishing of the gold fund special account," read a message on June 10 from the Ministry of Finance to a financial officer at the Japanese embassy in Berlin. The ministry also provided details about the gold: total weight, purity, fineness, and inherent value. GI-A commented: "Momi is the *I-52*, en route Europe from the Far East," and a pertinent remark appeared in a June 22 U/Boat Intelligence Summary from COMINCH: "Besides a number of Jap technical experts *I-52* is carrying two tons of gold; 228 tons of tin, molybdenum, and tungsten; 54 tons of rubber; three tons of quinine and opium."

It was at this point that the new attaché in Berlin, Admiral Kojima, sought to engage in a scheme—with the cooperation of German naval operations, whose idea it was originally—intended to divert Allied forces from the trail of Japanese submarines in the Atlantic, the *I-52* specifically. Kojima outlined the deception in a dispatch on June 5 to the navy minister and the chief of the Naval General Staff, the objective being "to give the enemy as well as our own people the impression that the Japanese submarines have already departed European waters." (The enemy was tuned in, as usual, and Kojima's scheme was compromised.) On June 15 it would be announced in Tokyo and Berlin that Imperial Navy ships had sailed to a German base, having completed Atlantic operations. (GI merely took note, then reported what it knew to be the *I-52*'s status. "The Momi is out in the Atlantic en route to Northern France where she should arrive about mid-July.")

The Japanese assertion that the *I-52* had abandoned Atlantic operations was contradicted by Kojima himself when he sent a detailed message to navy headquarters in Tokyo on June 22: "The German Navy has recently taken under consideration plans for loading the Momi, and we would like to have you open the negotiations . . . and send us instructions." He attached a "proposed order of loading," which had been submitted to the German navy and contained the esoteric elements of modern warfare, such as: vacuum tubes, luminous paint, electrical fuses for aerial machine guns, hemoglobin, balsam, spark plugs and electric generators, steel balls, lithium chloride, Wurzburg type electric transformer, Bosch jet nozzle and pipe for use in motors, B-2 type speedometer, industrial micromeasuring instrument. A GI comment was inserted at a later date: "*I-52* believed sunk 24 June en route Europe."

Radio traffic between Berlin and Tokyo involved a number of sources, not all of them traditionally official, as in the case of an

SRDJ, or diplomatic, file placed at the disposal of the Yokohama Specie Bank (Y.S.B.), an official financial institution of the government of Japan. These dispatches were usually attributed to a temporary employee named Yamamoto, though often they were the work of Kojiro Kitamura, the manager of the bank's Berlin branch, who used the radio to conduct business and to air his opinions about the progress of the war. Y.S.B. had its own code, though it had been broken, and its messages were routinely intercepted by the enemy.

Kitamura was in the habit of sending lengthy confidential messages to a vice president of the bank, Mr. Kashiwagi. On June 5 the subject was an overworked staff and the need for two additional employees—"first-class youngsters in their twenties, . . . mentally and physically sound and of good courage"—to be sent at once. "I would prefer them to come via Russia," Kitamura added, "but if that is out of the question, please do your best with the Navy Department to get them to come with Yamabuki." Kitamura had been informed by Kojima of a full waiting list for submarine voyages, so he asked Kashiwagi to use his influence with the Bureau of Military Affairs. "Please bear in mind that the Navy Department treats this matter as a secret," Kitamura advised, "even to the extent of avoiding telegrams." ("Yamabuki . . . is the flower Kerria Japonica," Allied intelligence added in a thoughtful analysis. "It could be a surname, but is not found in any of the lists of surnames available to this department, including the bank's own list of its employees. It may, like Yanagi, stand for a blockade runner or a commodity to be run.")

NORMANDY, JUNE 6, 1944

"Following is the enemy situation as of 1000, June 6," Kojima reported.

Beginning last night, the enemy carried out a severe bombing attack against the area of Ostend, Dieppe, Calais, and Boulogne, and then also bombed heavily the landing points in the Bay of the Seine. The landing point was the coast from St. Vaast to Deauville, and the main strength appears to be at St. Vaast and Ouistreham (at the mouth of the Orne River). At 0330 forces began landing from ships at Grand Camp, Port en Bessin, Ouistreham, and Cherbourg, and at the same time powerful naval forces shelled Le Havre and St. Vaast. In the attack on Le Havre there were apparently six battleships (or heavy cruisers) and 20 destroyers.

Kojiro Kitamura was also heard from. "Trains to Paris have ceased," he reported to Mr. Kashiwagi on the day after the Allied invasion, but in Berlin the people were relatively calm. Kitamura was mindful of the *I-52*'s secret mission, having participated in the purchase of a German miracle weapon, code-named *Yamabuki*. "If the enemy succeeds in establishing a bridgehead [he probably meant beachhead]," Kitamura reasoned, "*Yamabuki* will have to be conveyed by land." (The *I-52* was to dock at Lorient, on the Atlantic coast of France, and later proceed to Kiel, a German port on the Baltic, to load cargo. Allied control of the French coast would remove this option, making it necessary to transport the cargo overland, from Kiel to Lorient.)

On June 9, 1944, events coincided—the Office of Naval Communications in Tokyo reported that the *I-52* had crossed the equator, and Admiral Kojima informed Commander Uno via Tokyo of the Allied invasion of the European continent. "Anglo-American armies have been landing on the coast of France . . . ," Kojima reported, "and at present both sides are engaged in fierce fighting. Your port of destination is still Lorient, but depending on the situation it may have to be changed to Norway." And once again showing a dangerous disregard of radio security, Kojima briefed Uno on procedures of the rendezvous with a German U-boat, to occur at 2115 hours G.M.T. (9:15 p.m.) on June 22, and he repeated the coordinates of the meeting point: 15 degrees north, 40 degrees west. "Your ship will surface and proceed back and forth along the parallel of latitude with the rendezvous as center and await the German submarine. In case the rendezvous is unsuccessful, you will carry out the above operation at high speed during the first ten minutes of every hour from midnight to dawn on 23 June. The German submarine will be submerged during this time and will pick you up with its hydrophone. . . . If the rendezvous is unsuccessful the first day, it will be attempted in the same manner until dawn of the second day. If it is still unsuccessful, report by radio." While he inadvertently increased her vulnerability, Kojima showed sincere concern for Momi's safety. "Take special precautions against enemy planes," he cautioned. "Always travel submerged during the day. Recently an enemy aircraft carrier appeared in the vicinity in position 15 degrees north, 30 degrees west, and was sunk by two German submarines." (The USS *Block Island,* having relieved the *Bogue* on searches of southern waters, was torpedoed by the *U-549* on May 29, becoming the only U.S. carrier to be lost in the Atlantic in World War II.)

A MESSAGE FROM MOMI

The Office of Naval Communications in Tokyo reported on June 15 of having been contacted recently by Matsu and Momi, but there was concern for Satsuki II, who had not been heard from since May 12. On June 16, having heard directly from the *I-52*, Kojima relayed a message from Uno to Tokyo: "On 11 June we were in position 10 degrees north, 31 degrees west. We have enough fuel left for 12,000 miles at 11 knots and provisions for three months." This terse advisory prompted an interesting comment from GI: "The Momi (*I-52*) departed Singapore early in May for Lorient. Due to Allied landings in France, her destination may be changed to Norway. She is scheduled to rendezvous with a German sub on 22 June at 15 north, 40 west." Kojima sent a message on June 16, via Tokyo, updating the submarine captains on the situation in northern France. "The Allied Army . . . is gaining a foothold in the area of Caen and Bayeux between Cherbourg and Le Havre with strong naval preparations and under an airplane umbrella. The Germans, with a striking force . . . under the command of Field Marshal Rommel, are in the midst of a fierce attack. Losses have been heavy on both sides. Since the defenses of Le Havre and Cherbourg are very strong . . . there is violent fighting. From what can be seen at the present . . . the enemy still have forty to forty-five divisions in England, and taking advantage of the shift in the initiative may open new offenses at other points along the channel. Submarine captains should keep careful watch for two or three weeks."

Task Group 22.2 was taking a break in Casablanca when word came on May 29 of the sinking of the *Block Island*, a *Bogue*-class escort carrier. There had been 951 survivors, and as rescue vessels were arriving at the Moroccan port, Abe Vosseller conferred with a fellow skipper, Francis Hughes of the *Block Island*. The *Bogue* returned to action on June 2, engaged in convoy cover operations until being ordered on June 15 to an area 850 miles west of Cape Verde, where enemy submarine activity had been detected by huff-duff

surveillance. Furthermore, Fleet Intelligence had learned from Ultra intercepts of enemy radio transmissions—notably the one
from Kojima to Momi on June 9—indicating that two submarines,
one German and one Japanese, were scheduled to rendezvous. Details of the meeting were contained in a U/Boat Intelligence Summary dated June 22: "*I-52*, 2,500-ton Jap sub en route to Lorient,
will R/V the outbound German *U-530* 22 June about 900 miles
west of the Cape Verde Islands (15N, 40W). A German liaison officer and latest German search gear, with operators, will be transferred. *I-52* will then cruise west of the Azores to France via the
Spanish coast (or alternatively to Bergen)." The German navy had
been acutely aware of Allied advances in radar technology since
the sinking in December 1943 of the battleship *Scharnhorst*, which
had been tracked by British warships from a distance of twenty-
three miles. Of more immediate relevance was the recent success of
British and American carrier-based aircraft employing centimeter-
wave radar with an operative range of sixty miles against surfaced
submarines. German U-boat crews, having experienced attacks
lasting a week or more, were painfully aware of the risk of lingering on the surface for a prolonged period. The *U-530*, a late-model
boat of the IX C-40 class equipped with a snorkel, had sailed from
Lorient on May 22 on a routine mission as a menace to Allied
cargo vessels. On the way out she would keep an appointment with
a Japanese submarine whose code name was Momi—or in German, Tanne. Lieutenant Commander Kurt Lange, the veteran captain of the *U-530*, understood that the success of the I-boat's
mission depended on this meeting, for without a radar search receiver and a German officer at the helm, she would have little
chance of making it safely through the blockaded Bay of Biscay.
(The German navy had used a search receiver called Metox until
discovering that its radiation field was attracting enemy ships and

planes, so in the fall of 1943 Metox was replaced by an adaptation of the receiver used by the Luftwaffe, called Naxos.) Lange intended to make quick work of the rendezvous and transfer, realizing that the longer they lingered on the surface, the greater the risk of attracting the attention of the U.S. Navy. He was also planning on the advantage of a moonless night, though he knew that American ASW forces were equipped with devices that turned night into day.

A CLASSIC AMBUSH

As the *U-530* approached the rendezvous point on the evening of June 23, her crew stayed perfectly still, straining to hear a cadenced tapping on pipes. When this prearranged signal came from the expected direction of 280 degrees at 2120 Greenwich, the U-boat surfaced and sighted the *I-52* waiting nearby. The two submarines pulled abreast of each other, lines were secured, and men and equipment were transferred by rubber raft. The exchange was completed by 2340, with but one minor incident when a box of electronic replacement parts went overboard and was retrieved by an alert Japanese seaman who dove in after it. He was back on board, dripping wet, when at minutes after midnight an alarm sounded—the searchlight of an aircraft was fast approaching from the northeast. The seasoned German crew was prepared for an emergency, and the *U-530* dove immediately, then circled in hopes of hearing that the *I-52* had also escaped. "We had the advantage of experienced people coming together, which made it possible to submerge the ship at a faster pace," said Werner Hess, a *U-530* radio engineer, in a 1996 interview with National Geographic Television. "We were able to submerge in less than thirty seconds." The Japanese crew had wasted precious time manning antiaircraft guns to no avail, though the *I-52* appeared to have made a getaway dive when Kapitaenleutnant Schaeffer, the German officer who had gone aboard, radioed Lange that they had been under attack but were faring well. Lange then set a course for the Caribbean to prey on merchant shipping. Three days later, June 27, Lange notified submarine headquarters in Berlin that the Momi had safely completed the rendezvous, and Schaeffer and two technicians had been received on board. "All hands on the Momi were in good health," Lange reported.

AVENGERS ON THE ATTACK

Lieutenant Commander Jesse Taylor, the commanding officer of squadron VC-69, was at the controls of a TBM 20 Grumman Avenger on takeoff from the *Bogue* at 2203 hours (10:03 p.m., G.M.T.) on June 23. He set a prescribed heading of 180 degrees, due south, intending to fly seventy-five-mile legs, back and forth, slicing the southwest quadrant into pieces of pie. It was a routine ASW patrol for Taylor, a twenty-six-year-old Missourian whose squadron had yet to sink a U-boat, but at ninety-six minutes into the mission, "routine" was no longer the operative word. At an altitude of fifteen hundred feet on a heading of 220 degrees, radar operator Ed Whitlock reported a blip at ten miles to the east. Taylor immediately turned and flew in the direction of the radar target, and when within a mile of it he dropped a pair of parachute smoke lights and a sonobuoy search device color-coded purple for identification. As soon as it hit the water, the sonobuoy began to transmit the steady beat of a ship's propeller. At a half mile from the target, having slowed his speed from 145 to 125 knots, Taylor ordered gunner Andy Emmons to release a flare. It lit up the sky, and a very large submarine came into view—surfaced and headed west at ten to twelve knots, according to the wake she was churning. Taylor altered course to 275 degrees, and after turning to starboard passed directly over the submarine as she turned north in an evasive maneuver. She was diving, but Taylor could see enough of her marking to make a tentative identification of an enemy warship— most likely Japanese, from her leviathan dimensions. Taylor wheeled as he descended to three hundred feet, then accelerated to 175 knots as he approached head-on. The submarine was nearly submerged, but Taylor could see her stern and conning tower protruding above the surface. When directly overhead, he dropped two hydrostatic depth charges set at twenty-five feet, and looked back to see them detonate—one "close aboard" and one "about 75 feet abeam," as he would note in his action report.

At a thousand feet beyond the target, Taylor deployed a second sonobuoy, color-coded orange, and it also transmitted a propeller beat. He then did a tight turn to starboard, placing his aircraft on the submarine's track, which was where he needed to be to launch a Mark 24 torpedo, nicknamed Fido for its dependability. The top secret Mark 24 was the U.S. Navy's first fully acoustic target-seeking torpedo. It was controlled by hydrophones that translated noise into signals, activating steering mechanisms—rudders and elevators— which guided it to the source of the noise. A compact weapon only seven feet long and nineteen inches in diameter, the Mark 24 carried a powerful 124-pound explosive charge at a speed of twelve knots, meaning it could outrun most submerged submarines.

Shortly before midnight (2347 hours) Taylor prepared to launch a Mark 24, but he failed in his first attempt, forgetting to reset a selector switch. He quickly circled and approached again along a track marked by the submarine's wake. In order to make a precision drop, he reduced speed to 120 knots, then descended to 250 feet and let her go. The area was still illuminated by the flare

Emmons had released and a smoke light attached to the torpedo, so Taylor could see it hit the water 550 feet ahead of the target.

A propeller beat remained audible over the orange sonobuoy for three minutes, and then a loud explosion was followed by what Taylor would later describe as "the sound of a tin can being crushed." The propeller sounds seemed to cease after the explosion, but Taylor took the precaution of laying a full pattern of six sonobuoys. Three of them functioned—the orange, the yellow, and the purple—but all that could be heard by Taylor and his crew was splashing water and microphone noise. Heading back to the *Bogue*, Taylor called Whitlock on the intercom while pointing to an audio recorder: "Put that wire in your pocket and guard it with your life."

At twenty-eight minutes into the morning of June 24, 1944, an Avenger piloted by Lieutenant JG William Gordon took off from the *Bogue* to relieve Taylor on ASW patrol. Gordon, known in the squadron as Flash, after the comic strip figure, had been asked by Vosseller to test a state-of-the-art weapons system in combat conditions, and for that purpose he had made room in the cockpit for Price Fish, a civilian technician with the Underwater Sound Laboratory in New London, Connecticut. At 0100, as they approached the scene of Taylor's encounter with a presumed Japanese submarine, Fish reported that he was receiving faint but distinct propeller noises from the orange and yellow sonobuoys deployed by Taylor. Gordon reported this to Taylor, who replied he was not now hearing any sonobuoy transmissions of submarine noise. Taylor further informed Gordon that the sonobuoys had been laid on a 270-degree course, and at 0115 he departed for the *Bogue*. Gordon continued to circle the area, as did another Avenger, piloted by

Lieutenant Art Hirsbrunner, who reported hearing submarine noise over the orange and yellow sonobuoys. Gordon later described the noise as loud enough to be identified as propeller beats. Fish, an expert in marine acoustics, was able to tell from the high-pitched and irregular characteristics of the beats that the submarine was well below periscope depth. When three additional sonobuoys produced no new information, Gordon decided to place a Mark 24 between the orange and yellow sonobuoys. He fired the torpedo at 0154 from an altitude of 350 feet as reception was beginning to fade, but the beats became loud and clear when Gordon climbed to two thousand feet—from the yellow sonobuoy especially.

At 0212, eighteen minutes after launching, an explosion lasting a minute or so was transmitted by the yellow sonobuoy and recorded by Fish, as were the memorable words of Gordon: "We got the son of a bitch." For another two minutes or so propeller beats could still be heard over the yellow sonobuoy—then silence.

VOSSELLER'S JUDGMENT CALL

Destroyer escorts sent at daybreak to inspect the area of attack discovered a massive oil slick, and one of the DEs, the *Haverfield*, reported on the sort of debris that had been retrieved: several bales of crude rubber, fragments of silk, lumber thought to be Philippine mahogany, a rubber sandal with Japanese lettering, and human flesh. It was convincing evidence of the sinking of a submarine, in all likelihood Japanese, but for most of the men of Task Group 22.2 her identity would remain a mystery for years to come. Intelligence on the imminent rendezvous of the *I-52* and the *U-530* was something Captain Vosseller shared with only a few of his officers, the reason being that brand-new and highly classified navy weapons were put to the test in the engagement. As Vosseller expressed it in his report, dated July 3, 1944, "Report of Anti-Submarine Action by Aircraft": "This series of attacks is believed to be unique in that it represents the first successful use of sonobuoys, the Mark 24 and sonobuoy recorders in conjunction, and certainly the first such attack at night." Vosseller used the intelligence in preparing the ASW action report to the commander in chief, U.S. Fleet. (That Vosseller would report directly to Admiral King, bypassing Admiral Ingersoll, attested to the importance of this particular action.) "At the time of the attacks it was believed that there were two submarines in the area," he explained, "a Japanese and a German, probably trying to effect a rendezvous. From the evidence available it appears that there were in fact two present, that both were attacked, and hit, with the Mark 24 and that certainly one, the Jap, was sunk." Vosseller then expressed an opinion that would undermine the accuracy of his report. "It does not seem possible that a submerged submarine could survive the explosion of a Mark 24 in contact, and as shown by the sono recordings the propeller noise stopped in both cases after the explosions." Vosseller was forced to admit, however, that "no debris distinctive of a German submarine was recovered."

Vosseller determined initially that the original radar target was the *I-52*, although his best evidence of that was the impression Jesse Taylor gained from a brief sighting that she was "very large and very pointed at bow and stern." Her propeller beat, transmitted by sonobuoy and recorded, was consistent with the rate of a crash-diving submarine, 238 rpm and steady. And it contrasted with the propeller beat recorded by Gordon slightly over an hour later—232 rpm, high-pitched, and irregular. This might have been evidence of a second submarine present, although it also indicated a target—Taylor's target, still in operation—at greater than periscope depth, as the civilian sonar specialist, Price Fish, had

pointed out. Vosseller concluded—incorrectly, it would appear—
that by the time he reached the scene Gordon would not have been
able to pick up the *I-52*'s propeller beat because she had been sunk
by Taylor, and he proceeded with a reconstruction based on circumstantial directional evidence. The Japanese submarine was
very near the orange sonobuoy on a 95-degree heading—a little
south of due east—and submerging when she was attacked by Taylor. There was no sonobuoy information that she reversed course,
assuming that if she had she would have been heard by the yellow
sonobuoy, which was positioned to the west and slightly north of
the orange. When Gordon later listened to propeller beats, they
were equally loud on yellow and orange, but then became louder
on yellow, whereupon Gordon launched a Mark 24 from a position closest to that of the loud-sounding yellow sonobuoy.

> From the actual location of the buoys [Vosseller observed],
> it therefore appears that the second submarine was either
> north or south of the sonobuoy pattern when first picked
> up, and steered a course to bring it toward both yellow and
> orange but closer to yellow. This supports the supposition
> that the two submarines had made or were about to make
> contact at a rendezvous. One was sighted and attacked while
> the other dived and remained out of the way until the sounds
> of explosions, propeller noises, etc., had subsided, where-
> upon he took up a course for the last known location of the
> other sub. This was probably considered quite safe since the
> Task Group was still approximately 45 miles away, and its
> screw noises were inaudible at that distance. It is believed
> that the enemy is ignorant of our use of sonobuoys and
> therefore this submarine commander felt quite safe from
> aircraft while submerged. However the sonobuoys picked

him up as he approached the pattern and Lt. Gordon dropped a Mark 24 which undoubtedly hit and exploded.

It was a noble effort by Vosseller, but he was wrong to suppose that two submarines had remained on the scene. He might not have known immediately that the *U-530* had slipped quietly away; but Lange's report on June 27, based on a belief that the *I-52* had survived, was the subject of an intercepted message from the attaché in Berlin, Admiral Kojima, to Tokyo. GI's comment was that the *I-52* and the *U-530* were to make the rendezvous on June 22— a day earlier than when it actually occurred—at 15 degrees north, 40 degrees west, though there was no mention of the American attack. (The *U-530* returned from patrol in October, and when Germany surrendered in May 1945, she was on patrol off the coast of New York. Ordered by submarine headquarters in Berlin to return to port or surrender, her new captain decided instead to flee to Buenos Aires, where he and his crew were arrested amid reports in the Argentine press that Hitler and his mistress, Eva Braun, had been passengers on the *U-530*.)

When it could not be determined with certainty who deserved credit for sinking the *I-52*, the Distinguished Flying Cross was awarded to both Taylor and Gordon. Nevertheless, the wording of Gordon's commendation seemed to resolve the matter. "Skillfully tracking a hostile U-boat badly damaged in a previous operation, Lieutenant Gordon maneuvered into position and made an extremely accurate depth-bomb attack which resulted in the complete destruction of the enemy submarine."

4. WAITING FOR MOMI FOREVER

On August 28, 1945, two weeks after the war ended, an American naval intelligence officer, Jasper Holmes, asked a favor of a friend from their days at Annapolis, Bill Sebald. Holmes had been a line officer, but an ailing back ended his career in submarines, and on December 7, 1941, he was Lieutenant Commander Joseph Rochefort's deputy at Station Hypo in Hawaii. Sebald, who had served in Japan in the 1920s, left the navy to practice law, but he returned when war was declared, soon to become head of a special intelligence unit, F-22, reporting directly to the commander in chief of the U.S. Fleet, Admiral King. Sebald was an authority on Japanese naval hierarchy, and Holmes—he was still in Hawaii but now serving with JICPOA (Joint Intelligence Center Pacific Ocean Area)—was seeking an expert opinion on top-level Japanese naval officers and how they ought to be rated in regard to responsibility for the Pearl Harbor attack. As Holmes put it in a top secret communication to Sebald: "In reference to special list of

Japanese naval personnel . . . would appreciate your opinions as to what top men . . . were driving force in decision to make war." Sebald in his reply described Admiral Isoroku Yamamoto, the commander in chief of the Combined Fleet in 1941, as the most influential naval leader as Japan prepared for war, and his second choice was Admiral Osami Nagano, the chief of the Naval General Staff. Neither Yamamoto nor Nagano came as a surprise to Holmes, but that was not so with Sebald's number-three pick, Vice Admiral Katsuo Abe. Sebald's explanation was brief but definite: "Nagano believed primarily concerned preparations for fleet whereas Abe looked after political side of affairs." What was generally known about Abe at the time was contained in a brief biographical summary: naval attaché in Italy, representative to the Tripartite Military Commission, chief naval attaché in Europe. Left out of the official version was the Bureau of Naval Intelligence, which Abe ran as the ranking officer of Joho Kyoku in Europe.

Abe was a former warship commander (the cruiser *Tama* and a light aircraft carrier, the *Ryujo*). As naval attaché in Rome from 1941 to 1943, a largely diplomatic posting, he was a familiar figure in the capitals of certain countries—Axis Bulgaria, neutral Turkey, and occupied France—often as an attendant to Admiral Naokuni Nomura, his immediate superior. When Nomura was recalled to Japan in 1943, Abe replaced him as the naval attaché in Berlin and was officially declared the senior Japanese naval officer in Europe. He was his government's representative on the Tripartite Military Commission, a position of little influence by 1943, with Italy out of the war. When Abe was succeeded in March 1944 by Admiral Kojima as the attaché in Berlin, he was still recognized as the senior Japanese naval attaché in Europe, though it appeared to be an honorary title. (Kojima once remarked that as a member of the Tripartite Military Commission, Abe had little to do but play bridge.) It would turn out that his reduced stature was contrived to conceal Abe's intelligence role, while a probing analysis of what he was actually doing—specifically in meetings with the German high command on significant strategy matters—more accurately reveals the admiral's actual influence. Reading the radio traffic, it is difficult not to be impressed by Abe's influence with the commanders of Germany's army, navy, and air force, Alfred Jodl, Karl Doenitz, and Günter Korten, and their immediate subordinates. Abe met with these men on matters equal to their level of authority, as when he was briefed by Admiral Doenitz on May 24, 1944, on a new-model submarine whose huge batteries propelled it at better than double the speed of operational submarines in any navy at the time. "They are designed for almost exclusively underwater operation," Abe reported. "The battery capacity is about three times as great as before, which makes the underwater speed and cruising range correspondingly greater. They use ventilators and charge the batteries while submerged. There are two types, large and small. The large type . . . has six torpedo tubes, carries 14 reserve torpedoes and mounts four three-centimeter machine guns. It has a surface speed of 18 knots and an underwater speed of 15.6 knots. The surface cruising ranges are 15,500 miles (at 10 knots) and 28,000 miles (at six knots)." Abe was optimistic, perhaps overly so, in his prediction that enemy countermeasures would be ineffective against the sleek new boats. The German navy had determined in experiments that they were not susceptible to a radar fix, and the ability to escape depth charge attacks would be immensely improved by the increased underwater speed "and the safe navigable depth which can be increased to 135 meters." (A number of 1,600-ton Type XXI "electro boats" and the smaller version, a 250-ton Type XXIII, were delivered by the end of 1944, but none was combat ready before Germany surrendered in May 1945.)

When Abe asked if Japan might obtain blueprints of the new boats, Doenitz assented. "We must wait a while . . . ," Abe said in his report to Tokyo, "because the experiments are as yet unfinished." He then let Doenitz speak for himself: "The German Navy intends to give everything to the Japanese Navy, but it would only add to the confusion if we gave you things still in the experimental stage." (The plans were shared, and the first of a new Japanese type, the *I-201,* was launched in early 1945. It was one of six such ships that could do an amazing nineteen knots submerged, but none of them was operational by the war's end.)

Abe ended his report to Tokyo of May 26 with a comment on cooperation, one navy to another, as it tended to be shown more carefully and consistently as the war situation grew more serious for Germany and Japan. As if to endorse Abe's assessment, Doenitz summoned him and Kojima on May 28 to his headquarters at Cologne. On the anniversary of the inception of the Japanese navy, Doenitz announced, it was his intention to make available to the Japanese navy the most recent and most secret weapons of the German navy. He had in mind on this occasion the essential elements of an acoustic torpedo, the T-5, and he invited Abe and Kojima to a test of the weapon at a secret location on the Baltic Sea.

FIRST-STRIKE ADVOCATE

Abe tended to minimize the bad news in advisories to Tokyo, but in May 1944 he could not conceal an anxiety over reports from both sides of the world. In Europe, as the Russians advanced from the east, the Germans were anticipating an imminent Allied invasion on the coast of France. In the Pacific, meanwhile, Japanese-held islands were falling one by one. So Abe could be grateful for a ray of sunshine in the briefing by Admiral Doenitz on a new generation of attack submarines. In addition to much greater speed, the operational range of the Type XXI U-boat was three times that of the *I-52,* and when equipped with a snorkel it could hide from enemy radar for periods measured in days rather than hours. Abe was a visionary and no less an advocate of undersea warfare for having served on surface vessels. So within a year, as Germany faced defeat, he would be making a persuasive case for transferring German naval operations, submarines in particular, to East Asia. The gist of his argument was that if it appeared the war in Europe could not be won, submarines would become a weapon of last resort in an ultimate defense of the Japanese homeland. Submarines might also be used, Abe contended, in the delivery of a new type of weapon whose explosive force would be measured in thousands of tons of TNT. Abe was of course aware that the enemy was also proceeding with atomic bomb development, and in a report to Tokyo on July 24, 1944, he left little doubt that he was advocating a first-strike strategy against the United States. "The conviction is deepening that America is the principal enemy of Germany and Japan from the standpoint of being an arsenal for war materiel," Abe wrote. "A heavy blow at this time inflicted on America from both the east and the west would shake her foundations. . . . I feel that before enemy air raids on the empire become intense, we must inflict a severe blow on America. . . ."

Abe, like Ambassador Oshima, was an unwitting source of Allied intelligence. The naval attaché code, labeled Coral by U.S. Navy Op-20-G code breakers, was a machine code whose basic features were learned when Purple was broken in 1940 by the Signal Intelligence Service. (At the end of the war, Op-20-G files contained some fifty-three hundred dispatches from the Japanese admiral identified in Washington as "Honest Abe.")

* * *

Kojima sent a high-priority report dated June 20—Action: Navy Minister: "The German forces began to use their reprisal weapon at dawn on 11 June. According to reports they made a few trial shots on 12 June, and from the fifteenth on they fired about 300 daily. . . ." This was the V-1, the first of the rockets that would deliver deadly payloads to targets in Great Britain. "The reprisal forces are under fairly direct control," Kojima explained, "and they are surrounded by the utmost secrecy. . . . They fire missiles weighing at least two tons (including the weight of the explosive) from the French coast to points about 150 kilometers distant from London. Outwardly they resemble small fighter planes and have a speed of about 600 kilometers per hour. Depending on the range, they are adjusted for wind direction, wind velocity, air temperature, air pressure and the rotation of the earth. . . . It is discharged, simply, and at the trajectory apex, which is a fixed point about eight kilometers in altitude, the propellant charge is exhausted, after which it glides toward the target. Its accuracy is generally effective over an area one kilometer square, and it is considered very effective in destroying factories crowded into large cities. . . ."

On June 20, Kojima alerted the captains of Momi, Matsu, and Satsuki II to the German rocket assault, as he monitored war developments and advised the submarines accordingly. "Since 15 June," Kojima advised, "the German Army has begun attacking London and southeast England with a new weapon . . . a sort of rocket bomb with wings. It has had a great psychological and physical effect on the enemy." As for the Allied invasion of Normandy by twenty-five to thirty enemy divisions, Kojima reported that the Cherbourg peninsula had been cut off, and the German army had completed preparations for the destruction of Cherbourg harbor. "In the Caen area the German Army is resisting strongly and inflicting heavy losses on the enemy. In the St. Lo area, it has retreated little by little."

In addition to the action in Poland and France, Abe was observing a third European front, in Italy, where in June 1944 the American Fifth Army had driven north to the Arno River, between Florence and Pisa. When Abe became the attaché in Berlin he was succeeded in Rome by his deputy, Tooyoo Mitsunobu, at the time of the Italian collapse. In July 1943 Mussolini was overthrown, and the new premier, Pietro Badoglio, signed an armistice with the Allies. An outraged Hitler had Mussolini "rescued" by German commandos and installed as the puppet leader of a Nazi regime in northern Italy, centered in Milan.

On June 8, 1944, Captain Mitsunobu was traveling by automobile from Milan to German naval headquarters at Montecatini, and as the convoy passed through the Apennine Mountains, it was attacked by guerrillas loyal to Badoglio. "Mitsunobu suffered a bullet wound to the head," said a Japanese aide, "so serious an injury that there was no hope for him." Abe attended the funeral, having declared in a note to Tokyo that Mitsunobu had died heroically on the European battlefield.

When he returned from Milan, Abe notified Tokyo that he would leave Berlin on June 29 for a conference at Wolfsschanze (Wolf's Lair), the headquarters Hitler had established 350 miles east of Berlin (in a part of Poland reclaimed by Germany as East Prussia in 1939 and chosen by Hitler—when Germany invaded Russia in 1941—as the site of his underground redoubt). Hitler wished his field headquarters to be near the eastern front, but in

1944 he would be forced by the Russian offensive to evacuate quickly.

Wolfsschanze was located near the city of Rastenburg, a two-day drive from Berlin, and Abe would be traveling with Admiral Kojima and the army attaché in Berlin, Lieutenant General Mitsuhiko Komatsu. Abe enjoyed their company, and he welcomed an opportunity to collect his thoughts, as he anticipated merciless questioning by the Nazis about the war in the Pacific. He had requested an updating from the Bureau of Military Affairs in Tokyo, "especially the situation in the Marianas," for to be unprepared or to sound even slightly defensive would be beneath his dignity and not in keeping with his devotion to the emperor. But explaining Japanese misfortune since the Midway debacle two years earlier posed a problem for Abe. There had been notable victories—in August 1942 at Savo Island in the Solomons, costing the enemy four cruisers and a destroyer—but in the six-month battle for Guadalcanal the Americans had prevailed decisively. Whether the news was good or bad, Abe quite naturally tended to personalize the action, to accentuate the exquisite performance of Imperial Navy colleagues. It eased Abe's mind to remember battles won, and to dwell upon the exploits of contemporary heroes. Raizo Tanaka was one of them.

A WARTIME RETROSPECTIVE

A naval academy contemporary of Abe's, Rear Admiral Tanaka ran destroyers down the Solomons "slot" carrying reinforcements and supplies to a stranded island garrison. He had therefore gained the grudging respect of American marines, who called him "Tenacious Tanaka of the Tokyo Express." Tanaka commanded DesRon 2, a squadron of eight destroyers, six of which had been stripped of armament to make room for cargo. On the night of November 30, 1942, as his crews were preparing to deliver rations and medicines sealed in steel drums—they were to be dumped into the sea and towed ashore by small boats—Tanaka was forced to abort the delivery and fight off an enemy attack. In a brief but furious battle, an American cruiser was sunk, three others were put out of action, while just one Japanese vessel, a destroyer, was lost. But when Tanaka returned to Shortland Island and reported to the Eighth Fleet commander in chief, he was criticized for failing to carry out the supply mission. Tanaka made matters worse by declaring that the situation was hopeless and calling for the evacuation of Guadalcanal. He would be proven right, but as preparations were made to remove remnants of the Guadalcanal garrison, he was relieved of command and transferred to a staff position in Tokyo. At the end of the war Tanaka was in disgrace in spite of—or because of—the praise he received from the American commander, Admiral Nimitz. Naval historian Samuel Eliot Morison had this to say: "It is always some consolation to reflect that the enemy who defeats you is really good, and Rear Admiral Tanaka was better than that—he was superb."

As a graduate of Etajima, class of 1912, Abe had served as an officer of the Imperial Navy for going on thirty years when war with the United States was precipitated by the Pearl Harbor attack. So he was by virtue of tradition one of a chosen few who stood a step from the pinnacle—flag officers of great stature and responsibility, having reached this point in their careers by commanding flotillas and divisions, or by serving on four-star staffs. As in the model navies of Great Britain and the United States, there was a barrier at the rank of rear admiral, the result of a winnowing of lesser lights to make way for the best, which inevitably produced a leadership elite. The class of 1912 was no exception, and the names of its rear admirals appeared on the 1940 promotion list in the order of seniority. Abe was there, bracketed by two wartime immortals, Tamon Yamaguchi and Matome Ugaki.

Yamaguchi, the commanding officer of the Second Carrier Division, First Air Fleet, died heroically at Midway on June 5, 1942, aboard his flagship, the aircraft carrier *Hiryu*. It was told in eulogies how he ordered his crew to board a rescue vessel and then led them in a rousing three cheers for the emperor. "I shall remain on board to the end," he announced, and he and Tomeo Kaku, *Hiryu*'s captain, went to their deaths, gloriously, although the *Hiryu* did not sink but was found drifting and on fire. "Nothing could be compared with his supreme spirit, laying down his own life for his responsibility," Admiral Ugaki wrote in the diary he kept religiously throughout the war. Ugaki was the Combined Fleet chief of staff, Admiral Yamamoto's closest aide and confidant. It was Ugaki who issued the historic signal, "Climb Mt. Niitaka 1208," authorizing the Imperial Navy to take up arms on December 8, 1941 (December 7 in the United States). He had become chief of staff in August 1941, trading his position as Naval General Staff chief of operations with Shigeru Fukudome, also an Etajima classmate.

Yet another member of the class of 1912, Yukichi Yashiro, would lead the way to the rank of vice admiral, promoted posthumously when he became the first Japanese flag officer to be killed in action in World War II. Yashiro died when his Marshall Islands Defense Force on Kwajalein was caught off guard on February 1, 1942, by bombers from the USS *Enterprise*.

The Japanese were desperate in the spring of 1943, following the drawn-out defeat at Guadalcanal, and Yamamoto was determined to destroy enemy air and sea forces across a vast area, from the Solomon Islands to New Guinea. He directed the campaign from Rabaul, on New Britain Island, and before returning to Combined Fleet headquarters at Truk in mid-April, he decided to visit battle-weary troops on Balale Island, south of Bougainville. The itinerary of the detour was radioed in a JN25 version that had been in effect only since April 1, but U.S. Pacific Fleet Station Hypo in Hawaii had managed to decipher the message, and an ambush of Ya-mamoto's aircraft was ordered by Admiral Nimitz with the ap-proval of the Navy Department in Washington. On the morning of April 18, dressed for comfort in a green fatigue uniform, Ya-mamoto boarded a Mitsubishi "Betty" bomber for a two-hour flight to Balale, and an identical aircraft carrying Ugaki and other staff officers followed behind. Minutes from their destination they were under attack by a squadron of American P-38s, and Ugaki watched in horror as Yamamoto's aircraft, trailing smoke and flame, crashed in the jungle. Seriously injured when his own air-craft went down in the sea, Ugaki was rescued along with the pilot and another passenger by soldiers of the Balale base force, who also recovered Yamamoto's body.

The new Combined Fleet commander in chief, having been hand-picked by Yamamoto, was Mineichi Koga, a former vice chief of the Naval General Staff, and Shigeru Fukudome, Ugaki's good friend from Etajima days, was named chief of staff. But a year later, in an all-too-familiar incident, Koga presumably died when an air-craft taking him to his headquarters at Davao, on the southern coast of Mindanao, went down and was never found. Koga and members of his staff had been aboard his flagship, the battleship *Musashi*, at Palau in the Caroline Islands when he was warned—mistakenly, it turned out—that an approaching U.S. naval force had been sighted. Koga decided to return to his headquarters, and on March 31 Fukudome arranged for Koga and the Combined Fleet staff to leave that night by flying boat for Davao. But in what would be their final meeting Fukudome became concerned about Koga's frame of mind—specifically his preoccupation with a glorious death and how he seemed to envy Yamamoto for having died in a proper way at the right time. Still, Fukudome was not prepared for a remark by Koga as they waited to board separate aircraft for the trip to Davao: "Let us go out and die together," he said.

Koga got his wish, as the aircraft vanished without a trace. Fukudome meanwhile was one of nine survivors aboard the second aircraft, which was forced by heavy winds and a dwindling fuel supply to crash-land off the Philippine Island of Cebu.

MARIANAS, A COSTLY LOSS

On the journey to Wolfsschanze in late June, Abe knew only that a land and sea battle for the strategically vital Mariana Islands— Saipan, Tinian, Rota, and Guam—was in its third week, and the news was not encouraging. An enemy bombing of the islands on June 12 was seen by the new Combined Fleet commander in chief, Soemu Toyoda, as an attempt to lure his forces away from the Philippines so MacArthur could occupy Mindanao. Abe did not agree that the Marianas attack was a diversion, and reports from Saipan and Tinian of battleship bombardments, followed on June 15 by a landing of 125,000 American marines on Saipan, indicated a full-scale invasion was under way. Admiral Toyoda countered with his "decisive battle" strategy, rationalizing the delay as a means of assuring a full commitment of enemy forces, so they might be destroyed by massive attacks. But the Japanese suffered by far the heavier losses in both the Battle of the Philippine Sea (three Japanese aircraft carriers—*Shokaku, Taiho,* and *Hiyo*— sunk and 480 aircraft shot down) and the defense of the Marianas (eleven of twenty-six submarines lost). Abe was troubled by a report that Rear Admiral Takeo Takagi, the commander in chief of the Sixth (Submarine) Fleet, was stranded at Saipan, having moved his headquarters there from the endangered base at Truk. Then came shocking news of the night of July 6, when some three thousand Japanese, Admiral Takagi among them, died in a banzai charge, and the ranking Japanese officers on Saipan—Lieutenant General Yoshitsugu Saito and Vice Admiral Chuichi Nagumo— had taken their own lives.

June 1944 would be remembered as the worst month of the war for Japanese submarines, and the toll for the year would come to fifty-eight, which was greater than the number of subs lost by Japan in the two preceding years combined. Such statistics were indicative of a trend that applied in a report by Kojima dated June 21, 1944, on transport to Japan by various German vessels. At the beginning of the year five surface ships were loaded and ready to depart, but while awaiting orders in the vicinity of Bordeaux they were attacked by enemy torpedo bombers, and one was sunk. "After this it was decided to suspend all the sailings of the remaining four," Kojima wrote, "and they are now discharging their cargo at Bordeaux." Akira submarines—U-boats formerly belonging to the Italian navy—had fared no better: two had been loaded at Bordeaux, and one had sailed for Japan, only to be sunk. A plan to build submarines designed specifically for transport had been canceled by the German navy, so the only offer Kojima was able to obtain was for space aboard operational U-boats that would accommodate about one hundred tons of a certain type of cargo—mercury, steel balls, lead, optical glass—to be carried in the keel and in tanks fitted to the sub's exterior. "It is also intended that important commodities should be carried whenever there is any room inboard," Kojima explained. "However the storage capacity inboard is likely to be very limited, and I do not believe that it will amount to more than two or three tons."

Kojima and Abe inspected the German Navy and Air Torpedo Experimental Station in Gothenhaven (Gydnia to the Poles), and Kojima filed a report on July 5. Clearly a reason for the visit was concern for Japanese submarines at sea, whose protection prompted an urgent need to stay abreast of antisubmarine warfare developments. A briefing on the Zaunkoenig T-5—the German counterpart of the American Mark 24, designed to zero in on propeller sounds—was followed by a demonstration. The T-5 was a showpiece weapon, the subject of a briefing by Doenitz a month earlier, at which time he announced that he intended "to make available to the Japanese Navy the most recent and the most secret weapons of the German Navy." Doenitz explained that "such things as density, specific gravity, water temperature, and the circumstances of the sound's origin . . . have a tremendous effect on the acoustic efficiency, so I can't give accurate figures, but I am certain that this acoustic device will considerably increase the percentage of hits."

Kojima reported on the performance of the T-5 in the demonstration at Gothenhaven: "Six successive shots were all hits. It is to be noted that, generally, even if it misses the ship once, it will turn around and continue to follow the sound of the propellers. The torpedo has two sound detectors in the warhead, with which it picks up the sound of enemy propellers and follows in the direction from which it receives the sound-impulses most strongly."

Kojima and Abe were so impressed with the T-5 that they made a purchase on the spot. "We obtained the torpedo and plans," said Kojima, "and are making arrangements for their delivery in the next mail."

With three *Yamabuki* submarines strung across the globe, each in danger of attack at any given minute, Abe was understandably worried. He may not have dwelled on statistics, but he could not help but be greatly troubled by the loss of life that the numbers implied. He was the shepherd, and the submarines were his flock—two I-class fleet boats and a converted German U-boat, all navigating a vast expanse of three oceans: Momi (*I-52*), Satsuki II (*RO-501*), and Matsu (*I-29*). They were heroic boats with heroic crews on heroic missions, though Abe was also concerned about less-heroic losses—the *I-33*, for example. (The *I-33* was sunk twice by accident—at Truk in October 1942, and after being salvaged and towed to Kure for repairs, she went down on June 13, 1944, during a training cruise in Japan's Inland Sea.) Actually, it was just one of the liaison boats, the *I-52*, that now consumed Abe's full-time attention. Matsu and Satsuki II were headed for Asia, hopefully, and out of Abe's control, but Momi was due to land at Lorient before the end of July, and Abe and Kojima were banking on her to make that landing as if the future of Japan depended on it.

It is safe to say that Abe was fully aware of the great danger the *I-52* faced as she presumably entered the hostile waters of the Bay of Biscay, and of the likelihood that she would be the latest of the liaison boats to be lost at sea. The *I-52* would have been approaching the western coast of France as the Allied invasion progressed, and if German intelligence had penetrated the secrecy shroud of Operation Overlord—in particular the British-American naval element named Neptune—it would have learned of some twelve hundred Allied warships and 350 aircraft on patrol in the area.

THE AGONY OF SILENCE

The *I-52* disappeared from the airwaves in the week following her rendezvous with the *U-530,* though she was still the object of rapt attention day by day in Tokyo and Berlin. On June 28 navy headquarters issued a correction of an item in the cargo manifest due to an encoding mistake: the amount of opium was 2.88 tons, not 288 tons. Also on June 28 Admiral Kojima notified Tokyo of the message from the captain of the *U-530.* "On June 27," Kojima advised, "the Germans had a dispatch to the effect that Momi had safely made her rendezvous with the German submarine, and the liaison officer and others were received on board. All hands on the Momi were in good health." In the absence of direct word from Commander Uno, it was an encouraging message, certainly more than could be said for the *RO-501,* missing since May 11. "It is presumed that your voyage is proceeding smoothly," Kojima said by radio on June 28, addressing Satsuki II, though he knew there was little hope for her. The Naval General Staff in Japan had accepted the reality of Satsuki II's loss and indicated as much on July 1 by issuing a formal request for an answer from Berlin: "Please inform this office of the whereabouts of the Satsuki." Kojima did not have an answer, so he replied by evaluating German navy communications with ships operating in the coastal waters of South Africa and into the Indian Ocean, an area where Satsuki II would be if she had stayed the course. His conclusion was ambiguous—communications were not good, but they did exist, and the Germans were making a special effort to reach the *RO-501*. If they were successful, he added, "We expect them to communicate with us immediately." It was a hopeless situation, but on July 5 Kojima made another try to reach Satsuki II. "We have had no news of your ship since 11 May," he said plaintively. "Please try to communicate by both the Japanese and German communication circuits." On July 10, in a disconsolate advisory to Tokyo, Kojima recalled that in her message on May 11, Satsuki II had reported having been under attack for three days. "It seems that she was located first by D/F and later by radar and then subjected to continuous attacks. It is feared that she was sunk."

On July 7 Kojima advised the captains of Momi, Matsu, and Satsuki II on the fighting in France: "Although Cherbourg has fallen, there is no great change in the situation." The attaché then referred to "tremendous progress" in long-range direction finder development by the British. "There are countless stations in England, Africa and India working in cooperation with each other," he warned, "and a vessel that uses its radio in the Atlantic or Indian Ocean will most surely be located. . . ." (The failure of the Japanese to regard silence as a condition of submarine survival was demonstrated by Kojima using the radio to issue his warning.)

Commander Uno was an exception, remaining silent for days, though he had been heard from on June 16, giving his position— 10 degrees north, 31 degrees west—as of June 11. The status of the *I-52* was a subject of concern for the admirals in Berlin, who were beginning to doubt the U-boat commander's assurance that the rendezvous had gone as planned.

MATSU HOMEWARD BOUND

On July 14 Tokyo relayed a message to Berlin from Takaichi Kinashi, the commanding officer of the *I-29*, in which he simply reported: "Arrived Singapore." In a joint communication to Tokyo, Admirals Abe and Kojima expressed qualified satisfaction: "At a time when submarine transportation between Germany and Japan is becoming more and more hazardous, it is indeed gratifying to learn that the Matsu has safely arrived in Singapore. . . . We pray for her safe voyage to Japan." Their caution was justified, for the *I-29* made it only as far as the Luzon Strait, west of Manila. She had been tracked since leaving Lorient in April, but with passing interest, and her arrival in Singapore went unnoticed by the enemy until July 15, a day after it occurred. But that attitude changed when the importance of the *I-29*'s transport mission—as defined by the military value of her passengers and cargo—was realized by U.S. Navy Intelligence. An intercepted Berlin-to-Tokyo transmission on July 17 listed her cargo: various radar apparatus, twenty Enigma coding machines, ordnance parts, rocket-type launching apparatus, bombsight plans, pressure cabin parts and plans, parts of a British Mosquito aircraft. (Scientists and weapons technicians, passengers aboard the *I-29*, were flown from Singapore to Japan, carrying with them secret documents, including plans for two experimental aircraft built by Messerschmitt, the rocket-powered Me 163 and the twin-turbojet Me 262.)

U.S. naval forces in the Pacific were alerted to the presence of the *I-29* and aided immensely by Kinashi, whose detailed itinerary, radioed to Kure on July 20, was intercepted and relayed by Station Hypo to submarines in a position to intercept the *I-29*—*Tilefish* (SS-307), *Rock* (SS-274), and *Sawfish* (SS-276). On July 26, Pacific Fleet headquarters (CINCPAC) issued a bulletin: "*I-29* recently arrived Singapore from Europe carrying samples and plans of many recent German developments in fields of radar, communications, gunnery, aeronautics and medicine. Left Singapore 22 July en route Kure. . . . Will pass through posit 15 N, 117 E, at 251400 [25 July, 1400 hours], and through Balintang Channel at 261200, speed 17. . ."

"He did not pass," radioed *Sawfish* on July 26. "Put three fish into Nip sub which disintegrated in a cloud of smoke and fire."

The loss of the *I-29*—and all of her crew save one seaman, who swam to Sabutan Island—was announced by the Bureau of Military Affairs in Tokyo in a message transmitted on August 8 to the naval attaché in Berlin: "The Matsu departed Singapore on 22 July. On the twenty-fifth, while on her way to Japan, she reported a surfaced enemy submarine about 300 miles west of Manila. All her passengers had proceeded to Tokyo from Singapore by plane, but her cargo had been left aboard. Though it is indeed regrettable, we can no longer hope for her safety in view of developments up to now. Despite the fact that we received, through your great efforts and the understanding cooperation of the Germans, many articles which were to strengthen the nation's capacity to prosecute the war, our inability to use them owing to the loss of the ill-fated ship is truly unfortunate and will have a great effect throughout the Imperial Army and Navy."

And while the Japanese could still only wonder about the fate of Momi and Satsuki II, the Allies were virtually certain of the fate of the two submarines, and therefore enjoyed a significant psychological advantage. "Loss of the *I-52* (Momi)," read a U.S. Fleet U/Boat Intelligence Summary dated July 20, "considered sunk 24 June west of the Cape Verde Islands by planes from USS *Bogue,* is still unknown to ComSubs [German navy submarine command], who on 12 July estimated this Jap U/boat to be north of the Azores en route Biscay." As for Satsuki II, the intelligence summary took note of a "transmission in 5-letter group Jap code [which] was DFd [intercepted by radio direction finder] 2329Z/10 May. . . . *RO-501* may have been sunk in a subsequent attack . . . by U.S.S. *Robinson* of the *Bogue* group on 13 May."

On July 10 Admiral Kojima had sent to the Bureau of Military Affairs in Tokyo a summary of recent reports by German naval intelligence on enemy underwater and above-water methods of detecting submarines. The basic radar system was identified as the Rotterdam, nicknamed "Stinky" by the Americans, which was currently being installed in destroyers and smaller patrol vessels. "The same apparatus, when installed in a plane," the report noted, "has an effective radius of 20 to 50 miles. . . ." The report went on to describe a typical strategy by British and American patrol planes when they had confirmed the general position of a submerged enemy submarine. "[T]hey place buoys at the apices of a one to ten mile triangular area having this position as its center. At the three buoys they place transmitters, which begin to broadcast sound direction immediately. They receive the transmission in the planes, from which they learn accurately the position and carry out effective bombing." Without knowing it—the Japanese, too, were none the wiser—B-Dienst (the intelligence arm of the German naval staff) had provided a fairly accurate account of the sinking of the *I-52*.

And while the U.S. Navy perfected ways to capitalize on a submarine's great vulnerability, the sound of its propellers, the British, according to Kojima, "have made amazing progress in direction finding which Germany has not been able to equal." There were twenty-two direction-finding stations in England, an unknown number in Africa, "and from 10 to 20 stations collaborate in taking bearings on the same target." Ships in the Indian Ocean, he warned, "can also be d/f 'ed from India and Australia." Clearly this information was of particular interest to long-range submarines, and the attaché's report was directed on July 4 to the captains of Momi, Matsu, and Satsuki II. "Radio broadcasts of over 10 seconds duration or 25 beats in length," Kojima advised, "are certain to be d/f 'ed."

On July 14, four months after his arrival in Berlin, Attaché Kojima spoke candidly about day-to-day aspects of the German-Japanese alliance. He listed his criticisms in a report to Tokyo on July 14, clearly hoping that an airing of his views would get attention. "Possibly because the dictatorial powers are considerable," he wrote, "there are many inconsistencies in the organization of German Supreme Headquarters, and it cannot be said that cooperation is good. . . . The Germans do not like foreign attachés to be stationed where Supreme Headquarters are . . . but outside headquarters there are no influential Navy officers, and all key positions in the control of operations are held by Army officers." But Kojima reserved his toughest comments for an appraisal of Foreign Minister von Ribbentrop and his dominant role in the German government's information system. "The foreign minister's position is very exalted. He is practically a self-appointed premier and apparently has a finger in the guidance of the war and even in military matters. It is impossible to learn anything about the highest policy unless one hears it directly from the Fuehrer or the foreign minister. . . . Consequently, the only one of us who has a chance of an interview is Ambassador Oshima. Even so, I am considering the possibility of approaching the foreign minister through the ambassador and having an interview in his presence." Kojima's objective was to have "one of us"—a member of the naval attaché's staff—based at Supreme Headquarters, but he was not optimistic. "Even if I were successful, it does not by any means follow that we would derive much benefit." Kojima had raised this issue once before, on May 26, when he suggested that Germany "is mainly concerned with continental warfare and does not see its direct relationship to Japanese operations." And he added that the German high command "is inconsistent in some cases and often highly personalized."

A few days later, discussing the T-5 torpedo, Kojima seemed to contradict himself when he described Germany's willingness to cooperate to the satisfaction of the Japanese navy. "Her attitude has been to spare no effort in offering all sorts of manufacturing and technical help in permitting Japan to put this torpedo into practical use."

CRISIS POLITICS IN AXIS CAPITALS

Abe reported on July 20 about his meeting the day before with Admiral Meisel, the Navy chief of staff, who agreed that the appointment of Naokuni Nomura as minister of the Imperial Navy would benefit German-Japanese cooperation. Abe was personally pleased with the elevation of Nomura, whom he had succeeded as naval attaché in Berlin, but he soon would learn that naming Nomura to the cabinet had merely been an expedient move by Hideki Tojo. Realizing that his days as prime minister were numbered following the fall of Saipan, Tojo had attempted to retain power by inducing Shigetaro Shimada to step down as navy minister in favor of Nomura, though Shimada would stay on as chief of the

Naval General Staff. The maneuver failed, and Tojo was forced to resign, as were Nomura and the rest of Tojo's war cabinet. When a new premier, Kuniaki Koiso, formed a government, the navy minister was Mitsumasa Yonai, a former prime minister considered an opponent of the war.

At the same time in Germany, a government upheaval was averted. "Shortly after 6 o'clock on the warm, sunny summer morning of July 20, 1944," wrote William L. Shirer, an American radio correspondent, "Colonel Klaus Stauffenberg, accompanied by his adjutant, Lieutenant Werner von Haften, drove out past the bombed-out buildings of Berlin to the airport at Rangsdorf. In his bulging briefcase were papers concerning the new Volksgrenadier divisions on which at 1 P.M. he was to report to Hitler at the Wolfsschanze in East Prussia. In between the papers, wrapped in a shirt, was a time bomb."

When Admiral Kojima reported to Yonai, the new minister of the navy, his words were measured, his tone somber, as he warned that similar incidents may be in store if the war situation continued to deteriorate. "It is believed that the recent unfavorable war situation was taken advantage of in carrying out this plot," Kojima declared on July 21. "The affair was suppressed at once with rapid and drastic measures, and it is believed that the control within the country will become more and more severe from now on. If the war situation continues to deteriorate and the bad news spreads to the Army and the people, one must be on the alert for other similar incidents." Kojima had more to say on July 24: "If such influential high-ranking Army officers as Generals Beck and Fromm were behind the plot and are directly or indirectly connected with it, it cannot be considered ordinary or shallow. . . . Because this is not only a grave matter for

Germany but for Japan as well, Vice Admiral Abe and I presented our views to the Ambassador. He will warn the Chancellor directly. . . ."

Ambassador Oshima was briefed by Foreign Minister von Ribbentrop on July 23, and his reports to Tokyo reached certain officials in Washington in a top secret document, the Magic Diplomatic Summary. "The attempt on Hitler's life," Oshima advised, "is the most serious occurrence for Germany since the outbreak of the war. Of course, it has been apparent that ever since the Nazi regime seized power there has been discord between the traditional Prussian general staff group and the radical Nazi party element." On August 3 Oshima sent a second message on the crisis, reflecting the essence of his conversation with von Ribbentrop. "The plot against Hitler was hatched chiefly by Army officers dissatisfied with his strategy and leadership, but they were not necessarily motivated by . . . defeatism. According to assertions by Foreign Minister von Ribbentrop, there is no evidence of their having communicated with England. Many suspect them of being in league with Russia. . . . Since the defeat of Stalingrad there have been malcontents among the Army officers because of Hitler's strategy in prosecuting the war with Russia. . . ."

On August 3 Kojima offered a critical analysis of the conspiracy to assassinate Hitler, though he too was preaching the von Ribbentrop line, elaborating on what Tokyo had heard from Ambassador Oshima.

> While it is fairly well rumored that generals of staff rank in important positions were involved, two of them—Albrecht and Stauffenberg—were shot at once, and Beck committed suicide, so an investigation of the scope of the plot will be very

difficult. It is especially hard to decide whether those who acted at the time were under the mistaken impression that orders issued by ranking members of the conspiracy were lawful orders. At any rate, drastic measures were promptly taken, and wholesale arrests were made.

Since Stalingrad, there have been officers of the German Army who were discontented with Hitler's strategy in the war with Russia, and operations . . . ending in failure after failure have aroused the antipathy of a military clique. . . . Certain officers became obsessed with the idea that their present dilemma was caused by Hitler, whose strategy led to what they feared most, a two-front war. Furthermore, they felt that Hitler's uncompromising attitude ruled out any chance of a political settlement with the Soviet Union. The assassination of Hitler was attempted without any definite plans for the future, and while there were other means to the end the plotters sought, they ignored them, believing that the first step toward peace with Russia was the elimination of Hitler. In these grave times it was indeed an ill-advised move.

Kojima used the occasion to air some thoughts about Germany at war, showing himself to be remarkably astute and boldly candid. "To cope with the present chaotic situation, Germany has raised the age limits for workers to 67 for men and 50 for women, and has swept away waste in government offices. In all, an additional million troops have been found to defend the homeland, and all Germans deserve congratulations for their determination. We are further impressed by communication facilities only slightly disrupted and food distribution that has continued smoothly in the Berlin area even during air raids, which are now quite frequent."

"Since the early part of June," he wrote, "as many as twenty-six generals have been made prisoners. It is suspected that these men, having lost their self-confidence in the war against Russia, felt that they would be better off surrendering rather than be called to account in the future. In general, however, the young men under 35 or 36 have remained steadfastly loyal to Hitler." Kojima praised the SS Corps as an "intrepid fighting force" that maintained discipline and morale, and he admired the German navy attitude. "When a call went out for pilots of a one-man suicide torpedo," he recalled, "there were 10,000 volunteers."

ETERNAL HOPE

Admiral Kojima was handling the imminent arrival of the *I-52* with meticulous care, anticipating it would occur at the end of July at Lorient, which happened to be in a battle zone. "In view of the present situation," he said in a message to Tokyo on July 10, "all preparations are being made to shorten as much as possible the time she will be at anchor there. There is fairly general disruption of lines of communication because of operations in northern France, and railroad transportation between there and Paris is at a standstill." The Momi turnaround was further complicated by the fact that her cargo for the voyage home was to be loaded at Kiel, a major seaport and naval installation in northern Germany. But getting from Lorient to Kiel by sea had been ruled out due to Allied naval activity in support of the invasion. As the German navy chief of staff, Admiral Meisel, explained to Admiral Abe in their meeting on July 19, "The enemy is using the coast as an anchorage, bombarding the shore with naval gunfire. Many destroyers and other anti-submarine vessels are stationed off the coast, making it very difficult for submarines to break through." It was now clear that the enemy had established a beachhead, and the cargo item known as *Yamabuki* would have to be transported overland from Kiel to Lorient for loading onto the *I-52*.

Hope was running high that Momi, despite her silence, would make it after all, and Kojima radioed instructions along with a war report on July 27. "Estimating that you will enter port on 25 July at the earliest, the assistant attaché Fujimura as well as other necessary personnel and the German authorities in charge are waiting in Paris. For the sake of security and because of the danger of enemy bombing, transportation is by automobile only and at night. Enemy propaganda has exaggerated the recent plot to assassinate Chancellor Hitler. The matter has been partially cleared up by swift and resolute measures, and on the whole the nation is calm. There has been no important change in the situation in northern France; the German army is putting up a good defense. In addition, all arrangements have been completed for your arrival in port. In view of the changing situation . . . the need for security, etc., try to make your stay in port as short as possible. I hope that you arrive safely."

Kojima knew better than to take Momi's arrival for granted, but he was optimistic. In a dispatch to Tokyo on July 27, he stated an intention to ship T-5 acoustic torpedoes by U-boat to the Malayan port of Penang, but if this was not possible, "we shall send at least two torpedoes on the next trip of the Momi." The German navy was making occasional runs to Asia and had established a base at Penang, and Kojima welcomed an opportunity to bid for passenger and cargo space on U-boats as an alternative to the *Yamabuki* submarines. But they still figured prominently in Kojima's thinking, and he was planning to send technician Tadao Yamato, who had completed a course on the T-5 at the Torpedo Experimental Station at Gothenhaven, to Japan aboard the *I-52*. He was also sending sets of manufacturing plans for the T-5, a weapon he seemed to believe would tip the balance of the submarine war. "As to the effective life of this torpedo," Kojima assured his superiors in a moment of wishful thinking, "there is no indication yet of its having been captured by the enemy, and since the enemy does not know the details of this torpedo, they will not have taken any defensive countermeasures."

The torpedoes appeared to be lost but turned up eventually, and on August 24 Kojima forwarded to Japan a note from the commander in chief, Admiral Doenitz: "The two acoustic torpedoes which you requested some time ago are being delivered at Penang. Please let me know on what date and to whom they are to be transferred." Kojima had this to add mournfully: "In view of the lack of news regarding the *I-52*, negotiations should be made for the transfer to take place in Penang at once. . . ." Finally, on August 29, Kojima was instructed by the vice chief of the Naval General Staff to arrange delivery to the Japanese SubRon commander in Penang. "Please express fitting thanks to the commander in chief of the German Navy in the name of the Japanese Navy."

The code name of the *I-52* was changed to Ginmatsu (silver pine) at the request of the German navy, but it was not until August 6 that Kojima was so notified by the Bureau of Military Affairs in Tokyo. (A GI comment was inserted on the intercept: "Momi, here changed to Ginmatsu, is Jap sub *I-52* which was believed sunk by U.S.S. *Bogue* on 24 June about 800 miles west of Cape Verde Island. Berlin reported communicating with Momi on 30 July. There has been no other evidence of any transmission from *I-52* since 24 June.")

The *I-52* still failed to arrive, causing renewed anxiety, but on July 30 there was jubilation in Berlin when a prearranged radio signal, QWF, was received, indicating she would land at Lorient in approximately thirty-six hours. "We were in communication with the Momi yesterday . . . ," Kojima announced in a dispatch on July 31. "It is estimated that she will arrive on or about 3 August. The reception party has departed Paris for the port of landing." Kojima mentioned that the train carrying the eight-member party from Berlin to Paris had been targeted by enemy aircraft and subjected to a guerrilla raid, so the trip from Paris to Lorient would be by road at night and with the protection of a German security force. (GI was ready with a relentless reminder: "Momi is the *I-52*, thought to have been sunk on 24 June. It was scheduled to rendezvous with a German U-boat on 22 June. . . . On 24 June the USS *Bogue* attacked two submarines in the area 15.16 north, 39.55 west, considerable oil and debris appearing on the surface. After that date there has been no evidence of any transmission from the Momi, apart from the above item.")

On July 18 Kojima had visited the chief of staff of the German air force, Günter Korten, who presented what the attaché considered "a very frank explanation of the present situation in aerial operations in Europe. . . . We also saw some motion pictures marked 'Military Secret' of the German revenge weapon, the V-I. . . ." Korten then offered a general assessment of the war. "The situation of the German forces on all fronts is not good," he said. "On the eastern front, in view of the success of the Soviet offensive, they have moved the Air Force staff headquarters some 120 kilometers back from the front lines, to avoid coming under attack by the advancing Red Army."

Just two days later, on July 20, Kojima was notified that Korten had died, an innocent victim of the attempted assassination of Hitler.

FUJIMURA AT THE DOCK

Lieutenant Commander Yoshiro Fujimura, a hero of the war—he was awarded a sword by the emperor for exemplary performance in combat aboard the aircraft carrier *Akagi*—and now an assistant naval attaché in charge of the *Yamabuki* program, led a party of Japanese naval officers sent to Lorient for the arrival of the *I-52*. Long after the war, in a 1985 interview with NHK, the Japanese national television network, Fujimura talked about the experience. It was not his first trip to Lorient. A year earlier the *U-180* had landed there following an Indian Ocean rendezvous with the *I-29*, and Fujimura was on hand to receive a shipment of gold and transport it to Berlin for deposit in a Japanese account at the Reichsbank. "It was to cover our operations," Fujimura explained. There was gold to be received this time as well—eight tons of it, Fujimura believed, though only two tons had been reported officially. And the naval officer who had come with the gold aboard the *U-180*, Lieutenant Commander Hideo Tomonaga, was now a member of the greeting party. This time, though, things would not go according to plan: to begin with, Lorient was in an area of intense combat.

Fujimura's account was recorded by NHK:

> We used a big bus, a new German Navy bus, which had a capacity of . . . 50 passengers. . . . We hired [20 German soldiers] as security guards, who protected us while traveling. . . . The . . . submarine was scheduled to arrive in Lorient on August 1, 1944. . . . In Paris we waited, carefully observing the situation. It was late in July. There we found that the submarine was going to arrive in Lorient on schedule. So we left Paris for Lorient. It took us two days to get there. . . . So we . . . arrived in Lorient in the evening on July 31.
>
> The next morning, August 1, we waited for the submarine to arrive. However it never came. The reason was that it was bombed by a British airplane when it arrived at the mouth of the Bay of Biscay. We found out later that it got as far as the mouth, but it sank.
>
> We decided to wait one more day. . . . We came back from the harbor to the base. . . . However that day, Patton's tank battalion . . . broke through German lines and advanced. . . . Patton's tank battalion commander was leading the advance. Then the U.S. and British troops went to the other side of the base. Therefore, the German submarine base was surrounded. . . . What happened then was a great turmoil, a huge confusion. It was as if the hornet's nest had been attacked. . . . Finally, we were invaded by the enemy and could not do anything to protect ourselves.

What to do? A German commander suggested they could flee by submarine to Norway, but that was little comfort for Fujimura and his men, who were already so far from home. "We submitted another idea," Fujimura recalled, "that is, there was no way except performing hara-kiri. . . . When I said to my juniors, 'What do you think?' they were rubbing their bellies and saying it would hurt." There was another possibility, and it was to use the German navy bus that had brought them to Lorient. After thinking it over Fujimura announced his decision. "We will return to Paris by bus."

Of course, the route to Paris meant risky encounters with the enemy, as Fujimura vividly explained. "During the daytime we could not advance, so we drove at night. But when we were seen regardless of day, night, or dawn, combat planes flew toward us. Four or five of the soldiers were sitting on top of the bus as lookouts. As soon as they saw planes they stomped on the roof, and the bus immediately stopped. All of the passengers got out and scattered like birds. One plane after another shot its machine guns, and two German soldiers, our security guards, were killed. . . .

"We finally got out of the enemy's territory. We safely passed through the war zone and entered the forest. It took a week for us to arrive in Paris. All of us returned without injury, however the submarine . . . is still under water in the Bay of Biscay, loaded with eight tons of gold."

As he delved deep into the past, forty years or so, Fujimura seemed to be filling in the facts the best he could, speculating where necessary. "Before I went to Lorient from Paris," he remembered, "I received a telegram, an encrypted telegram. It said that the submarine would arrive on August 1. Thinking of it later, you know, the telegram was a fake made by Great Britain. They successfully read Japanese codes, copied and used them. The encryption looked somewhat strange. At that time, I did not really suspect anything amiss, therefore I went there. When I arrived, Great Britain had already stolen all the gold. They sent the telegram saying that the submarine would arrive on August 1. After all, the submarine did not come. I do not regret losing the eight tons of solid gold. Rather, I regret that we lost about 100 soldiers. Even now, I wish we could salvage the bodies."

Fujimura was mistaken about where and when the *I-52* went down, though his suspicions have been shared over the years by shipwreck salvagers and naval historians. One such doubter was Nigel Pickford, a British researcher whose *Atlas of Shipwrecks & Treasure* was published in 1994. "German records refer to the *I-52* sending a radio signal requesting new routing instructions on July 24," Pickford writes, "a whole month after it had supposedly been sunk southwest of the Azores. Another radio signal received on July 30 gave its position as 36 hours from Lorient." Reviving a theory that Momi was sunk by an aerial bombardment in the Bay of Biscay, as Fujimura proposed, Pickford suggests she was only damaged in the attack by aircraft from the USS *Bogue* on June 24, and debris gathered by U.S. destroyers had been purposely released by the submarine to make it appear she had been fatally hit. "The *I-52* and its cargo have not been found," Pickford concluded, but when she was discovered in 1995—very near where navy records had placed the attack—he sent a note congratulating the successful searcher, Paul Tidwell.

GIVING UP THE GHOST

Kojima kept at it, taking care not to sound defeated, but by August 6 doubt and disappointment were creeping into his radio calls to Momi. "Although the German escort vessels waited for you on August 1st, 2nd, and 4th at the rendezvous point outside of Lorient

Harbor as per instructions of 23 July . . . they did not meet you. Was there not some error? Please inform us again of your expected date of arrival at the rendezvous point." (GI, in its comment, was sounding a little less certain than previously: "Momi is the *I-52*, thought to have been sunk on 24 June, although Berlin reported that they were in communication with Momi on 30 July. . . .") Kojima tried again on August 8, this time informing Captain Uno of a destination change: "Although we are not in contact with your ship, we trust that she is safe. In consequence of the sudden developments in the war situation in northern France, it is no longer safe to enter Lorient or any other port on the French coast. You are therefore requested to sail for Norway. Your port of arrival should be Trondheim or Bergen. Whatever happens, please report subsequent developments . . . immediately. . . ."

In a report on August 9 to the Japanese Naval General Staff, Kojima cited a dispatch from the German submarine *U-530* on June 27.

The Ginmatsu safely completed her rendezvous with a German submarine on 23 June. Thereafter she was instructed as to her movements by direct radio from the German Operations Department to the liaison officer. . . . Though she was to report three or four days before reaching the [Lorient] rendezvous point, this was not done; however on 30 July she unexpectedly transmitted the agreed call, QWF, meaning that she was 36 hours from an indicated point on her route. Accordingly German escort vessels stood by off Lorient at 0430 and 2315 on 1 August but did not effect rendezvous. Meanwhile they received the same prearranged signal, QWF, on the morning and again in the afternoon of 1 August. . . . Thus they stood by in a similar manner on 2 August but did not effect rendezvous. Thereupon the German Navy radioed to the Ginmatsu that escort vessels would stand by at the rendezvous point at 0430 on 4 August, and in case she did not join them she should report her condition. The escort vessels acted as scheduled, but, as before, failed to effect rendezvous.

Since it seemed from the circumstances that there might have been some sort of error in the operations, I again radioed instructions concerning her movements directly to the captain of the Ginmatsu and asked for her expected date of arrival at the rendezvous point. However I have received no reply to date, and doubts have been raised here about the ship's safety. Perhaps the QWF was a dummy call sent by the enemy, but no enemy operational action accompanied it. Moreover, on previous occasions when the enemy has attempted to attack submarines in the Bay of Biscay, they have generally transmitted dispatches before and after the action. The German Navy can decipher those, but since there have been no such reports lately, they say that it would not seem that she was attacked in the Bay of Biscay. Therefore it is difficult to make assumptions concerning her condition, but the German Navy appears to have despaired of her safety in view of the fact that no news has been heard from her to date. . . .

The party sent to the port of landing to handle affairs connected with the Ginmatsu . . . stood by at Lorient, but when circumstances evolved . . . and because of the rapid development of the war situation in northern France, they went down to Angers, site of submarine headquarters. When communications with Lorient were cut off, they withdrew to Paris and returned to Berlin yesterday, 8 August. The trip from Paris and return was fraught with great difficulty. Only four hours after they left Nantes, enemy armored units entered the city. Though they ran into danger innumerable times, all came through safely.

· · · · · · · · · · · · · ·

On August 9, coincidentally, the final days of waiting for Momi were the subject of a U.S. Fleet U/Boat Intelligence Summary.

> The enemy apparently is still confident of the arrival in Lorient of *I-52* (Momi). In a signal made on 31 July the Jap Naval Attaché in Berlin reported to Tokyo, "We were in communication with Momi yesterday, the 30th. It is estimated that she will arrive on or about 3 August. The reception party has departed Paris for the port of landing. . . ." However on 6 August the Naval Attaché radioed to Momi that German escorts had waited for her at the R/V off Lorient on August 1, 2, and 4 without making contact. He added, "Please inform us again of your ETA." (Note: No Jap transmission has been intercepted in the Atlantic since 23 June, when *U-530* . . . reported that his R/V with Momi west of the Cape Verde Islands had been carried out. It is still considered that Momi was sunk by *Bogue* a/c [aircraft carrier] early the following morning.)

More than anyone, Admiral Abe understood that the loss of three key submarines spelled the end of *Yamabuki* and dimmed the prospect of a strike-America strategy that for the time being depended on the *Yamabuki* boats. His dejection was reflected in a brief but eloquent message to Tokyo on August 11. "In addition to our former loss of contact with the Satsuki and the recent report of the loss of the Matsu, we have failed to receive word from the Ginmatsu. The disaster which has befallen these liaison submarines, one after another, at a time when they were playing such an important role in transportation between Japan and Germany, is indeed an extremely regrettable loss to both countries." He then added a thought about where to go from here. "We will enter into negotiations with the Germans and press them to commission transport submarines. Since those which have already been planned are unable to avoid attack satisfactorily, construction of them has been suspended in favor of a plan to reconvert operational submarines for the assignment. And for the present, since our transport capacity is very meager, no other alternative is seen but to utilize the German submarines operating in the Indian Ocean."

THE VIEW FROM BERLIN

The war in Europe was also not going well, as Admiral Kojima was forced to report to the central authorities in August. The American army had penetrated the Brittany area—the invasion force of twenty to thirty divisions supported by thirty divisions of mechanized infantry, twelve tank divisions, and about four hundred fighter aircraft operating from captured bases in Normandy. "They have caught the Germans off guard," Kojima wrote, "and are swiftly pressing toward Paris along the Loire." The British were also sweeping across France, having broken through in the vicinity of Caen. As for German forces in Brittany, Kojima reported, they consisted of six Army divisions, thirty thousand naval personnel, and another four divisions in the area between Nantes and Paris. "On 8 August, however, the German army was finally forced to make a general withdrawal from the area, which has been the scene of heavy fighting since the invasion."

The Allied buildup was awesome, as Kojima described it. "To provide a steady flow of supplies for its forces on the continent, the enemy has constructed enormous landing facilities along the coast north of Caen and Bayeux, near the mouth of the Orne. The capacity of these artificial docks is such that the ports of Cherbourg and Le Havre are said to be superfluous. On the other hand, almost all important railroads in France, particularly those west of Paris, have been badly damaged by air attacks, and the network of rail transportation around Paris is in considerable disarray due to bombing raids that have occurred every day for three months."

Kojima had obviously been checking out transportation options, by rail or road, for the purpose of moving personnel and cargoes overland from one submarine port to another. "Trains running to and from Germany," he said, "generally require from 12 to 24 hours in traveling within a hundred kilometers of Paris, so the German Army west of Paris must depend chiefly on motor vehicles. Supply units travel in 100-truck convoys, and they station guards to defend against guerrilla attacks. During the day they hide from enemy aircraft, and at night they repair roads damaged by bombings and remove debris before continuing on their arduous and dangerous journey at 20 kilometers per hour."

Kojima also reported on activities of the French underground. "According to estimates by German headquarters in France," he wrote, "there are some 120,000 Frenchmen, most of them in the southeastern part of the country, armed against the Germans and collaborating with the Allies. In addition, the American thrust into Brittany in early August encouraged the Bretons to rise in revolt and display open good will toward the enemy. Furthermore, there are thousands of people in cities west of Paris who have no utilities—no gas, water, or electricity. Rationing is becoming increasingly difficult in Paris, and the anti-German sentiment of most of the populace has been inflamed by circumstances of the occupation. About 600,000 young men are in hiding to escape forced labor in Germany. . . . All in all, the problems of the occupation are undermining the German Army's ability to defend against the American and British invaders."

Kojima clearly was in a quandary, his loyalty at odds with the reality of Germany's dire situation, and he did his best to conclude on a positive note. "Morale is high among frontline troops in France, the SS Corps especially, and even though it has frequently been necessary for German Air Force units to move their bases in France, they are showing determined resistance against heavy odds. And it appears that the recent assassination plot at Supreme Headquarters has had little effect on the German fighting spirit. But in addition to their overwhelming power, the Americans have been taking the German Army by surprise. They have also been working secretly with the French, making it doubtful that the German army will be able to rally."

Finally Kojima was forced to speculate on when, not if, the German army would be defeated in France. "Germany's ability to prevent the enemy from reaching Paris depends on whether reinforcements can be moved continually from the fatherland and whether air power can be increased. However, if American supply units can keep pace with the rapid advance of the frontline forces, the enemy's arrival in Paris may be imminent. It is even possible that they will arrive there this month."

Allied forces reached Paris on August 25, 1944.

In September 1944, Vice Admiral Matome Ugaki, commander in chief of the First Battleship Division, heard from classmate Katsuo Abe, who said he had considered requesting combat duty after three years in Europe, but he had decided to stay on in view of the importance of the war. Ugaki wrote in his diary that he was sorry for Abe, "stuck in a desk job for so long, but he would just have to put up with it."

5. MOMI MEETS THE MIRS

In November 1998 Paul Tidwell returned to the I-52 for the first time since his discovery in May 1995. Richard Billings was one of thirty members of the expedition party.

It is fifteen hundred nautical miles from Las Palmas in the Canary Islands to where Momi lay hidden at 17,400 feet in the foothills of the mid-Atlantic ridge, a five-day journey for our floating laboratory, lumbering along at twelve knots. But there would be a detour, we learned, to a hydrothermal vent site, some "black smokers" discovered years ago by a geologist on board, Yuri Bogdanov, and we agreed it was not a bad idea to warm up the Mir submersibles and check out the systems in advance of deeper dives to the *I-52*. We quickly sensed the excitement of the Russian complement at the prospect of doing basic science. Notwithstanding a murky Cold War history, when a KGB mission was supreme, the

Akademik Mstislav Keldysh is the flagship of the Russian research fleet. She is owned by the P. P. Shirshov Institute of Oceanology of the Russian Academy of Sciences, and her calling is scientific when she's not on a treasure hunt or filming the *Titanic*. With that in mind, one wondered how the Russians regarded this voyage to nowhere, or rather, to a destination known only by Paul Tidwell, for it was a treasure hunt that meant money in a Moscow bank, if nothing more. (For Tidwell it was much more, hopefully, in the form of secret orders regarding the *I-52*'s return to Japan with nuclear material.) And what was the attitude of Anatoly Sagalevitch, the "head of expedition?" He had been here before, searching for the *I-52* in 1995 with Orca Ltd. of London, and he no doubt recalled that the failure to find the submarine was due to purposely misleading guidance from Tidwell. Until the Cold War ended in 1990, Sagalevitch and Tidwell were enemies in the strictest sense, and their business relations since had been cordial but distant. That was until September 1998, when at a meeting in England they settled their differences over a bottle of vodka and agreed to join forces in an expedition. Anatoly even suggested a name for the Mir submersible to be assigned to Tidwell: "Hero Sub" it would be called, out of admiration for an American who dared to try.

As we left Las Palmas, Tidwell seemed out of sorts and dispirited, though it had little to do with Sagalevitch, with whom bygones were bygones. Nor was he anxious about being able to locate Momi, whose position he had carefully recorded and would provide to Anatoly at the appropriate time. It was the investor, said Tidwell in a conversation out on deck. "If the gold isn't in the debris field but was stored in the sub, quite possibly in a torpedo tube, we're not equipped to recover it." He was alluding to the budgetary elimination of a $40,000 pneumatic tool designed by Deep Sea Systems of Falmouth, Massachusetts—a dirt blower that could be converted into a metal cutter by changing heads. "It's Philippone's doing, and Zajonc's," said Tidwell in a rare display of agitation. Jim Philippone was the principal financial backer of Operation Rising Sun, as the project was named by Tidwell in 1995, and Zajonc (it rhymes with "science") was secretary-treasurer of Cape Verde Explorations and the project coordinator. An attorney from Spokane, Washington, Zajonc specializes in start-up corporations and taking them public, and he was the only officer of the company in addition to Tidwell.

Treasure hunting is conducted by and large with other people's money, which may not distinguish it from other businesses, although the reward is often substantially greater, as is the risk. Since his discovery of the *I-52* and the founding of Cape Verde Explorations, a good bit of Tidwell's time had been devoted to courting investors and considering their suggestions patiently and respectfully. Relations with financial backers had at times been difficult. Fred Neal Jr. of Harrison, Arkansas, a cellular telephone manufacturer who bankrolled the *Yuzhmorgeologiya* outing in 1995, filed suit over his right to raise his stake, and a group of Texas investors failed to meet a $3 million commitment. In his dealings with the Texans Tidwell met Jim Busch, an attorney in Atlanta with a sharp eye for sources of capital. When Busch proposed an Asian millionaire (born in China and educated in Japan, he had become a leading businessman in Indonesia) with shipbuilding and other properties, Tidwell caught a flight to Bali. The meeting went well, and Tidwell was promised a letter of intent to put up $3 million, but it was December 1997, and when the rupiah plummeted in the economic crisis, the offer was withdrawn. It was then that Busch put Tidwell in touch with Philippone.

A trial lawyer in Rochester, New York, Philippone expressed interest, which was reciprocated by Tidwell when a financial profile routinely obtained on a would-be investor showed a $100 million line of credit at the Chase Manhattan Bank. Tidwell flew to Rochester, and while he later would say that Philippone "blew hot and cold," an agreement was formalized in a contract signed in March 1998. Philippone would receive half the gold that was recovered from the *I-52* on an expedition later that year; in return, he would put up $3 million in the form of a loan, payable in March 1999, virtually reducing his risk to zero. Nevertheless, when Philippone heard that the expedition was to be a survey of the wreck site with no recovery of gold unless it was found in the debris field, he reduced the amount of his investment-loan to $2 million. It was not until late in the summer—shortly before the meeting with Sagalevitch in Falmouth, England, to plan the expedition—that Tidwell became aware of the reduced investment. He heard it from Busch, the mutual friend and attorney, and when presented with an addendum to the contract, Tidwell refused to sign it. It galled him all the more to discover that Philippone had informed Zajonc of the cut a month earlier, and the two of them had agreed on budget adjustments to accommodate the reduction. The pneumatic blower-cutter was red-penciled, as were other high-tech items crucial to the success of the expedition: a $133,000 digital camera, custom-made by Benthos of North Falmouth, Massachusetts, for which $75,000 had already been paid; and a prototype metal detector of such sensitivity that its design was a tightly held secret, although Tidwell was confident that his industry connections would have enabled him to lease it.

In late September, Tidwell was inclined to postpone the voyage and said so in a memo to Philippone, who emphatically resisted the slightest delay. So in an e-mail to Zajonc, Tidwell suggested at least waiting until they could agree on what tools and equipment were required. Zajonc e-mailed back that he and Philippone were ready to go without him. It was then that Tidwell recognized a test of his prerogative as project leader. He again considered calling a halt, but there was too much at stake, including a National Geographic documentary on prime-time television, and he was confident he could handle Zajonc and Philippone.

Tidwell had other urgent concerns that came under a general heading of security. He worried about his competitors in the salvage business, who would stop at nothing to beat him to the *I-52*'s cargo of gold, and there was the more imminent threat to thirty Americans whose safety was his responsibility. Not that he wanted to dramatize the situation unduly, but the terrorist threat could not be ignored. The sinking of the *I-52* occurred in a faraway part of the world, eight hundred miles from anywhere, and was ideal for a hijacking. It was hard to discount rumors that the Russian Mafia had a grip on the docks in Kaliningrad (formerly Konigsberg, the capital of East Prussia, which was annexed by the Soviet Union in 1945 and remains part of Russia), home port of the *Keldysh*. Tidwell was also fearful of the ship's crew. "A gang of angry seamen, jealous of rich Americans getting richer on Japanese gold, is something I worry about," he confided. "It may sound far-fetched, but I don't think so." Following his protective instincts, Tidwell had hired a security firm founded by retired navy officers who had served in Vietnam as SEALs (Sea Air Land), combatants skilled in hit-and-run attacks. Two of them—Larry and Jim, nicknamed the "Bookends" for the way they stationed themselves on the flanks of people in their charge—were on board as bodyguards and ready at a moment's notice to call in parachute reinforcements.

There were some who objected to the SEALs. Zajonc, for one, was offended by their swagger, and a test of wills was inevitable between diametric extremes: a lawyer from the enlightened Northwest and Larry, a born-again Christian from the Florida Panhandle. As for Tidwell, he was all the more grateful for the presence of the "Bookends" when word got around that the *I-52* manifest, in addition to two tons of gold, listed 2.88 tons of opium with a street value in the millions on the criminal market. Tidwell had notified the Drug Enforcement Administration and received assurances that a U.S. warship would be positioned over the horizon, just in case.

ONLY THREE MILES TO GO

As the *Keldysh* neared the *I-52* site on the night of November 19, Tidwell briefed Anatoly on the location of the submarine. He also supplied the frequency of radio transponders left behind in 1995 to guide a return visit; however, a two-year life expectancy of the signaling devices put their usefulness in doubt. They were never put to the test, as it turned out. The coordinates supplied by Tidwell were precisely right, and we were due for a pleasant surprise at breakfast the next morning.

The voyage had not been all that enjoyable thus far. We were soon to realize on this adventure that while inspired by anticipation of rare excitement, maybe the experience of a lifetime, there were those of us who went from day to day with little to do. How the search for the submarine and her precious cargo would turn out was something most of us did not control, and all we could do was hope that Neptune would smile on us; meanwhile, to greater or lesser degree, we sought palliatives for time hanging heavy on our hands. The designers of the *Keldysh*—she was built in Finland, as were the Mirs—did their best with diversions, no doubt anticipating long and tedious voyages. A small gym on the seventh deck was outfitted with weight-lifting devices, rowing machine, and a Ping-Pong table; through a door toward the stern there was a miniature salt-water pool next to a sundeck beneath a volleyball court, which was enclosed by a net to stop the ball from being blown into the sea; and another door led to the most popular Finnish invention, a sauna, though there were tight controls on its use, and often confusion as to which gender had it reserved for which night. With all this and tropical breezes, who could complain?

The answer was that just about everyone experienced ennui at one time or another, and the common cause was the humdrum routine of daily life. All of us were cast in similarity: we breathed the same air, thought the same thoughts, and had little that was new and interesting to impart at the dinner table. Prolonged periods would sometimes be marked by the exchange of nary a word.

It was quite possible aboard the *Keldysh*—for thirty-eight days, in all—to barely realize that we were at sea. The four-hundred-foot ship is tall (seven decks plus the bridge) and square, with a pair of parallel hallways connected by wide and sturdy staircases and running the length of air-conditioned living quarters and work space. It was not unusual in the course of this unique nautical experience, especially for those victimized by a peripatetic virus, to remain cooped up for days. Seasickness should not have plagued us: the equatorial waters were calm, and the only perceptible motion of the ship was the vibration of her four Wartsila Vaasa 1,460-horsepower diesels. But behind-the-ear patches were in vogue, and there were some who suffered from chronic mal de mer. There was a doctor on board, rather a pharmacist, and when the symptoms were feverish and flu-like, he would administer an antibiotic shot that worked wonders. As it turned out, we were extremely fortunate with regard to illness and injury. That thirty landlubbers could go for nearly six weeks in a nautical environment with but one accident—a *National Geographic* writer bruised his foot playing volleyball and was hobbled for days—is remarkable. Of course, we had been warned: a set of rules signed by A. Titov, the chief mate, and posted in each cabin was designed to prevent mishap. They had been translated for the English-speaking clientele, and the result was as amusing as it was confusing. Example: "It is forbidden in dark time of day to make any work at bad illumination for one person on external decks."

The ones who suffered the most physically and psychologically were three septuagenarian naval veterans of World War II, members of VC-69, the carrier-based torpedo-bomber squadron that accounted for the sinking of the *I-52*. Invited by Tidwell to witness his discovery and help put it in historical perspective, Bill Gordon, Wilbur Yarrington, and Jack Gamble soon realized it was a long time with little to do from one ceremonial activity to the next. The one who handled it the most creatively was Yarrington, a chief machinist in 1944 known to his mates as "Snuffy," due to a likeness to Snuffy Smith of the comics page, just as Gordon, one of the pilots credited with sinking the *I-52*, was nicknamed "Flash." Snuffy Yarrington was a self-appointed collector of incidental intelligence, such as the fact that a silver sleeve used to attach a Mir submersible to a cable as it was lifted by crane to and from the sea was called a bullcock. Snickers around the breakfast table showed the degraded state of our collective sense of humor after a few weeks at sea.

There had been growing signs that we were not a group in the all-for-one and one-for-all tradition, and as we got closer to the wreck site the choosing of sides intensified. There was a palpable dividing line, based on loyalty to Tidwell or to Philippone. It was depicted in trivial yet telling ways—in the dining hall, for instance, where the protagonists always sat at separate tables. Each was accompanied by his wife; but this was not a pleasure cruise, and Jo Anne Tidwell and Mary Ann Philippone were more like seconds in a boxing ring, quietly advising while pretending to be above the fray. Also lined up with Tidwell were his son Steve, the "Bookends," VC-69 veterans Snuffy, Flash, and Jack, and Harry Masson, a computer expert and friend of Paul's from their Louisiana boyhood. The Philippones were regularly joined by Zajonc, his friends Rich and Kathy, a vacationing couple from Spokane, and a handful of engineering contractors who tried but failed to remain neutral. Then there was the National Geographic contingent, a director and film crew, and a magazine writer and still photographer, who attempted with some success to sympathize with both sides and keep a journalistic distance. And there was Jeff Simon, a cameraman under contract to make a large-format movie for theater distribution.

The weather was balmy on the morning of November 20, as might be expected at 15 degrees north of the equator. The *Keldysh* is uniquely equipped with a propulsion unit and thruster that enable her to "stand still," and she seemed to be hovering in a certain spot. We were finishing breakfast when an excited Jeff Simon called Tidwell and said Sagalevitch had something to show him in the Russian sonar lab, which was only about twenty-five feet away. Sure enough, there was something of interest on the screen, though it took a practiced eye to see it for what it was, a sonar image of a submarine. We were "loitering" over the target, Tidwell explained, therefore the image was what is known as a bathymetric irregularity, or a bump on the bottom, which bore only a faint resemblance to the sub's hull. But Tidwell had studied sonar images of the area from his 1995 expedition and was thoroughly familiar with the landscape. "That's Momi, all right. No doubt about it."

Philippone and Zajonc had gotten there ahead of Tidwell and could see from Anatoly's expression what was not all that clear on the sonar monitor. "Right on the money," exclaimed Philippone— an impromptu remark that was quite in character for a money man to make. It disturbed Tidwell that because he was backing the expedition, Philippone felt that others on board, Tidwell included, were in his employ. "I don't pay you to take unnecessary chances," Philippone said during preparations for Tidwell's first dive. Tidwell replied that on this expedition no one paid him to do anything.

On that Friday morning, though, the mood was joyous as we celebrated with a second cup of coffee. Philippone congratulated Tidwell: "You know, you were at this very spot three and a half years ago," and Tidwell responded by saluting the VC-69 vets. "They were here forty-four and a half years ago." For the moment, levity prevailed. When Zajonc wondered who was making sandwiches for the next day's dive, Tidwell said he planned to order a pizza. He seemed about to make a speech, then smiled. "Three miles to go," he said. "Straight down!"

It was just then that Sara Page Roth, the producer of the National Geographic film documentary, appeared. She was usually affable and friendly, but she had a hot temper at times (as Jeff Simon learned when he was fiercely rebuked for walking into her line of sight as she viewed a videotape), and this was one of those times. Sara fixed Tidwell with a steely glare and said she wished to re-create the event that had just occurred in the Russian sonar lab. Tidwell said okay, but she was clearly not appeased. "Next time something like this happens, we would appreciate being told in advance."

Some events had to be re-created, such as Tidwell's first glimpse that morning of the *I-52*, which he botched by uttering a loud "Holy shit!"

GOLD PANDEMONIUM

Harry Masson was the only one of us who had worked with Tidwell prior to the discovery of the *I-52*. He had been on the trip to Biloxi, Mississippi, when Paul was seeking data from the navy's oceanographic office at the Stennis Space Center. Harry recalled that as a result of that trip, Tidwell was nearly indicted for espionage, though there were discrepancies in their respective versions of the incident. The Office of Naval Intelligence was conducting the investigation, not the Naval Investigative Service, as Paul remembered (Harry agreed that they could both have been right). And when ONI officers interrogated Harry, they voiced suspicion of Tidwell for having chartered a Russian ship and using search facilities of the former Soviet Union, an aspect of the investigation that Tidwell did not recall. There had been other differences between Harry and Paul, serious enough to prevent them from working together for quite a while, but now that he was back, Harry was dedicated to Tidwell and his mission.

Harry was the first to express fear of a psychological danger, calling it the "*Sierra Madre* Syndrome," for the Academy Award–winning motion picture about gold and greedy men. "It wasn't long ago that the gold was actually secondary in Paul's mind," he explained. "He was very sensitive about the sinking of the submarine, the loss of life, and about returning personal effects to Japan. In fact, as it was originally planned, this trip was not for finding gold. That would come later, though I know he hadn't figured on so much pressure from Zajonc and Philippone. His purpose on this trip was to come out here with the VC-69 veterans and maybe some Japanese kinfolk, visit the submarine and survey the site, and take pictures for IMAX and National Geographic. It was going to make him famous, and that's what Paul cared about. He was hoping to see his name up there with Beebe, Piccard, Cousteau, and Ballard."

It was suggested that Tidwell's initials might imply courage, as in PT-109 of the John F. Kennedy mythology, but they also evoke an image of Phineas T. Barnum, the circus impresario. Harry simply replied: "That's Paul. If he wasn't a master showman, we wouldn't be here."

Harry Masson had done engineering jobs in the offshore oil fields of the Gulf of Mexico, so he was acutely aware of the risk involved in diving to great depth in a manned submersible. The Mirs were rated for six thousand meters (19,685 feet), and Momi was on the bottom at fifty-three hundred meters (17,389 feet), which would be called "pushing the envelope" in test-pilot jargon. The ratings are based on the shear level—defined in physics as the level of lateral deformation produced by an external force—of the nickel-steel sphere of the submersible. There were, however, systems outside the sphere whose reliability worried Harry because they had a history of failure. These were the electrical and hydraulic systems that regulated the water level of ballast tanks, which in turn determined the submersible's buoyancy—that is to say, its ability to submerge and rise to the surface. Harry had read the documentation report based on test dives of the Mirs and learned of hydraulic problems beginning at sixteen thousand feet. "They kept telling the pilots to go deeper," he said, looking troubled as he spoke. "Then certain other things didn't work, until they finally reached twenty thousand feet. Just reading about it was scary as hell."

A *mir* was a village in czarist Russia and a commune since 1917; today it is a colloquial term for exploratory vehicles— spacecraft and submersibles. In the case of the latter, *Mir 1* and *Mir 2* are the only two of a kind, so it is a name as well as a generic descriptive. Built by Rauma-Repola of Finland, the Mirs were tested in December 1987, eight hundred miles south of the Canary Islands in the mid-Atlantic. Anatoly Sagalevitch, our head of expedition, was a designer of the Mirs for the Shirshov Institute and one of the test pilots. Problems were encountered at five thousand meters when a high-pressure ballast pump failed. "The test dive wasn't interrupted," according to the report, "because the crew calculated the buoyancy of the vehicle at different depths, and after a discussion with the surface officer, decided to complete the dive." *Mir 1* reached bottom at a depth of 6,170 meters, but a return to the *Keldysh* was only achieved by activating an emergency system in which metal pellets were jettisoned. When *Mir 2* was tested on the following day, and a similar emergency occurred, it was again necessary to jettison pellets.

Harry had given Paul a copy of the report and assumed he had read it, but they had not discussed the early testing of the Mirs and mechanical failures at five thousand meters, as they might have in preparation for Tidwell's dive on Saturday, November 21, aboard *Mir 2*. We would realize our mistake in not paying close attention to the Mirs' early history, especially the test dive record, for it would have prepared us for what happened aboard *Mir 1* that Saturday. Understandably, it was not something Tidwell wanted to discuss as he prepared for an experience he expected to be quite frightening. He readily admitted that he looked forward to what the French call *la vieillesse*, or old age, and the only time he had thought about dying was when he purchased life insurance—for his family's benefit and for Philippone's, as stipulated in their contract. "I'm certainly looking forward to my first dive," Tidwell commented a day or so before he was to go, "and I hope to be looking forward to my second dive as well."

Tidwell thought it over on the night before his first dive, wondering why, first of all, he was willing to squeeze his fifty-year-old body into a cabin seven feet in diameter with two burly Russians and descend to a region of the planet far less traveled by humans than outer space. The answer was easy enough—this was a personal quest, and for Tidwell not to go down to her, not to pay his respects personally to Momi and the men who died with her, would leave it unfulfilled and was unthinkable. As he explained: "I cannot see myself as a nonparticipant in this final leg of the journey. I might as well abandon the project, trade it off in some way, but that is not an option. I decided long ago I would finish what I started, though it has taken longer than anyone expected. As we said good-bye to our daughter in Virginia, I was really touched by her parting remark. 'Please hurry,' she said."

Tidwell acknowledged there was a ceremonial ingredient of trips to the site, on the first dive especially, but he was unapologetic and brushed aside suggestions that it was for the benefit of the cameras. He was also plagued by practical concerns, such as procedural discipline. "We have to complete a navigation survey in the first two days of diving, which may sound easy but won't be," he explained. There would be a tendency to stop and look and try to pick up items of interest, such as metal ingots that appear in photos taken in 1995. "We don't know yet what they are," said Tidwell, "whether gold or tin or whatever." But when a Mir lands to pick something up, it creates a billowing cloud of dust that will make it impossible to discern objects and features of the bottom for the remaining hours of the dive. "One good reason we need to complete the survey," Tidwell added, "is so when we see something we want to retrieve, we can mark its location and come back for it at the end of the day." Thinking about retrieval led to another prominent concern: How much in the form of relics, personal effects, and precious metals, hopefully, could be brought to the surface? "See how they screwed up?" said Tidwell, referring to Philippone and Zajonc. By canceling orders for materials without consulting Tidwell, they had severely limited what could be recovered by the Mirs. It wasn't so much a weight limitation, he explained. "We brought along about a ton of syntactic foam to increase buoyancy, and if we jettison some heavy equipment and reduce the number of passengers from three to two, we can lift five hundred pounds on each Mir." But volume is another matter, and this had not been taken into account. "The Mirs are limited to what can be stored in a pair of sample baskets about two feet wide by four feet long." Tidwell drew a sketch as he spoke. "We originally ordered steel plate to build boxes that would hold five hundred pounds of gold, but it too was eliminated by the budget cut."

Tidwell said his greatest worry was Philippone's unpredictability, which had been demonstrated more than once since he became the primary investor. "He agreed to finance the search with a three-million-dollar loan, for which he gets half of whatever treasure we find. That was last March, and a couple of months later he said he wanted to join the expedition." There was a meeting in August in Seattle, to settle with Anatoly on the charter of the *Keldysh*, and Philippone was there, as well as Ted Brockett of Sound Ocean Systems. It was Brockett's opinion, which he expressed to Philippone, that the expedition in the fall was to be a survey trip, with no ex-pectation of recovering gold. On the strength of that information, Philippone did three things: he reduced the amount of his invest-ment loan to $2 million, he took charge of the finances, and he sought the right to participate in a future operation if gold was not recovered on the one coming up. From then on Tidwell did not see a check signed by Philippone because payments were made di-rectly to the Shirshov Institute and other contractors.

Tidwell admitted that he agreed to Philippone's demands "as the only way to get here," but he never signed the piece of paper that formalized the amended agreement. As for Philippone want-ing an option to invest in a future expedition, Tidwell was inclined to say no. "I say Philippone's interference doesn't bother me," he explained, "but it's there. He has no idea what's going on. He watches and says it's marvelous, without understanding how com-plex it is, or how dangerous it's going to be when we dive into a black abyss with only battery-powered lights and sonar to see and navigate."

Tidwell was asked why, in the original deal, he was willing to offer Philippone four times his investment (based on $12 million for a ton of gold) and to treat the $3 million as a loan. He thought a minute before he answered. "It's true that I was taking a risk, but I retained the so-called entertainment rights—the TV documen-tary, an IMAX film, and a popular motion picture—as compensa-tion. I won't feel badly about his reducing the loan to two million dollars if we make a recovery. I'm okay with that."

Every other day for two exhilarating weeks the main events were the launching and recovery of the Mirs, and from a spectator's point of view, these activities were simply magnificent. The sendoff always occurred in midmorning, between nine thirty and ten thirty, for reasons the Russians kept to themselves. We could speculate to our hearts' content and even voice an opinion that it might be better to go off at the crack of dawn, but to no avail. The timing of the dives was up to Anatoly, who seemed to be a creature of ritual and possibly more than a little superstitious. When he was a pilot on the first test of the Mirs in 1987, the launch time was nine a.m., which apparently established a pattern for subsequent operations. A dive normally lasts from twelve to twenty hours, meaning a return to the deck of the *Keldysh* early the following day— between two and five a.m., it was not important. Now that the time had finally come to visit Momi, what difference did a few hours make? We had been waiting for months going on years, and Tidwell had been dealing with an *I-52* obsession for nearly a decade. On dive day one, he was to ride aboard *Mir 2* with Evgeny Chemiaev, genial Genia, deemed the most proficient of the Mir pilots. *Mir I*, with Anatoly Sagalevitch at the controls, would depart first—always, for an obscure reason—with Marco Flagg, a navigation consultant, aboard. Sagalevitch had insisted on two pilots in each Mir on this first trip to an uncharted region, though on subsequent dives two observers with one pilot would be permitted.

The mood was cheerful and optimistic that morning. Tidwell hugged Jo Anne good-bye, as cameras whirred and clicked, and word got around that it was the day before their thirtieth wedding anniversary. "They are cheering for you," the dutiful wife said of the crowd that had gathered. "They're counting their money," Tidwell replied.

Mir 1 was over the side and away, and it was time to board *Mir 2*— Genia Chemiaev, Tidwell, and copilot Sergei Smolitski. All were wearing blue flight suits with a Mir emblem above the right chest pocket, but the uniform look ended there. While Genia seemed the model pilot in every aspect, Tidwell might have been a visiting V.I.P., and Sergei, bearded and black-hatted, looked to be a natural for the cast of *Fiddler on the Roof*. One by one, they climbed a ladder and slithered through a hatch at the top of the sphere, stopping to place their shoes in a yellow toolbox. They would be attending to Momi in stocking feet, which seemed fitting in light of Japanese custom.

As *Mir 2* was lifted over the side and allowed to float in the rolling sea, it was quickly towed clear of the *Keldysh* by a high-powered tender, the *Koresh*, which in Russian means friend. Enter the Zodiac, an inflatable craft that is remarkably seaworthy and skims the waves powered by a 40-horsepower outboard motor. A Zodiac crewman, one of three, was standing in the bow, poised to board the Mir. His name is Anatoly Osadsky, called Tolia, a former officer of Soviet Special Forces, who has also been a Mir pilot and a diver. Tolia was quite a performer, leaping from the Zodiac to the orange-and-white Mir, and how he kept his footing on the slippery fiberglass superstructure was anyone's guess. His job was to disconnect the bullcock, which he did as waves nearly washed him from his perch, and with the Mir no longer tethered but still under tow by the *Koresh*, Tolia dove into the water and swam to the Zodiac a few yards away.

Mir 2 was ready to depart on its long journey to the bottom, which was described in detail by Tidwell upon his return.

> As the weight of water pumped into the ballast tanks overcame its buoyancy, the submersible slowly descended, and in three and a half hours we reached the bottom. It was

a soft landing, not even a thud. Genia had been watching a sensor, and when we reached a certain depth, he turned on one of the 1,200-watt exterior lights so he could see through the main viewport, a window 200 millimeters in diameter in the center of his control panel. There are two smaller viewports, 120 millimeters, to either side, but I could get a better look at what was out there using the monitor of the Zeus, a high-resolution video camera.

Once we landed, the trip to the *I-52* took but about fifteen minutes, and I could look through crystal-clear water at a desert surface with gentle slopes and ridges two or three feet high. We now know from having retrieved articles covered with the material that it's more like a silt or mud, but it had a sandy look from twenty feet above. Genia was using the hydraulic thrusters, one at the rear and one on each side, to propel our vehicle at five knots or so. Pretty soon I could see debris—pieces of metal as much as eight feet square that had been shorn from the outer hull of the sub. I thought I'd prepared myself for what I saw next, a shoe, but it came as a shock. I fully realized that I had intruded upon a sacred place, a World War II graveyard, and I was awed.

The debris got thicker, and I knew it was forming a path to its source, guiding us inevitably to the *I-52*. I spotted a sweater and wanted to pick it up but decided against it, for fear we would damage it without the proper tools for handling. We did try to retrieve a tin ingot, but it slipped from the grasp of the Mir's manipulator just as it was being placed in the basket. I had seen ingots in the 1995 photos and could not say for sure what they were, though now it was obvious from the size and shape that they were not gold. We know from Japanese records that the *I-52* was carrying 228 tons of tin, molybdenum, and tungsten, which explains why ingots were strewn all over the place.

We approached from the southeast, running abreast of the starboard bow, forward of the conning tower. I was struck by the stark enormity of the looming shape before me. I knew she was big—over 350 feet—but from now and forever I'll remember Momi as the leviathan of lore. She was listing to port, almost lying on her side, and we could see the length of the hull, all the way to the stern. Then I noticed *Mir 1* perched on Momi's bow, hanging by its manipulators. I would not learn the details until later, but *Mir 1* was in trouble.

My attention was fixed on the *I-52*. Sure, she was a wreck, but the damage was confined to three main areas— much of the bow had been blown away, a section of deck forward of the conning tower was missing, as was a piece between the conning tower and the stern. Other than that, Momi seemed to still be a ship, a ghost ship that will never reach port. Parts of her are intact, in nearly perfect condi-tion. This is surely so of the conning tower, only slightly corroded and standing in behalf of those who died in the sinking. I took note of the bridge, imagining signs of long-lost lives, and it occurred to me once more that war is so stupid, and Momi is a monument to the millions who have died.

As he surveyed the damage further, Tidwell relied on his expe-rience as a salvage engineer in finding clues to the status of the cargo, more specifically to where the gold might be located. "I wanted to know as much as I could about what occurred," he explained. "I needed to understand what happened while the *I-52* descending and when she hit bottom—what cargo spilled out and what was still stored inside. *Mir 2*'s navigation system was not operating because a computer was out, so we were free to roam on dead reckoning." Crossing the debris field in an X-shaped pattern, they set a course and ran along until they stopped seeing debris, then came back around and did it again. It was just a quick survey, but it showed what could be done.

At this point, as they returned to the *I-52* for a closer look, the experience was just a bit hair-raising. "We got a little too close," said Tidwell, "and suddenly realized we were inside the submarine, having entered through a hole in the hull probably caused by an internal explosion. Genia was peering straight ahead and failed to notice these 'rusticles' that caught my eye out the right viewport. I tapped him on the shoulder, pointed at the 'rusticles,' and suggested by my motions that we get the hell out, which we did by reversing the rear thruster. Genia's skill at the controls was very impressive." (Genia Chemiaev later explained that when not piloting a Mir he drove a taxicab in Moscow, and Tidwell thought what a waste of talent that was.)

When *Mir 2* returned to the deck of the *I-52*, *Mir 1* was still sitting there, and Genia learned from Anatoly that they were stuck, unable to pump water out of the ballast tanks. There was more radio conversation, in Russian, and Tidwell decided not to complicate matters by asking questions. When *Mir 1* eventually began a slow ascent, *Mir 2* stayed a thousand meters behind. "It was customary for *Mir 2* to follow *Mir 1*," said Tidwell, "but this was not a matter of protocol. There had been a serious problem, and we remained in position to assist in a rescue, if it came to that. As soon as he knew that *Mir 1* was safely aboard the *Keldysh*, Genia powered up the side thrusters and we sped to the surface."

Expectations were running wild aboard the *Keldysh* that afternoon, based on a misconstrued report from Tidwell that he'd reached an area littered with boxes. They were cargo boxes, larger than any made to hold three thirty-pound gold bars, each bar about the size of a building brick. The cargo boxes were more than the Mir's manipulators could handle, and they were not recorded on videotape because the pan-and-tilt mount on *Mir 2*, the mechanism that aimed the Zeus camera, was not operating. Nevertheless, it was too late to quell a belief that the Mirs were bringing back gold, or to prevent Priit Vesilind of the *National Geographic* from calling by satellite telephone to let his editor know "the good news." We were in the grip of "gold pandemonium," and Harry Masson was quite serious, albeit premature, when he predicted the SEALs would soon summon reinforcements. The Mir control center was a scene of giddy celebration. Philippone put in a radio call to Tidwell and was elated when he got through: "Paul, are you bringing me a souvenir?" Tidwell had little to say, but it didn't dampen Philippone's enthusiasm.

We were crammed into the control center, ordinarily called a navigation lab but now the center of activity, when there was an abrupt change of mood. The Mir communicator was speaking in Russian, but we could sense his anxiety over trouble below. We would learn later of a policy not to let us know if something went wrong, and that policy was in effect. A Mir was in trouble—that was certain—and the mission was being aborted. But which

Mir? What was the trouble? Confusion reigned, and Jo Anne Tidwell was beside herself.

Full details of the trouble on *Mir 1* would not be generally known until seen in the light of day, and there would be serious repercussions. For the moment all that mattered was the safe return of the crew. *Mir 1* was on the deck by one a.m. Sunday, and Anatoly brushed aside questions about the emergency, offering instead his succinct impressions of the *I-52*. "Submarine destroyed, nowhere bow," he said. "Machine guns sighted, stern intact, very small pieces in debris field." *Mir 2* followed close behind, though it took a good hour to bring the submersible alongside so a crane could lift it from the sea. Coming down the ladder into the arms of Jo Anne, Tidwell was delighted with his day's work and happy to admit he was at a loss for words. "Unbelievable," he said, as he proceeded to offer a steady stream of mind's-eye images: "A whole side of the submarine was destroyed when she slammed into the bottom like a meteorite. There is cargo everywhere. Lots of ingots, but they appear to be tin." He pointed to a couple of samples in the basket—a tin ingot and a metal box containing liquid opium. And yes, he had seen personal items, pieces of clothing, a few shoes, and he had been reminded of the tragic consequences of war. Again, groping for a way to express heartfelt feelings, he did the best he could. "It was overwhelming."

Tidwell was thirsty—he had gone easy on liquids on account of primitive toilet facilities on the Mirs. Offered water, he said: "I'd rather have a Heineken." (Tidwell was aware that the National Geographic film crew had raised the issue of commercialism over Hewlett-Packard emblems decorating his equipment, and his ad-libbed beer commercial was to show he got the point.)

WE'VE MET THE ENEMY—US

The day of Tidwell's close encounter with Momi—a crowning personal achievement, for all the world to see—was followed by a day of adversity in the search for her cargo of gold. It was not something Tidwell could have foreseen as he sailed around the wreck site observing cargo spillage that made it appear likely that there was gold in the debris field. As it turned out, the trouble could be traced more readily to Cold War animosities than to anything that had happened here and now, yet the all-too-evident differences between Tidwell and Philippone offered an old apparatchik like Anatoly Sagalevitch the chance to play one American against another. The immediate issue was the mechanical reliability of the Mir submersibles, about which there was no disagreement since the safety of the crew was paramount. But as the debate proceeded, it encompassed expedition objectives, ultimately leading to the question: Who's in charge here? At the end of the day Tidwell's position was intact, but he had resorted to autocratic management, ruling by fiat rather than bowing to an apparent majority will. Finally, he scolded his minions. He was tired of the petty bickering, and he noted a comment by Anatoly. "He has sensed our problem," said Tidwell. "He says we are not a family."

Marco Flagg did not appear to be a man who frightened easily. As a scuba diver he had once encountered a great white and would have been a fast lunch had the shark not taken a bite of Marco's oxygen tank and found it hard to digest. It was a terrifying experience, but to be expected by anyone who dives the dangerous depths off California, and when a friend proposed to Marco doing a movie about it, he trusted his luck and returned to the great white's habitat. Born in Germany, Marco came to the United States in his twenties, settled in California, and founded a company that makes ocean survey systems. His job on this expedition was to survey the *I-52* site and make it navigable—that is, once we located something of interest on the bottom but had to leave it behind, we could find our way back. It stood to reason that a navigator would be on the first dive to the *I-52*, and he was aboard *Mir 1* with Anatoly as pilot. With all the excitement of Tidwell's trip on *Mir 2* that Saturday, insufficient attention was paid to Marco's harrowing experience on *Mir 1*. When it was over, he was congratulated for a difficult job well done, though we had no way of knowing how difficult. If he seemed distraught, it was attributed to fatigue, and he was forgiven for rushing off to bed. But eight hours later Marco was back on deck in an angry argument with Anatoly.

The fourth deck of the *Keldysh* is where the action is. The Mir submersibles are housed along the starboard side toward the stern, and adjacent to their garages is a maintenance lab and offices for the pilots. Over on the port side is the *Koresh,* the twenty-five-foot fiberglass auxiliary launch, and the Zodiac inflatable craft that is used by divers who tend the Mirs at the beginning and end of each dive. There are also cables of varying lengths and capacities, one of which is capable of reaching a stranded Mir at six thousand meters, although it has never been put to the test. (The *Keldysh* was featured in James Cameron's epic film *Titanic,* and it was from the cable platform on the stern of the fourth deck that the hundred-year-old survivor of the tragedy dropped her "Heart of the Ocean" diamond necklace into the sea.)

What was said between Marco and Anatoly was lost in the wind, but the gestures and facial expressions spoke clearly enough, and when Anatoly turned heel and went into the Mir maintenance lab, he slammed the door behind him. The film crew had been meeting nearby, and their anguish was evident. "People's lives are at stake," said Mark Stouffer, the director, who could be forgiven in a stressful period for such an obvious remark. Paul Ilinsky, a Russian translator in the employ of National Geographic, had been admonished by Anatoly for reporting radio communications from the day before that indicated a mechanical failure with one of the ballast tank pumps. "It's the old Communist way of threat and denial," said Ilinsky. "Now they claim it was a false radio transmission." "Bullshit," said David Huie, a lighting technician. "Marco thought he was going to die." And he added: "If there was no problem, why are they out there now draining all the hydraulic systems?"

On the day before, as *Mir 1* approached Momi, Marco made a scuba diver's assessment. "It would make a good diving wreck if in shallow water—busted open, so you could swim inside, and there would be lots of fish." More to the point, Marco was concerned about the way the Mir kept bumping into the submarine. It didn't make the job any easier, deploying three transponders and doing some initial navigation, and the noise of the thrusters made it hard to record ranges. Marco was busy with his work and unaware of another problem until *Mir 1* came to rest on top of the *I-52*'s hull, its manipulator arms clinging to the edge of the deck. From the angle of tilt Marco could tell that the Mir had lost its balance, which was maintained by pumping water in and out of the ballast tanks. After sitting on the *I-52* for maybe ten minutes, Anatoly checked his gauges and clasped his face in his hands. He could release enough water to move off the deck of the submarine, and did so, but the tanks were still half full, and *Mir 1* sank to the bottom.

"I knew for sure there was a problem," said Marco on Sunday. "We were stuck, and the pumps weren't pumping. I tried to help, but the language barrier made it impossible. The ballast readings just wouldn't go down. I asked Anatoly if we had a problem, and he replied in English: 'No problem.'"

Still it was serious enough that Anatoly turned to an emergency system consisting of 350 kilograms of nickel-steel pellets that are held in place in two funnel-shaped canisters by an electromagnet and are dumped when the magnet is switched off. He had coped with this situation at least once before—on the first test dives of each of the Mirs in 1987, when the emergency systems worked—which may explain his confidence. But nothing happened when he hit the off switch, and now he admitted, again in English: "Problem."

"Anatoly got on the radio with Genia in *Mir 2*," Marco recalled. "It sounded as if Genia was making a number of suggestions, and one of them seemed to work. We began to rise very slowly, at about ten meters a minute. And when we got to three thousand meters the ballast pumps were operating normally, meaning the problem had been caused by pressure at a greater depth."

Asked about the argument out on deck, Marco said Anatoly had asked him to be silent about what had happened because it would be bad for business if it got out. "I said he really ought to come clean about it, and that's when Anatoly got angry. It's too bad. They have an old submersible system, and old systems develop problems."

A meeting in the seventh-deck conference room on Sunday afternoon was a chaotic free-for-all, an airing of attitudes that ended in a muddle. Flagg could be forgiven for dismissing Sagalevitch's assurances that any problems with the Mirs had been corrected: "I need to know that the system is fail-safe." Larry Barrett, one of the SEALs, was sympathetic: "It looks a lot different when you get down there and look right into the eye of the elephant." The National Geographic people did not refrain from exerting their considerable influence, as Stouffer laid it on the line: his crew would not dive while safety was an unresolved issue. An all-Russian crew on *Mir 1* was discussed and all but dismissed by Vesilind, the *National Geographic* writer, who argued for an American aboard *Mir 1*, "to keep the Russians honest." Photographer Jonathan Blair said he'd be happy if Anatoly would just take him aside and admit to a problem, whereupon the National Geographic contingent departed en masse so it could meet in the hallway and adopt a unified position. Zajonc spoke in favor of a dive mission on Monday, even if the *Mir 1* crew was all Russian, and Philippone, a self-appointed arbiter, weighed the options. He was asked to explain company policy on minimum safety requirements, and rather than admit he was not authorized to speak for Cape Verde Explorations, he declared it was an individual issue, not a company matter.

Tidwell said little, but as the meeting was ending, he promised an announcement based on a discussion he'd had with Anatoly. When he returned to the conference room after dinner to narrate a videotape of his dive on Saturday, Tidwell seized the opportunity to make a few observations. It was getting late, and the room was only half full, but Mary Ann Philippone was still there and could be depended on to carry a message to her husband.

Tidwell skipped polite niceties. "There are some things I can't stand," he said. "One is the kind of crap that has been going on around here. You know what I mean, the sniping, the cheap shots. People are entitled to their opinions, but enough is enough. I want it to stop." He then announced Monday's dive assignments. They were in keeping with his objectives, operational and photographic. National Geographic would occupy seats in both Mirs—Blair in

Mir 1 and Bill Mills, the television cameraman, in *Mir 2*. Tim McGinnis, an ocean engineering contractor, was also in *Mir 2* to complete the site survey. There were still signs of unrest, which Tidwell chose to ignore. As far as he was concerned, we had weathered the storm.

Monday, November 23—at breakfast Marco Flagg announced that he was satisfied with the repairs to the ballast system and was ready to dive on *Mir 1* again. Why the abrupt turnabout? He'd had a long talk with Genia Chemiaev while they were installing laptop navigation computers on the Mirs, and he had finally gotten straight answers. The pump problem had been the result of a faulty electrical connector that reduced hydraulic pressure, causing the system to quit at a depth of three thousand meters. The connector had been replaced, and the system was functioning normally. As for the drop weights, the nickel-steel pellets to be jettisoned in an emergency, Genia's explanation was even simpler. The system had been recently modified; to prevent the pellets from dropping a few at a time as water rushed into their container, the power of an electromagnet that holds them in place was increased. To do this, a second switch was added, and deactivation of both switches was required to release the pellets. Anatoly had forgotten about the second switch, said Genia, and was able to correct the problem when reminded of it. Again, Marco was satisfied, though it occurred to him that Anatoly might have spared him a lot of grief by admitting to a poor memory.

Marco still had a question, and Genia seemed anxious to restore his confidence. Did releasing the drop weights guarantee a return to the surface? The answer was no and could be explained by simple arithmetic. The Mirs' ballast tanks hold a thousand kilograms of water, and the submersible is neutrally buoyant at between four hundred and six hundred kilograms. To achieve positive buoyancy and thus enable the submersible to rise, the weight of the water must be less than that of the drop weights, 350 kilograms. But even if the emergency ballast release failed to rescue a Mir, as it did for so long on Saturday, there is a red-button escape mechanism that activates a life-support system and releases the batteries from the undercarriage of the submersible. "The only way to get a one-way ticket on a Mir," Marco observed, "is to keep the ballast tanks full and run out of battery power."

Marco would remember those words as prophetic when he made a second dive on November 25, again with Sagalevitch on *Mir 1*. He was more familiar with the system, thanks to Genia's briefing, and he knew to pay attention to ballast water level and battery power. For that very reason—Marco was a man who knew too much—the experience was all the more harrowing.

Mir 1 reached the *I-52* at two thirty in the afternoon, and when *Mir 2* arrived, with McGinnis aboard, they tried running both Mirs on one navigating system. But the system, which depends on radio signals from transponders, was disturbed by the noise of the thrusters. A problem with the rudder made it necessary for *Mir 1* to steer with its side thrusters, so Marco directed Anatoly to a point south of the *I-52*, where it was possible to navigate by dead reckoning. He would pick a starting point and ask Anatoly to proceed on a selected heading, and by applying elapsed time to the speed of the Mir, he computed the distance to a visual target. He worked on the survey until after six thirty, when Anatoly said it was time to go home because the batteries were running low. "Just before we began pumping water out of the ballast tanks to make our ascent," Marco recalled, "we picked up a tin ingot. It was six fifty-six, and I made a note that we had used five hundred ampere-hours of electric power and had only two hundred left. We appeared to be in trouble." Having pumped for over an hour, *Mir 1* was able to leave the bottom at eight eleven only by dumping some emergency drop weights. "It should have taken about fifteen minutes to pump enough water to begin our ascent," said Marco. "We had used another eighty-eight ampere-hours of power and were rising very slowly. We then got rid of the tin ingot."

Mir 1's headway was very disturbing—a hundred meters in twenty-four minutes, barely four meters a minute—and battery power was being expended at an alarming rate of more than one ampere-hour per minute. Marco then noticed something that was all the more ominous. When Anatoly shut off the pumps, water flowed back into the ballast tanks. "We had only about one hundred ampere-hours of power left, and water kept coming back in about as fast as we could pump it out."

Anatoly kept releasing drop weights, struggling to reach the three-thousand-meter level, where he knew the pumps would function more efficiently. Meanwhile, Marco made computations to see if the battery, now dangerously close to its seven-hundred-ampere-hour limit, would get them to the surface. "As the voltage of the nickel-cadmium cells started to drop, I remembered a feature of NICAD cells. They hold at 1.2 volts for most of their life, then the voltage drops rapidly. Ours was at 1.1, about gone. There were other batteries on board, but this was the main one and the only one that powered the pumps. If the main battery died, our only hope would be to dump it. It weighed a ton, so we would have reached the surface quickly, at a cost of a million dollars."

In the angry aftermath of his first dive, Marco told Anatoly that it was a strain on his relations with the Americans to keep denying problems. This time Anatoly promised not to do that, and true to his word, when they were safely on the deck of the *Keldysh,* he offered a logical explanation for water flowing back into the ballast tanks. It was caused by a worn seal on a filling plug that was promptly replaced, and that was that. Or was it? Tidwell was disturbed enough about the latest life-threatening incident that he confronted Anatoly, who proposed pulling *Mir 1* off the line and sending *Mir 2* by itself on Friday's dive. Tidwell was losing patience. He wasn't worried about mechanical systems, which he believed to be basically sound, but about careless maintenance that had allowed a worn seal to go unnoticed. A reason for choosing the Mirs over other submersibles, manned and remotely operated, was the quality of photography they could produce by lighting the scene for one another. And as Anatoly well knew, there was a safety advantage of the Mirs working in tandem.

The dive assignments were still bargaining chips in a contest for control, and while Tidwell had prevailed to this point, he was seeing his authority diminish in proportion to the prospect of finding gold. The dives were also a source of dispute and animosity in conference room planning sessions. Zajonc had been blunt in admonishing Blair, who had stopped taking pictures only long enough on his first dive to retrieve a single box of the *I-52* cargo. Zajonc informed Blair that he was at the rear of the line for dive assignments, which was a hollow threat because Blair was covered by a contract with Tidwell Entertainment, not Cape Verde Explorations, and he would make two more dives whether Zajonc liked it or not. "I left my ego at the dock," Blair said when asked if he was offended by Zajonc's rebuke. He had studiously tried not to take a side in the political war, although he had probably helped Tidwell's cause by subordinating himself to the mission. He voiced no objection to being assigned to *Mir 1* for all three of his dives, and was reluctant to report that on the third one, on December 3, there were suspicious signs of an electrical fire.

Philippone was beginning to worry Tidwell. Every time the Mirs returned at an early-morning hour, he would be out on deck waiting for a chance to peer inside the sample baskets, looking for gold that was not there. Then he would walk away, wearing an expression of dejected disbelief. Tidwell had seen the look before, when he worked with Mel Fisher searching for Spanish treasure off the Florida Keys. People are strangely affected by gold, he theorizes—they become obsessed with it and even dream about it. They act irrationally, making inconsistent decisions and acting in ways they cannot explain. They take to heart the wondrous characteristics of gold, as did Lois De Lorenzo, the author of a chatty little book called *Gold Fever: The Art of Panning and Sluicing* (Gem Guides Book Company, 1970). "It has a low melting point and is malleable and more ductile than any other metal. It can be hammered into sheets as thin as 1/250-thousandths of an inch, and has been drawn without breaking into a 35-mile wire. It is heavy: 19.3 in specific gravity. It is soft: 2.5 on the hardness scale. It occurs almost everywhere in the world. The Bible refers to 'gold' at least 25 times. Archaeologists have uncovered hoards of gold in the ancient ruins of Greece, Egypt, Mexico and Peru; and Egyptian monuments show that gold has been panned, melted, and pounded to fit mankind's wants and needs as far back as 2900 B.C." But the author of *The Treasure of the Sierra Madre* (Alfred A. Knopf, 1935) took a decidedly dimmer view. "Gold is for thieves and swindlers," B. Traven wrote. "For this reason they own most of it. The rest is owned by those who do not care where the gold comes from or in what sort of hands it has been."

6. THE SECRET MISSION
OF THE *I-52*

Resigned to the fate of the *I-52* but still sounding tentative, Admiral Kojima posed the question of alternative passage in a dispatch to Tokyo on August 14. "In the event that it becomes necessary to acknowledge the loss of the Ginmatsu, I should like to negotiate with the German Navy for transportation to Japan . . . of the several officials . . . who were scheduled to return on the next trip of the Ginmatsu." He attached a priority list, and passenger number one was Commander Inaba, identified as a navy paymaster, which was misleading since Inaba was a financial officer who negotiated with Japan's Axis partners for major weapons systems, paid for with the tons of gold being transported to Europe by submarine. Number two was Technical Commander Genzo Syozi (spelled Shooji in transcribed radio transmissions), who actually was an air force colonel and aeronautical engineer, an expert on rockets and jet engines. (Syozi had been scheduled to return to Japan in April aboard the *I-29*, bringing plans for two

Messerschmitt prototypes, the Me 163 and the Me 262, but his orders were abruptly canceled.) Next in line was Technical Lieutenant Commander Hideo Tomonaga, a naval architect and inventor of a submarine depth stabilizer, who had come from Japan by submarine in 1943 and had just returned from Lorient, as a member of the reception party that waited in vain for the *I-52*. It soon became clear that Inaba, Syozi, and Tomonaga worked as a team, most recently in June 1944, traveling to Milan for negotiations with the Italian designer-builder of a one-man submarine.

YAMABUKI TRANSFER

There was an unspoken reason for Syozi's sudden reassignment and his teaming with Tomonaga when he did. It was connected with the item of cargo referred to as *Yamabuki* by Kojiro Kitamura of the Yokohama Specie Bank, who said in a dispatch to Japan on June 7, the day after the Normandy invasion, that if the enemy succeeded in establishing a strategic position in France, the item would have to be conveyed by land. The cargo was at Kiel, and the *I-52*, if and when she arrived, would be at Lorient, unable to reach Kiel due to a concentration of enemy air and sea forces in support of the invasion. So it is quite likely that the cargo item called *Yamabuki* was hauled from Kiel to Lorient, which might explain why a reception party of ten Japanese naval officers needed a fifty-passenger bus. Bearing in mind the circumstances, all that is required to identify the item is a careful review of the *I-52* loading plan transmitted to Tokyo by Kojima on June 22. The item in question appeared in the radio dispatch as "(13) uranium oxide, 500 kilograms," but "uranium" was deleted in a hard-copy Ultra intercept, the censorship having occurred during a review of the document by U.S. Fleet Intelligence. A radio message could not have been censored, though the uranium reference could have been omitted or identified by its code name, *Yamabuki,* had the Japanese wished to do so. They did not, probably because they did not see the necessity of concealing the purchase of uranium oxide in radio communications, as indicated by previous references to uranium purchases (army secret wire, Tokyo to Berlin, November 15, 1943). U.S. policy, on the other hand, was to delete any mention of a fissionable material that might insinuate nuclear development, probably because such a development proceeding in the United States was a closely guarded secret. U.S. intelligence agencies had no reason to believe that the Japanese were nearly ready to build an atom bomb (in which the uranium itself is the explosive element). But they were clearly capable of scattering radioactive material over a vast area with devastating effect, using a conventional explosive such as TNT.

Three additional technical officers rounded out Kojima's top-priority list for passage to Asia—Technical Commander Kuroda, Technical Lieutenant Tarutani, and Tadao Yamato, the civilian technician who had been quickly trained on the T-5 acoustic torpedo and was now its custodian. Other departments as well—Kojima referred to them as "the Army, etc."—were heard from in the clamor to arrange transit, and not all of them were Japanese. A ranking German officer—Lieutenant General Ulrich Kessler, the designated air attaché in Tokyo—was trying to reach Japan, and Admiral Abe made a special plea in his behalf. The German air force was seeking to secure closer Japanese-German cooperation,

Abe advised on August 4, "by getting the general quickly to Japan by . . . some means or other . . . The war having now entered into a really decisive stage, the need for ready liaison between Japan and Germany will never be more pressing. . . ." Abe and Kojima were vocal advocates of an air route between Germany and Japan, although German-Soviet hostilities were a serious impediment. Nevertheless, Abe took this opportunity to press the case. "I consider it . . . advisable," he argued, "for Japan . . . to take steps . . . to cooperate in an early fulfillment of this flight by some means or other. . . . I may say that the Ambassador and Military Attaché entirely agree."

Three German submarines—the *U-180,* the *U-195,* and the *U-219*—were dispatched from France in August 1944 loaded with new weaponry: V-series rockets, target-seeking torpedoes, radar sets and accessories. The *U-195* and the *U-219* reached Indonesia following a four-month voyage, but the *U-180*—the boat that rendezvoused with the *I-29* and brought Lieutenant Commander Tomonaga to Europe—got only as far as the Bay of Biscay, where she hit a British mine and sank. These departures occurred too soon to meet Japanese needs, but Kojima reported on August 27 to the Navy Department in Tokyo that a U-boat was scheduled to leave Kiel for Penang in early September: "We are negotiating the passage for some of those who are scheduled to return to Japan in view of the current war situation." He further explained that the German navy would be sending one or two submarines a month to the Indian Ocean, if conditions permitted. "I shall try to procure transportation each time for about three men and purchased goods to the amount of 15 tons on surface and 50 tons submerged."

A "DEPLORABLE" STATE OF LIAISON

Abe and Kojima met on September 3 with Admiral Meisel, the chief of the German naval staff, to discuss "the growing serious- ness of the war situation," as Abe put it; but if they were hoping for specific proposals, they came away disappointed. Meisel was con- sidered a man of little imagination, who functioned, according to a Doenitz biographer, as a "transmitting organ of Doenitz's ideas." The best he could offer on this occasion was an assertion that as unfavorable as the war situation might be, "it was of vital impor- tance that they should be resolved to continue the fight to the end." He did discuss the U-boat war, conceding that the loss of coastal ports in France had disrupted operations, but he promised that the policy would be to continue U-boat activity "to the utmost . . . by making use of bases on the German . . . and Norwegian coasts." The plan now, said Meisel, was to intensify U-boat operations, which he acknowledged were Germany's "sole means of carrying out aggressive operations." Accordingly, seven boats presently in the Bordeaux area, together with other boats on the French coast, were being ordered to proceed to North Sea bases. How would the enemy respond? Probably by moving antisubmarine forces— aircraft carriers in particular—from their present positions in the Mediterranean and the Bay of Biscay to the coast of Norway.

On September 6 Kojima sent Tokyo an advisory on where the en- emy was concentrating its ASW strength in the Atlantic, based on intelligence obtained by the Operations Section of the German air force. The information differed entirely from what was heard three days earlier from Meisel: instead of assembling off Norway, the Anglo-American antisubmarine groups were headed south.

"Britain and the United States, having completed anti-submarine measures in the North Atlantic," read Kojima's summary, "have now set about to make plans for anti-submarine defense of the South Atlantic routes, which are menaced by numerous German submarines. This is confirmed by intelligence reports, which indicate the new establishment of air bases on the northern coast of South America and the western coast of Africa." The intelligence also suggested that the enemy "is studying methods whereby he can seek out and attack submerged submarines from airplanes. In one of the methods which we know to be used, special buoys are dropped in a triangular pattern in the area where the submarine is thought to be, and an 'impulse' is then sent from the plane. . . . The distance from each of the buoys [to the submarine] is measured . . . and the position of the submarine is determined."

The hypothetical strategy of the German air force against submerged submarines was remarkably similar to that of the U.S. Navy in its actual attack on the *I-52*.

Conditions still did not permit a U-boat departure from Kiel as of September 7, and Kojima so informed Tokyo. "With regard to the scheduled transportation of men and materials now in Europe to Japan, we have had since the disappearance of the Ginmatsu no means other than German submarines. An agreement was negotiated with the Germans, and departures were scheduled. However, as a result of the recent heavy bombings on Kiel, the situation has become such that departures cannot be made. . . . I am also afraid that the increasing heavy bombing attacks on Kiel and other submarine bases are turning western Germany into a battlefield. Moreover, the enemy is certain to increase his attacks against submarines in the North Sea–Norway area with planes, ships, mines, etc. In making plans about transportation by submarines, one cannot look lightly upon the true significance of these events. In addition, the war situation is developing very cataclysmically, and even though there might be a change in conditions, one should not fail to give heed to the fact that the time at sea would be at least three months." Kojima at this point spoke, as Abe had done, in favor of an air route via Siberia. "Since Finland has fallen, might not our former contacts in Turkey serve as a channel?" (Finland, in 1941, had joined in the German invasion of Russia, but was forced to withdraw in September 1944.)

Kojima was sounding frustrated, even desperate, when he addressed the transport issue and viewed it in the context of victory or defeat. "The war situation is indeed grave," he lamented on September 14, and to the specific issue he addressed day by day, he offered a bleak assessment: "The state of liaison by sea between Germany and Japan is deplorable. Increasing difficulties may be expected. . . . Although a one-way flight could be made by German planes over the northern route . . . if the Germans should suspend the manufacture of large-type planes, this hope too would prove to be ephemeral." The attaché offered a quick solution: "Japan could purchase a suitable plane from Germany, and based on an understanding with Russia . . . send it to Japan. At least we would be able to transport important Japanese personnel. . . . If the Russians object to this, I believe it would be well to have . . . [them] select the route, arrival and departure points, and carry out inspections." Tokyo did not respond directly, but did so upon hearing from Kojima that General Kessler was about to receive his orders and would depart for Japan in four to six weeks, either by submarine or aboard a Junker 290 long-range bomber. The central authorities replied on October 10 that while the Germans planned to avoid Soviet territory, "it is to be expected that when it comes to actual practice they will (for reasons connected with the capacity of the aircraft) take the short-cut over Siberia. . . . Hence, taking into account the critical states of relations with Russia . . . we desire most emphatically to be free of any affairs which might . . . give rise to trouble. The U.S.S.R. has recently been taking a particularly serious view of any violations of her territorial water and air, and appears bent on making an issue of them. . . . It almost looks as though the underlying motive is to use such cases as a means of stirring up trouble against Japan, and over here we try to be most circumspect. . . . [I]n the case of the journey to Japan of the Air attaché and his party, if their dispatch is a matter of urgency please do your best to persuade the Germans to make use of submarines for this."

Kessler's appointment was "temporarily canceled," Kojima reported in December, and the general attributed it to the inability of the air force staff to "free itself from a continental point of view." Tired of waiting, Kessler appealed to Oshima, and the ambassador convened a meeting in early January of Abe, Kojima, and Lieutenant General Komatsu, the army attaché. While an advocate of air routes still, Abe spoke for his government, explaining that the plan to fly Kessler and his entourage to Tokyo raised "important problems . . . which concern Japan's conduct of the war," and he advised the general "to depend as far as possible on submarines scheduled to depart in the near future." Abe would summarize the situation in a report to Tokyo on January 13, 1945, adding cryptic yet revealing thoughts about another aspect of the five-month transport freeze. "There have been left behind here for an extremely long period of time," he explained, "important weapons and techniques (for example: radar, anti-tank guns, and rocket guns) and essential personnel, all of which can be relied upon to make immediate contributions to the present-day Greater East

Asia war situation. Utmost efforts were made ... to transport them by submarine, but because of the successive losses of last year, few arrived in Japan. Since then blueprints have been used, and equipment is being set up after various plans are sent in the form of small-scale photographs. In view of the need for the early return of the men who are essential to technical and cooperative operations, this plan is earnestly to be desired, but it does have some delicate aspects."

U-BOATS TO EAST ASIA?

The central authorities in Tokyo reacted immediately to the disruption of U-boat operations by bombing raids of bases in France and Germany, directing Abe to propose to the Germans a transfer of submarine operations to East Asia, where there was "comparatively little enemy anti-submarine activity. . . ." It was pointed out that "the strategy of destroying enemy commerce can be carried out everywhere," and since these submarines "could be restored to pre-war strength . . . it seems to be an appropriate action for the naval operations of both countries." Abe knew better than to discount enemy ASW activity in the Far East, given the number of Japanese submarines lost in Pacific battles, but he would press the case with increasing determination as the situation in Europe deteriorated. The idea would be resisted, Abe knew, so it eased his qualms to realize that Tokyo was aware of that, and Abe was pleased to learn that his friend and former mentor, Naokuni Nomura, might be involved in the endeavor. "In view of our supposition that the Germans harbor some misgivings with regard to the submarine transfer operation," said the central authorities in the directive dated September 7, "we are studying plans for having them engage in joint operations under Admiral Nomura. . . ."

* * *

Abe knew all too well that any hope of a victory at sea—and in the war itself, needless to say—depended on locating the hub of German and Japanese submarine operations in East Asia. But if he expected a prompt and positive German response, his illusions were soon dispelled. On September 26 Abe and Kojima met with Admiral Doenitz, having sent documents in advance, "setting forth the main points of our request." Doenitz did not hesitate to respond, and his tone was challenging, a bit irritable. "To date twelve German submarines have been dispatched to the Indian Ocean," he remarked. "Two of them are assigned to transportation duty between Japan and the Singapore area. Moreover, the German Navy is dispatching six more submarines to the Indian Ocean, which are already on their way. . . ." Enough is enough, his position seemed to be, and he would prefer to continue operating from ports on Germany's Baltic coast. "Bunkers for submarines are all set up in places like Kiel, Bremen, Bergen, and Trondheim," he said, "and there is very little to be uneasy about from the standpoint of defense." Abe and Kojima might have argued about the effect of Allied bombings on those German and Norwegian ports, but Doenitz was clearly determined to continue his U-boat operations from North Atlantic bases. He was also angered by the failure of the Japanese navy to provide adequate security in East Asian ports. "Today a report to the effect that another German submarine was sunk off Penang . . . ," he said, "torpedoed by an enemy submarine and most of the crew made prisoner." Abe and Kojima were hearing a candid commentary by the German navy's commander in chief, realizing how firm he would be in opposition to the Japanese plan. "It is regrettable," said Doenitz, "that while there are no losses on the high seas, arriving and departing from ports should involve

as much danger as it does. . . . The frequent occurrence of such un-
toward events discourages the dispatch of additional submarines."

On a brighter note, Doenitz announced that the first of the new
Type XXI and Type XXIII boats, noted for high speed underwater
and a long cruising range, were due to be dispatched, though further
details would remain a closely guarded secret. Abe and Kojima had
recently visited the shipbuilding facility at Danzig, and Kojima reported on September 12 with reserved enthusiasm on their inspection of construction models of the Type XXI sixteen-hundred-ton
boats. "There are four vessels at present undergoing official tests at
the acceptance-trial station," he explained. "Apart from these we
saw seven or eight vessels on which post-launching fitting-out is
in progress, and inspected one of them." He added a few positive
points: the underwater speed of sixteen knots could be increased to
seventeen or eighteen, and underwater maneuverability was rated as
"good." As for a production schedule, Kojima predicted an output of
thirty vessels a month "before very long." But this remarkable efficiency depended on a "one fits all" system of similar pieces, he cautioned, and if a piece is damaged the whole work will be delayed.
This was what Kojima called "the chief defect of this method," and
he related it to an even more serious cause for concern. "Since enemy
air raids are likely to get heavier," he warned, "while the German antiaircraft defense measures are inadequate, there is room for considerable doubt as to whether construction will in fact proceed
according to plan." In a manner that was polite yet demanding and
skeptical, Kojima offered his conclusion: "Admiration is due to the
Germans for the determined way in which they have gone ahead in
this matter in spite of . . . difficulties, but when we reflect that, with
this thorough changeover coming all at once, the construction of
submarines has been suspended for nearly a year while at this most
crucial stage of the war the new submarines have not yet been able to

join battle. . . . With regard to the tactical value of these vessels, we have only inspected one that was moored, and have only a general description of its performance in the official trials, and many experiments are as yet incomplete. But it could be seen at a glance that it is an epoch-making submarine. . . . Though it will no doubt need certain improvements, I felt that the tactical value would be great. But I think that, as it is intended exclusively for underwater operations, it should as a rule be used in harbors or at key points of shipping routes, and if used in the open ocean, the cooperation of an aircraft would be essential."

The "war situation," as Abe and Kojima described it in periodic reports, was progressing inevitably to a German defeat, though it would take months of heavy combat to convince Hitler and his commanders, whose fighting spirit Abe would continue to commend when there was nothing more to hope for. At the end of September he noted with alarm that the war in Europe was now confined to German territory, and the western front line was the German-French border. Abe was worried about German supply lines, which had been reduced—largely by enemy air attacks—to a third of what was consumed at the front. The German army was a massive force to support—eighty-four divisions and a total of 1.2 million men—facing sixty American, British, and Canadian divisions of some 850,000 troops. The telling enemy advantage, Abe believed, was an air force of six thousand heavy bombers and six thousand fighters based in Britain and France, against three thousand German aircraft. And Abe was openly critical of the German air force, as he put it to Admiral Doenitz when they met in mid-December, for failing to see "the importance of attacking enemy supply lines in the rear." Speaking for himself and Kojima, who had been present,

Abe said: "We suggested that Admiral Doenitz, whose voice would bear weight, would endeavor to arouse the interest of the Air Force. . . . He said that he was entirely in accord and that recently the Air Force had begun to move in that direction. They had actually sunk three enemy ships . . . with torpedo planes." Abe then balanced his criticism with high praise for German navy submarines for sinking seven enemy ships—two destroyers and five transports. "Does this mean," he inquired, a resumption of "all-out submarine warfare?" Doenitz in his reply was cordial, in contrast with his mood in September, but serious: "It was carried out by old-type submarines. It was not as yet an all-out operation using the new-type submarines."

In the December meeting Abe brought Doenitz up to date on the battle for the Philippines, where, in a losing cause, the Japanese had introduced the kamikaze tactic, sinking two enemy escort carriers in the Battle of Samar in October and attacking convoys in the Leyte Gulf in December. Success of the tactic, of course, came at the expense of the pilot's life, and it was this element—described by Abe as "the unswerving loyalty and magnificent results of the kamikazes"—that "caught the fancy" of Doenitz and his aides, Admiral Meisel, the chief of staff, and Admiral Wagner, the chief of operations. Just a month earlier the Germans had requested from Kojima information on the kamikazes, beginning with the delicate matter of selecting personnel. "Because of the present severe condition of the European war," explained Kojima on November 5, 1944, "the German Air Force is establishing storm-battle units." The German intent of a suicide-attack strategy was confirmed by Field Marshal Wilhelm Keitel, the chief of the Combined German General Staff, in a meeting with Abe on December 1. Keitel at first offered the usual assurances of ultimate victory. "This war is a matter of life and death to Japan," he proclaimed, "just as it is to Germany." He then became specific and declared: "There is nothing but admiration for the sincerely inspiring operations of the special attack forces in Japan." There were similar groups of patriots in Germany, Keitel promised. "Not only are there one-man submarines for surprise attacks by the Navy, but also there are many volunteers for comparable tasks in the Army and Air Force." (Air defense groups flying the Messerschmitt Me 262, a twin-turbojet fighter, were being formed in Germany, and collision attacks on enemy bombers were under consideration.)

Abe renewed his campaign for joint submarine operations in Greater East Asia, citing the imminent arrival of a British fleet in the region as an urgent reason to send submarine reinforcements. Sounding vastly more cooperative than he had in September, Doenitz assured Abe he had given the plan special consideration, and submarines were on the way: three U-boats had recently been dispatched. Abe thanked the commander in chief, but he was less than satisfied as he shared his thoughts with his superiors at Imperial Navy headquarters. "It is essential that we check the advance of the British Fleet in East Asia; hence an immediate increase in the activity of the new-type German submarines is needed. To date the operations of the German Navy have not always been at their fullest."

In turn, Doenitz had a proposal for the Japanese to consider, and Abe summarized it on December 15:

> The German Navy wishes to dispatch eight line officers and two engineering officers to the Japanese Navy. These officers are all lieutenants or lieutenant commanders, and each has been chosen as a specialist in a given field (tactics,

torpedoes . . . gunnery, communications, radar). Germany wishes to do this, first, to improve German-Japanese cooperation in a war that will decide the fate of the two countries; and to perpetuate this cooperation after peace is restored. A point to consider: the German Army was given priority due to the demand of land defense on the European continent; rebuilding the Navy therefore lagged, and it became engaged in war in that condition. In the war the German Navy has relied principally on submarines and has conducted surface warfare with small vessels in coastal waters. However, when looking to the future the necessity of a Navy is obvious, and what the German Navy now requires of the Japanese Navy, based on its valuable battle experience, is the training of these promising young German naval officers, who have much to contribute to the future of the German Navy. The German Navy therefore wishes to have these officers assigned to Japanese surface forces and naval air forces, working toward the end of German-Japanese cooperation. Both Hitler and I feel certain that these officers will strengthen relations of the German and Japanese Navies, and it is a matter which arouses a great deal of hope as far as I am concerned.

. . . .

For the first time in many months there was good news from the western front, as Abe reported: "The enemy is suffering from a great lack of supplies, and the German Army is exploiting this weakness with its great offensive. The war situation is favorable at present." This was the Ardennes counteroffensive, otherwise known as the Battle of the Bulge, in which the Germans drove deep into enemy territory in northern Belgium. The American line bulged but did not break, and the Germans were repulsed in January

1945. As Abe put it on February 3: "About 12 divisions of front-line troops, mostly from the American third Army, were knocked out. Since then, the western front has been generally stabilized. The German army abandoned further advances."

Abe took stock at the end of 1944. The almost simultaneous sinking of three strategic submarines had made it all too clear that the *Yamabuki* program had failed, leaving tons of essential weapons and supplies in German naval warehouses. On June 22, as the *I-52* was approaching her ill-fated rendezvous with the *U-530*, Admiral Kojima had broached the complex subject of cargo allotment in a radio message to Tokyo. The German navy was planning the loading of the *I-52*, Kojima advised, and he attached a "proposed order of loading," which had been submitted to the German navy and which contained one very significant item: "(13) _____ oxide 500 kilograms." The cargo was at the German naval base in Kiel, as indicated by the Japanese navy's chief inspector in Berlin, who advised in July that hundreds of tons of special steel and mercury were to be loaded aboard the *I-52*. Of course, the loading of the *I-52* with these and other materials—including a half ton of uranium—was an academic matter, as U.S. intelligence noted on a copy of the intercepted loading list: "*I-52* believed sunk 24 June en route Europe."

The German plan to send two U-boats a month to the Indian Ocean did not materialize, as Kojima had informed Tokyo on September 7. And he predicted that relentless enemy bombing of Kiel and other German submarine bases on the Baltic Sea would prevent the situation from improving any time soon.

THE FALL OF DANZIG

Kojima's dour outlook in September 1944 proved to be accurate, as the situation did worsen, and in November all U-boat departures to Asia were canceled. In December, however, a special commission of the German navy, the Marinesonderdienst Ausland, paid heed to urgent Japanese needs and ordered a series of U-boat missions in the early months of 1945. There were to be five at first, led by the *U-864*, whose passenger list included Tadao Yamato, the T-5 torpedo technician, and Toshio Nakai, a rocket plane engineer with Mitsubishi. But soon after reaching the North Sea the *U-864*, code name Caesar, reported she was under enemy surveillance. Ordered to return to Kiel, she was not heard from again. (It was later learned that on February 9, 1945, the *U-864* was sunk off the coast of Norway by the British submarine *Venturer*.)

On March 16 the German navy notified Kojima that Japan could count on only two more submarines heading for the Far East in the next four months, and only one, the *U-234*, managed to "break out" into the Atlantic. The two Japanese technical officers, Syozi and Tomonaga, were among her passengers.

It was a "sudden change in the war situation in the east," Abe reported on February 27, that forced the German navy to assign war missions in the Baltic and North Sea areas to all but three of its old-type U-boats. Thus, the plan to send five submarines over two months was reduced to three, and of those only two—the *U-864* and the *U-234*—ever left the dock. As for the new high-speed submarines, the Germans had offered only promises since August, when Abe and Kojima visited the shipyard in Poland where Type

XXI boats were being tested. With Danzig now about to be under siege by the Russian army, it was doubtful they would ever be deployed. In preparation for a meeting with Admiral Doenitz on February 15, Abe and Kojima had been briefed by Rear Admiral Wagner. "The way in which the war on the eastern front develops," he said, "will have a very direct influence on the German Navy," pointing out that in addition to shipbuilding, the Baltic coast was where naval training bases were located. "The emphasis of the war in Germany today is on land fighting, and there are many who believe that submarine warfare should be stopped." Instead, Admiral Doenitz had ordered "the continuation and strengthening of submarine warfare." As for the new-type submarines, scheduled to begin operation by the end of 1944, Wagner stuck to the script: "They will begin operation at an early date."

Abe again pressed his case with the commander in chief, reminding him of "the necessity of sending German submarines to East Asia from the standpoint of cooperative operations between Germany and Japan."

Abe and Kojima met again with Wagner on March 5, and little had changed since mid-February. All eyes were still on the eastern front, where the Russian army continued its offensive through the Pomerania region of Poland to the Baltic coast, heading for Danzig. As for submarine warfare, Wagner was confident the new high-speed boats would soon "begin to operate in the open ocean," but they had not been sufficiently tested and would not be ready for large-scale production until May. On a hopeful note, Wagner reported that two of the 250-ton Type XXIII subs were operating off the coast of England, and reports on their performance were encouraging. Abe and Kojima sent a joint report to Tokyo on

March 24, telling of a tenuous plan for a German counterattack against the Russians. Forty newly organized divisions added to twenty pulled from the western front and Norway were ready to go, though hampered by damaged communication lines, transportation failures, and a production shortage of basic weapons. The Red Army, meanwhile, was massing for an attack on Berlin. "Defensive operations and reconquest are becoming more difficult for the German Army," Abe observed. "There is even fear that the new troops, prepared at great effort for the counterattack, will be gradually expended. . . . We are forced to conclude that the chances of a . . . counterattack are unfortunately small."

At a meeting with Doenitz on March 26, Abe and Kojima were again briefed by Wagner, who described the situation as "worse than at the time of our previous conference [on March 5]." The Russians were exerting great pressure on the coastal region around Danzig. (Known as Gdansk prior to annexation by Germany in 1939, Danzig was captured on March 30 by the Russians, who proceeded toward Berlin against a collapsing German resistance.)

These were the bleakest of times for Japanese officials soon to be stranded in Europe—in enemy-occupied Berlin especially—and Abe aired his concerns in a dispatch to Tokyo on March 31:

> In spite of the strong determination of German authorities and their great effort, the general trend of the European war situation is day by day more disadvantageous for Germany. Moreover, the situation in Greater East Asia is going the same way. . . . It is to be surmised that if Germany is defeated, Japan will be in the very difficult situation of having to oppose by itself the great powers of the world. At this time, as our functions in Germany become more and more important, we feel strongly that there are great obligations. . . . With

accurate estimates of the situation we are doing our best to have the Germans contribute to Japan's prosecution of the war, indirectly, by having them fight on . . . and we are doing our best in regard to appropriate countermeasures. . . .

In this situation it is most troubling . . . that Japan's situation is unknown, that is, not knowing the results of the Greater East Asia war, estimates of the general situation . . . and the plans and methods Japan will take, basic to our assignment. In the matter of . . . liaison and communications between Germany and Japan, it seems there is nothing to do but await word from the Central Authorities (we have often reported our opinions on ways of carrying this out). Though we realize that the Central Authorities are very busy at this time when the war situation has become so serious, please consider our position here and at least give us an outline of the above matters.

ABOARD THE *U-234*

Warrant Officer Wolfgang Hirschfeld, the *U-234* chief of communications, observed the loading of the submarine at Kiel and dutifully took note of items being brought aboard, including: optical glass, percussion caps, cameras, binoculars, an antitank gun, the crated components of an Me 262 twin-turbojet aircraft. And he was more than routinely interested in two Japanese officers who were supervising the insertion of cube-shaped containers into shafts used for storing mines when the two-thousand-ton *U-234* was fulfilling its original function of laying them. Out of curiosity Hirschfeld had identified the officers, Genzo Syozi and Hideo Tomonaga, and he wondered out loud why they were writing "U-235" on the brown paper wrappers of the fifty-odd nine-inch lead cubes. It was because they were to have been shipped to Japan on another submarine, the *U-235*, Tomonaga explained, but it had been rerouted. It took just a phone call to Fifth Flotilla Headquarters for Hirschfeld to confirm that Tomonaga was lying: the *U-235*, a training ship, had never left the Baltic. When he mentioned the incident to Lieutenant Commander Johann Fehler, the *U-234* captain, Hirschfeld was told to forget it. Instead he checked the ship's manifest and found the entry in question: "uranium oxide, 10 cases weighing 560 kilograms, consigned to the Japanese Army." Hirschfeld also noted that the loading of the uranium had been observed by a Japanese army officer from the embassy in Berlin.

The importance of the uranium load was further confirmed for Hirschfeld when Syozi and Tomonaga were honored at a flotilla commander's reception just before the *U-234* sailed from Kiel. It was attended by Hiroshi Oshima, the Japanese ambassador, who conducted a solemn ceremony. Tomonaga was a Samurai, and his sword was entrusted to Fehler for safekeeping.

In September 1944 the *U-234* had returned to the factory of F. Krupp Germania Werft in Kiel for as overhaul and functional redesign. Launched in 1942 as a minelayer, she was a Type XB, the largest class of *Unterseeboot* at 295 feet; and by inserting containers made to match in diameter her sixty-six vertical steel mine shafts and held in place by the mine-release mechanism, she was converted to a transport vessel capable of carrying 240 tons of cargo plus fuel and provisions (including nine hundred bottles of liquor) for a six-to-nine-month voyage. Once the cargo was in place, the passengers came aboard, all but Luftwaffe Lieutenant General Ulrich Kessler, who was finally heading for Tokyo to become the

German air attaché. Accompanying Kessler were three air force and four navy officers, each of them a technical specialist of some sort, and two civilian employees of Messerschmitt. The Japanese officers, Tomonaga and Syozi, were treated cordially, but the Germans, to a man, were conspicuously unaware of their purpose and pointedly knew nothing about the uranium shipment. Two of them, who occupied a cabin adjacent to that of Syozi and Tomonaga—Kai Nieschling, an air force lieutenant colonel, and Gerhard Falck, a navy lieutenant commander—appeared to know more than they were willing to admit.

The passengers had been a troubling issue for Fehler since he was summoned to Kriegsmarine headquarters in Berlin and informed of a passenger list of twenty-seven. Out of the question, Fehler protested, as it would require leaving eighteen members of the crew behind, endangering the mission. A compromise was reached, calling for twelve passengers and a crew reduction of eight. (Fehler recognized one of the passengers, Lieutenant Commander Richard Bulla, with whom he had served on the raider *Atlantis,* and he alleviated the situation somewhat by appointing Bulla first lieutenant of the *U-234.*)

Early in the morning of March 26 the *U-234* slipped out of the harbor at Kiel escorted by two Type XXIII boats, the smaller (250-ton) version of the high-speed and long-range "electro boats" still not ready for deployment. (This bit of irony was not lost on Fehler, who secretly had little faith in the success of the mission due to the general war situation.) The initial destination was a German naval base at Horten, in Norway—a two-day voyage—and enemy ASW patrols were encountered off the coast of Denmark. The *U-234* remained on the surface, under alert, and as an aircraft made a radar-guided approach, Hirschfeld, whose duties included electronic countermeasures, beamed back and apparently caused the pilot to disengage. As Hirschfeld noted in his diary, "I have never discovered exactly what effect this trick caused on the enemy radar screen."

A collision with another U-boat during snorkel exercises tore open a port-side bunker, causing the release of sixteen tons of diesel fuel, and the *U-234* limped into the Norwegian port of Kristiansand to find no drydock available. They could go north to Bergen, at the mercy of the enemy, but Fehler chose a do-it-yourself option. He obtained a sheet of steel plate, anchored the boat in a quiet fjord, elevated the stern by submerging the bow, and put his men to work. It was a tedious task, cutting and welding with electrical power supplied by the diesel engines, and progress depended on the winds being calm and not causing the boat to rock.

On April 15, having stopped at Kristiansand to bring General Kessler aboard, the *U-234* was under way. As she cleared the harbor, a launch came alongside, and the regional commander of U-boats came aboard for a farewell ceremony. "When you return from this mission," he said, "we will have our final victory." Fehler's expression was one of disbelief, Hirschfeld thought, as he sealed the hatch and trimmed the boat at periscope depth in preparation for the long underwater voyage. The official destination was Batavia, the Indonesian capital.

A day out of Kristiansand, a bilge pump motor caught fire, and while the flames were quickly extinguished, the crew was sickened by "an appalling stink," as Hirschfeld put it, and breathing was difficult. The *U-234*'s position was in the North Sea, and she was running submerged as a defensive measure against Allied ASW patrols. The foul air had been exhausted, using the snorkel, and Fehler brought the boat to within fifty feet of the surface to receive radio messages and do a precautionary periscope sweep. He was momentarily startled by the sight of a low-flying aircraft that had eluded the submarine's radar and was approaching head-on. Fehler sounded the alarm and dove the boat to three hundred feet to await a depth-charge attack, which soon came.

"Despite the excellent audibility," Hirschfeld would recall, "we heard nothing but three gentle splashes. . . . By intensive hydrophone observation I located the emission of an occulting beam consisting of a five-second hum and a longer period of silence from three different bearings. This was consistent with a conclusion that the aircraft had dropped three sonar buoys capable of transmitting data to the aircraft, whose navigator could then pinpoint our position by means of triangulation." There was only one way to escape, and it was by diving even deeper in the hope of finding a warm water layer that would cause the sonar beams to refract. "Fehler took us to her maximum operating depth, 550 feet, and we found that we were not attacked." There were additional aircraft alerts that night, Hirschfeld reported, "but our radar detected them"—the *U-234* was equipped with a new Luftwaffe device, called a *Hohentwiel*—"long before they could get a fix on us."

(The ASW encounter appeared in a book by Hirschfeld and is remarkably similar to events surrounding the sinking of the *I-52* ten months earlier. In fact the event he describes is a near repetition of what occurred—except for the outcome—on June 24, 1944. But due to the secrecy surrounding the *I-52* sinking, it is highly unlikely that

Hirschfeld could have known of this coincidence at any time prior to the publication of his book by the Naval Institute Press in 1996.)

SURRENDER AT SEA

The *U-234* proceeded submerged at snorkel depth for sixteen days, reaching the Atlantic on April 30—it was on this day that word came of Hitler's death and the appointment of Admiral Doenitz as chancellor—and coming to the surface in the midst of a severe storm. From there a pattern was established—two hours on the surface at night, the rest of the time submerged to depths of forty to one hundred feet. Under no-attack orders, there was a near collision with a large vessel of undetermined type and nationality, but the *U-234* managed to steal away, unnoticed. Radio failure was the first indication that all was not well in the homeland; then the signals stopped coming from the station at Nauen, near Berlin, and radio contact ceased altogether, in part because Fehler insisted on running submerged. He briefly surfaced to receive radio signals on May 4, just in time to hear that all attack U-boats were to return to Norwegian ports. Fehler took note, but the *U-234* would proceed with her mission, staying submerged except for periods at night when she would rely on the *Hohentwiel* radar for protection. On May 8 a message told of Germany's capitulation, and that evening the *U-234* received an order from U-boat headquarters in Norway: "Continue your voyage or return to Bergen." Fehler was adamant, Hirschfeld recalled: "I'm not going back." They continued to head south, though Fehler was having second thoughts about her destination. Japan had severed relations with Germany, according to a news broadcast on May 8, and he was now inclined to accept the order to surrender. His immediate problem was the two Japanese officers, Syozi and Tomonaga, who had been placed under arrest for fear they might act to prevent the uranium from falling into enemy hands. They made a strenuous protest and said they could vouch for the gratitude of the Japanese people for bringing this precious cargo to Japan. Fehler heard their impassioned plea with a sympathetic smile, indicating that his mind was made up.

Syozi and Tomonaga were making their way through the boat, Hirschfeld remembered, "taking their leave of the crew," though he insisted it was not realized "what all this might portend." Early in the morning of May 15 a German passenger, Colonel Nieschling, reported that Syozi and Tomonaga were lying in adjacent bunks, arms linked and breathing but not responding to attempts to revive them. An empty sleeping pill container was found nearby, along with a note to Fehler:

> *It was a great pleasure for us to be able to be together at all times with you and your boat, whether in life or death.*
>
> *But because of fate, about which we can do nothing, it has become a necessity for us to separate ourselves from you and your boat.*
>
> *We thank you for your constant companionship and request the following of you:*
>
> > *1. Let us die quietly. Put the corpses in the high sea.*
> >
> > *2. Divide our private possessions among your crew and please take the largest part yourself also.*
> >
> > *3. Inform Japan of the following as soon as possible:*
> > > *Cmdr (Freg. Kapt) Genzo Syozi*
> > > *Cmdr (Freg. Kapt) Hideo Tomonaga*
> > > *committed suicide on ___ May 1945 on board U-234.*

In closing we express our gratitude for the friendliness of
you and your crew and we hope that everything will go well
for the Commanding Officer and all of you.

(signed) Genzo Syozi

(signed) Hideo Tomonaga

. . . .

Fearing that when officers of the U.S. Navy came aboard they would try to revive Syozi and Tomonaga, Fehler ordered the ship's doctor to make sure they died in peace. The bodies were sewn into weighted hammocks—Tomonaga's Samurai sword was strapped to his chest—and committed to the deep at dawn. Preferring the American navy to the Canadian when surrender was imminent, Fehler had acted to this end by sending false reports of his speed and bearing to Halifax, Nova Scotia. The USS *Sutton,* meanwhile, a destroyer escort from the U.S. base at Argentia, Newfoundland, was ordered to intercept the *U-234.* Fehler had seen to the disposal overboard of some sensitive materials—T-5 acoustic torpedoes and microfilms of classified documents—but other items were not jettisoned for whatever reason, such as the 560 kilograms of uranium oxide.

A boarding party from the *Sutton*—three officers and thirteen enlisted men—boarded the *U-234,* and the one in charge inquired about the two Japanese officers. "They've gone to Davy Jones's locker," Fehler replied.

The *Sutton* escorted the *U-234* to Casco Bay, along the coast of Maine, and turned her over to a Coast Guard cutter for the final four days of her interrupted voyage, which ended at the Portsmouth, New Hampshire, naval base on May 19. With as little ceremony as possible, the six officers and fifty-one crewmen of the *U-234*, looking shabby and fatigued, were taken to a naval prison and would soon be sent to prisoner-of-war camps. The German passengers, meanwhile, were put on a bus and would be flown to Washington for extensive interrogation. They were as disheveled as the crew, showing the effect of a two-month ordeal—all but General Kessler, who seemed bent on fitting the Hollywood stereotype, à la Erich von Stroheim. In a U.S. Navy photograph released to the Associated Press, Kessler even had a monocle fixed to his left eye. He was comfortable in the role, as if he knew, as William Blair of the *New York Times* wrote, "that aside from Kessler no one of any importance was bagged when the U-boat gave up. . . ." Kessler did intend to present himself as a heroic Prussian military figure, a Rommel look-alike, but there was an anti-Nazi twist that he expected would impress his American interrogators. To be of value, Kessler had to be believed, so the interrogators who listened to him throughout the summer of 1945 would need to distinguish fact from fiction. It was clear from the content and tone of the interrogations that instructions had been issued to allow the general to speak his piece.

THE GENERAL'S LIKELY STORY

The questioning began in late May, and Kessler immediately tried to establish that he had sacrificed his military career by standing up to Hermann Goering, the German air minister and a Nazi leader. In 1938 he had met with Goering in expectation of being sent to England as air attaché, but first Goering wished to know if Kessler agreed that in a war that seemed imminent, England would be crushed by the mighty German army. The answer he gave was no, Kessler explained, because America would support

England, and the whole world would support America. Goering said bluntly he had no use for someone who felt inferior to the British, so the London assignment would be withdrawn. (Kessler's career did not end in 1938, and when Goering met with Admiral Kojima in January 1945, he praised Kessler and expressed satisfaction with his appointment to Tokyo.) Kessler also claimed that he never intended to go to Japan, and was using the *U-234* mission as a means of escape from Germany. He had participated in the plot to assassinate Hitler on July 20, 1944, and was fearful of the Gestapo. His plan had been to go ashore when the U-boat reached the coast of Argentina and seek asylum at the U.S. embassy in Buenos Aires.

An unfortunate incident at the naval prison on the day the *U-234* arrived in Portsmouth would complicate the Kessler interrogation and embarrass the navy. Petty theft by naval personnel aboard captured German warships had become a serious problem, but this was a case of wanton larceny. At four on the afternoon of May 19, luggage belonging to General Kessler was placed in the lobby of the prison, presumably for safekeeping, and in a two-hour period, it was stripped of Kessler's belongings. The items could be identified only by awarding possession of anything not of intelligence value to those who had stolen them, and they included the general's cap, campaign ribbons, decorations, watches, a pair of binoculars, a Leica camera, and a wallet containing twelve hundred Swiss francs and papers of possible importance.

An investigation was conducted by naval intelligence officers led by a civilian, Jack H. Alberti, who wrote a report on the incident. Alberti and his team were mainly interested in papers the general said were in his wallet, including a list of people in Chile and their addresses and a second list containing contacts in Argentina. Lieutenant Commander Fehler was angered by the looting and issued what might be called a retrospective threat. Referring to when the *U-234* was being escorted to Portsmouth, Fehler remarked, "All I had to do was pull a lever, and every one of the mine shafts would have been emptied."

WORRIES GALORE

Fehler's remark—and the consternation it caused among navy interrogators—raised the delicate issue of safety in connection with the *U-234* cargo, also a topic of the report by Jack Alberti to Captain John L. Riheldaffer, dated May 22. Mine-shaft controls, hydraulic and manual, were chained and padlocked, and flexible connections to the mine-shaft manifolds were disconnected. The boat was relatively secure, Alberti declared, though there were worries galore. When it came to removing the steel tubes from the vertical mine shafts, he was advised by the *U-234* engineer that it would be necessary to defuel the boat and raise it to a point that outside lugs holding the tubes in place would be above the water level. There was a danger, said the engineer, of tipping a release trigger if the lug removal was attempted underwater. Alberti notified the officer in charge of unloading, who said he saw no reason why the lugs could not be removed by a seaman wearing a diving helmet. Alberti could do nothing but call attention to another potential danger: "It is believed possible that some of the tubes contain hydrostatic scuttling charges designed to blow up the tubes in case of jettisoning. The tubes are sealed shut and will have to be opened with an oxyacetylene torch."

An important item not stored in the steel tubes and ready for immediate removal was the Me 262 jet fighter. Its several components, individually crated, were off the boat within a day or two of docking (the aircraft does not appear in an English translation of the ship's manifest dated May 23), and shipped to Wright Field in Dayton, Ohio, where its first flight occurred before the end of the month. August Bringewald, a Messerschmitt engineer assigned to the Kessler mission, accompanied the aircraft, and in due course would return to the United States as the Republic Aviation project manager of the F-105 Thunderchief.

THE REACH OF THE MEDIA

Fehler had neglected to honor a request by Syozi and Tomonaga that he inform Japanese authorities of their death by suicide. It would have been an appropriate gesture, but the fear of the Japanese officers that their passing would go unnoticed failed to take into account the reach of the international news media. A Reuters report from Washington caught the attention of the Japanese naval attaché in Sweden, Mr. Mishina, who notified Tokyo on May 17. Two Japanese officers were aboard the German submarine when it surrendered five hundred miles off the coast of Newfoundland on May 13, and they had committed suicide when the American navy arrived. "We believe the two Japanese officers may be Technical Commanders Syozi and Tomonaga," Mishina added. Yoshiro Fujimura, the naval attaché in Switzerland, also sent an advisory on May 17, citing Reuters and also an announcement by the commander in chief of the U.S. Atlantic Fleet. "Judging from all circumstances, this is the submarine which departed Kiel with Technical Commanders Syozi and Tomonaga." The American news release identified the aircraft aboard the *U-234* as a "rocket plane" and stated that General Kessler and a German air force party had been taken prisoner. Mishina in Stockholm then cited the current issue of *Time* in his follow-up report to Tokyo on June 4: "After the Americans boarded the vessel, the bodies of two unidentified Japanese who had committed suicide were tossed into the sea by the German crew. Consequently we believe that it is certain that the above two men were Technical Commanders Syozi and Tomonaga."

Admiral Abe, who had fled to Sweden when Germany surrendered, was heard from on May 28.

Although we have obtained no conclusive information since the enemy broadcast, 17 May, as to the . . . matter of the surrender to United States forces of the submarine carrying General of the Air Force Kessler and his party, a synthesis of intelligence reports indicates that it is unquestionably true. Consequently, the two Japanese naval officers were Technical Commanders Syozi and Tomonaga. Both officers heroically took their own lives in a pre-determined resolve. The two officers at the time of their departure embraced the following resolution, that is to say, no matter what changes in the situation they might encounter . . . to the very end they would try to get the German vessel to Japan. In particular, in case Germany should fall to the Allies, and German submarines should be ordered to enter the ports of other countries, they would endeavor to persuade the captain to continue the trip and fulfill their purpose. If they did not succeed . . . and seemed in danger of falling into enemy hands, they would take the decision into their own hands. They had made their preparations, and though both officers made every effort possible in accordance with their resolution, they were unsuccessful, and not being able to accomplish their objective, they committed suicide. Both officers were noble minded . . . and their glorious attitude was truly a model for soldiers. Accordingly, I shall give a full report, supposing the surrender of the submarine to be true, indicating that the two officers died . . . during operations and ought to be accorded the treatment of those who die in battle. . . .

From March 1939 to August 1944, as an inspector in Italy, Technical Commander Syozi was in close contact with influential persons and acquired effective technical data and other general intelligence. He made great contributions to the improvement of our fighting strength. In particular, recently, he made tremendous efforts to obtain data on rocket planes and one-man submarines, proposing invaluable engineering improvements without regard for receiving credit, and finally succeeding in the production of manufacturing plans.

Since his arrival in Berlin in September 1943, Technical Commander Tomonaga developed a close relationship with officers of the German navy, enabling him to acquire effective technical data based on actual submarine warfare situations. Specifically, he obtained data on the new Type XXI and XXIII high-speed boats, which he recently succeeded in transmitting to Japan.

Abe was careful not to say too much about the activities of Syozi and Tomonaga from August 1944 to March 1945, as they waited to complete their sensitive assignment of transporting the uranium to Japan. From their temporary duty stations, said Abe— Syozi in Sweden and Tomonaga in Switzerland—they made "great contributions toward the increase of our fighting strength."

7. TOUCHING BOTTOM

Paul Tidwell was confident of his right to salvage the *I-52*, having found the abandoned submarine in international waters. He also understood the position of the government of Japan and was prepared for a challenge in international court, based on a nation's right to recover a warship. Tidwell was aware of a poor prospect in international court and wanted to make a deal with the Japanese—they would get the boat and human effects, he would get the cargo. Above all, he hoped to avoid a court confrontation, and he had let it be known to the Japanese government that raising the ownership issue would call attention to the origin of the gold. This having been said, Tidwell placed a high priority on working in concert with Tokyo. Whenever he could, he emphasized his respect for the sensibilities of the Japanese people and his sympathy for the families of those who died on June 24, 1944. And on November 29, 1998, toward the end of a monthlong expedition, he presided over a unique ceremony at the bottom of the Atlantic Ocean. On a second visit to the wreck site, he placed a Japanese flag on the conning tower of the *I-52*. (It was an authentic Japanese war flag, red rising sun on a white background, which had been donated by a collector of military memorabilia in Massachusetts.) This was Tidwell's way of paying tribute to a onetime enemy in the interest of reconciliation and world peace. When questions were raised as to his purpose, he dismissed them as cynical carping. There were even those loyal to Tidwell who were dismayed by his theatrics, but he believed that if it was theatrical to honor a heroic crew and restore to a lost warship her national emblem, so be it. The *National Geographic* was there to preserve the moment for worldwide distribution.

It took quite a while for Genia, using the manipulators, to lift the flag from where it was fastened to the Mir's undercarriage, unfurl it from a pair of aluminum poles, and set the poles in such a way that the flag was splayed across the side of the conning tower. The photography was even more time-consuming, as magazine photographer Jonathan Blair and TV cameraman Bill Mills, in *Mirs 1* and *2* respectively, coordinated their moves and assisted each other in lighting the scene. Preoccupied by their work, Tidwell and the photographers were not fully attentive to the time, but aboard the *Keldysh*, when it got to be seven p.m. and time for dinner, there were those who were impatient and angry because the Mirs had not begun searching for gold in the debris field. Having just come to the dining room from the navigation lab, Guy Zajonc was asked if anything had been found at the site. "To find anything, we first have to look," he replied.

PHILIPPONE TAKES CHARGE

On that Sunday night, while Tidwell was still aboard *Mir 2,* Philippone was angry. It was his $2 million that was financing this expedition, and with five dives down and two to go, the prospect of finding gold was fading fast. The Mirs were due back at one or two in the morning, as usual, but this time Philippone altered his habit of appearing at the last minute to check the sample baskets. He was sounding off to anyone willing to listen. Tidwell had wasted $400,000 of his money, Philippone maintained, and he served notice that he intended to take action. This was Philippone's way of announcing that he was taking charge of the expedition.

The computer room—it was known as Harry Masson's lair—was down in the bowels of the ship behind the National Geographic workshop, and there was a risk of being locked in late at night if the TV people forgot you were in there. This was where Tidwell and Masson were meeting on Monday morning when Philippone came to carry out his promise. "He showed me a list of dive assignments," Tidwell recalled, "and when I said they didn't suit my strategy, he said it wasn't up to me anymore because he was assigning the dives. He wanted the debris field covered, and that was the way it would be. I tried to explain that I intended to go down again with Genia, that we had a plan to do some light cutting and reach into the submarine for some likely looking objects we had seen. Philippone shook his head. He had made up his mind. I told him that any dives he assigned were not coming out of my budget." It was quite a row, according to others present, and as it reached its

186 BATTLEGROUND ATLANTIC

peak, Anatoly Sagalevitch walked in and witnessed the latest episode of "family feud."

What did Philippone say? Tidwell was asked after the dust had settled.

"He just said there were some things he didn't like about me and some things I didn't like about him."

That was the size of it?

"Not quite. I wanted to show him how the search ought to be done by studying videotapes of earlier dives. Simon was there, so I asked him to play a tape of *Mir 1*'s first dive. Simon couldn't find the right tape, so I left, saying they could let me know when they found it. I went to my cabin."

Later on Monday Tidwell stated his position for the National Geographic cameras. "A financial backer has taken it upon himself to assign dives to the submarine without consulting the project leader," he said simply. Tidwell had decided to omit the detail of an earlier draft in which he said Philippone had taken advantage of an incorrect interpretation of his authority. In their contract it was stated that Philippone's $2 million investment had been in the form of a loan, which technically speaking left Tidwell in charge of the expedition. He did not condone Philippone's seizure of control, but in the interest of safety and the well-being of everyone aboard the *Keldysh,* he would stand aside.

He also had prepared a press release.

The thirty members of Operation Rising Sun soon will be wending their way homeward, expecting to reach Las Palmas on December 10. Overall, the voyage has been a success: in the course of seven dives by the twin Mirs, ten

American adventurers and their Russian pilots have entered the once prohibited region of 17,000 feet, where a Japanese submarine, the *I-52*, has rested for over half a century. It was a challenging experience for Paul Tidwell and his party of engineers and photographers.

The voyage has not been without risk. Reaching the *I-52* was by manned submersibles called Mirs, which are intricate vehicles that can fail mechanically when subjected to deep-sea extremes of temperature and pressure. On two occasions, hydraulic failure made it necessary to resort to emergency procedures to bring one of the Mirs up from the bottom. There have been other troubles as well, though most were quickly overcome by ingenuity and persistence. But eventually a lust for riches became a dominant theme and motivating force, and when an investor in the project, an attorney with no experience in ocean exploration, insisted on making dive assignments, it was deemed sensible to suspend the activity. Salvage of the submarine had been successful to that point: tin ingots and empty metal boxes (some of them had contained opium and were destroyed) were recovered. But to find the treasure that had become the source of obsession, it would be necessary to regroup and return another day.

The monthlong expedition has accounted for other major accomplishments. The *I-52* was easily located by means of navigation data from Tidwell's 1995 discovery of the submarine, and the site was completely mapped and surveyed. The sub also was pictured in clearly detailed photographs, videotape, and film footage—all adding up to what is probably the most complete set of deep-sea disaster images ever displayed. Samples of cargo brought to the deck of the Russian research ship *Keldysh* included personal articles that

Tidwell will return to the families of crew members, fulfilling a pledge he made, and a Japanese flag was placed by Tidwell on the *I-52*'s conning tower. Finally, a computer record that integrates photo images and mapping data was prepared for future use in exploration and salvage.

The *I-52* has retained most of her secrets for now, and her cargo of gold lies somewhere within.

•••••••••••••

Six slots were open for two remaining dives—two on *Mir 1* with its two pilots and four on *Mir 2*—but the enthusiasm of the engineers was waning. Tim McGinnis, who had ridden *Mir 2* on successive dive days a week earlier, answered point-blank when asked by Philippone if he'd go again: no, he'd rather not. Marco Flagg, recalling emergencies on two earlier dives, had his doubts about safety but felt obligated to finish his navigation. Geoffrey Howe, having pressed a point of having faith in the pilots, now had a chance to prove it. To round out the list, Philippone made an unlikely choice. He picked Zajonc and his nephew, a precocious twenty-year-old with unusual mathematical skills.

Even though he was Napoleon at Elba, Tidwell was quite satisfied with what had been accomplished, as he explained: "We're going home with just about everything we had hoped for. We rediscovered Momi, went down to her, honored her, and we have the most magnificent shipwreck pictures ever taken. I regret not finding the gold, but we'll be back."

SAYONARA, MOMI

Unaccustomed to having time on his hands, Tidwell was determined to put it to good use. He and Jo Anne found an isolated spot on deck near the bow, where they could be alone, at least until the TV crew asked, with unintended irony, if they might record their solitude on film. Tidwell did some reading, but mostly he thought about his situation. A year ago he had traveled to France to meet with IFREMER (*Institut français de recherche pour l'exploration de la mer*), an agency of the French government. While he decided against working with the French because their surface ship was too small for his purpose, Tidwell was impressed with their role in the discovery of the *Titanic*, which has gone largely unnoticed. IFREMER is the owner of the Nautile, a deep-diving submersible in a league with the Mirs and the U.S. Navy's Alvin. From 1993 to 1996 the French made many dives to the *Titanic*, collecting artifacts for George Tulloch, an American promoter who owned salvage rights to the world's most famous shipwreck. (Competitors of Tulloch's company, RMS Titanic, Inc., were banned by a U.S. federal court from trespassing on the wreck, and the Shirshov Institute was specifically named in the suit, based on evidence of an accident in which the *Titanic* was littered with pieces of one of the Mirs.) Tidwell had another reason for rejecting IFREMER. He was not convinced that manned submersibles were superior to remotely operated vehicles for his purpose. The Mirs and the Nautile were ideal for search, survey, and photography, when a human factor can be significant, but ROVs were probably better suited for a salvage operation.

When Tidwell signed a contract with Philippone in March 1998, he had a commitment from Sub-Sea International, a New Orleans subsidiary of Dresser Industries. Sub-Sea had designed and built the Hammerhead, a versatile heavy-duty ROV, and Tidwell's planning had been geared to using it. So when problems developed with an electronic cable that controlled the Hammerhead, it came as a serious setback. It had been three years since he discovered the *I-52*, and Tidwell did not want to let another year pass. Besides, he had an offer of a $3 million loan (from Philippone), and he had already spent $250,000 on underwater TV cameras and other essentials.

Tidwell had a decision to make. He could try to come to terms with Oceaneering Technologies, whose office was right down the road from Tidwell in the Washington, D.C., area. But he was leery of doing business with the ROV industry giant. This was a company that liked to flex its muscles, and on a recent occasion at Tidwell's expense. The navy had offered to lease him a submersible, but Oceaneering cried unfair competition, killing the deal. But let's face it, Oceaneering's Magellan was the Cadillac of ROVs, in a class with Nemo, which was used to retrieve gold worth millions from the wreck of the *Central America*, discovered off South Carolina in 1988. Owned by an Ohio salvage company, Nemo was not for hire, whereas Oceaneering was in the business of leasing its two Magellans. However, both were spoken for in Tidwell's period of need, the summer and fall of 1998, and his list of choices was narrowed to one: the Shirshov Institute in Moscow.

Tidwell learned that the *Keldysh* was in the vicinity of the North Pole, so he sent word to Anatoly Sagalevitch via Moscow, and when he heard back, the letter was postmarked St. John's, Newfoundland. This was disturbing since it meant to Tidwell that Sagalevitch intended to return to the *Titanic*, and a bit of investigating confirmed the suspicion. Having teamed up with an enterprising travel agent in Germany, the Russians were turning the *Titanic* into a tourist attraction, offering round-trips aboard the Mirs at $35,000 a head. This defiance of a U.S. court ruling indicated that Sagalevitch might show a similar disregard for measures that would enable Tidwell to protect his exclusive right to salvage the

I-52. There would be no way to prevent Sagalevitch from learning the exact location of the submarine, and Tidwell was reluctant to file for a court order similar to one obtained by RMS *Titanic*. It was obvious that the Russians would ignore it, and it was likely to disturb the Japanese, whose cooperation was so important. "We have a lot more to gain by working with Japan, securing their trust, than by going into court over the sovereign rights issue," Tidwell explained.

The solution Tidwell devised seemed suitable if not ingenious. He would stipulate that the Russians could only make return trips to the *I-52* when licensed to do so by Cape Verde Explorations. "Licensing means they are required to obtain our permission and pay us a fee if they wish to return to the site," said Tidwell. "It is also a more practical way to go. If we were to rely on a court order and someone decides to test it, jurisdiction becomes an issue, and we might lose." Tidwell knows to be careful, for in the ship salvage business, lawsuits are filed at the drop of a hat, and even when you win, there is a loss of precious time to be considered. For quite a while after the 1998 expedition, Tidwell expected to hear from Orca Ltd. in London about a clause in their contract with Sagalevitch, prohibiting anyone but Orca from using the Mirs to dive on the *I-52*. It was not Tidwell's problem, but his previous dealings with Orca had taught him to watch his step. He had recently heard about a new book telling of how months were spent aboard the *Keldysh* in 1995 in an unsuccessful search for the *I-52*. There are several references to a "Mysterious American" who for a fee provided a location of the submarine. Tidwell knew the "Mysterious American" to be the creation of his intermediary as a means of passing erroneous information to the British. Tidwell was especially interested in an accurate account of how he found the *I-52* shortly after Orca had failed. He also noticed there was no mention of his offer in early 1995 to put up $250,000 for a minority partnership in the Orca venture, which was rejected.

At the meeting in September 1998 in Falmouth, England, where the *Keldysh* was in drydock for insurance recertification, an agreement was reached on the charter. Philippone put $300,000 in escrow to cover a down payment, and the *Keldysh* was scheduled to sail to Las Palmas for an expedition that would begin in early November. It was right after the Falmouth meeting that Tidwell had serious second thoughts, having learned that Philippone had cut his investment-loan to $2 million and would be making direct payments for all major charges against the reduced budget. Philippone was also showing his hand on personnel matters—"meddling" was Tidwell's word for it—and in one important case he actually overruled Tidwell. Mike Lowther, an experienced ocean systems engineer from California and a friend of Tidwell for twenty-five years, attended the Falmouth meeting, expecting to be the project manager. But due to a personality clash, he was quickly out of a job. "Mike pissed off both Philippone and Zajonc," Tidwell recalled. "They didn't want him on the trip."

We were heading back, due to reach Las Palmas on December 9, and Sagalevitch was worried about an overdue $162,000 payment for the charter. He feared it might become a bargaining chip in a Tidwell-Philippone standoff, and how right he was. The Americans met, and Philippone said he would fax immediate instructions to his banker to wire the money. Tidwell had just told

Sagalevitch the news when Philippone asked him to come to his cabin. "Paul," he said, "I will not have that money wired until you sign the contract addendum." Tidwell was affronted but tried to cooperate, and after a series of discussions with Philippone and Zajonc, separately, agreement was reached on a draft addendum to the March contract. "I was ready to sign it when Philippone made a further demand I could not accept," said Tidwell. "He insisted that his two-million-dollar loan be repaid by proceeds from the National Geographic television documentary. I said no. As it was, he would be paid by the earnings from an IMAX movie or from salvage of the submarine. I even suggested that we call his two-million-dollar loan an IMAX investment. That way he could tell his friends he came out here to shoot a movie, not just to find gold."

What did he say to that?

"He didn't bite. He kept repeating his demand for the TV money, and if I didn't sign the addendum, he wouldn't pay Anatoly the $162,000. I said fine, it was his call, and I walked out."

In a memo to Tidwell, dated December 4, Philippone did an abrupt turnabout:

> *After careful reflection, I am satisfied with the agreement made in March 1998 as modified by our discussions in Falmouth and action taken pursuant to those discussions. Consequently, I am faxing Republic Bank to release the final payment of $162,000 to the Keldysh account. . . .*
>
> *You are too pessimistic about your ability to move forward. This trip was a great success as a documentary and IMAX film. It was also a success as a debris field search.*
>
> *Hopefully by March 1999, when the note comes due, your prospects will look better and we can avoid a conflict.*

We should both strive to make the balance of this trip a success. I will do what I can to make it a good project for all of us.

· · · · · · · · · · · ·

Tidwell was not very satisfied with Philippone's latest move. "He claims we made an agreement in England, a verbal agreement. We did agree on certain issues in Falmouth, but not on all that he says we did. That's why we have an addendum that's signed by him but not by me, an addendum he then wanted to change even further. Now he wants to come somewhere in between, but I'm going to get legal advice before I sign anything."

When he heard on Tuesday, December 8, that the "final" payment of $162,000 to the Russians did not cover a port fee in Las Palmas, Tidwell went to Sagalevitch to offer a camera and a couple of his custom-made twelve-hundred-volt underwater lights in lieu of the $30,000 fee. Sagalevitch seemed agreeable at first, but then thought again about his own financial situation and insisted on payment of the port fee. Then on Wednesday, with the *Keldysh* due to land that night, Tidwell got a note from Zajonc saying the port fee was still unpaid and there was no money for it in Philippone's budget. Tidwell knew better, but he paid another visit to Sagalevitch, who was unyielding. "The *Keldysh* could be arrested for not paying these port charges," he told Tidwell, who promised to do what he could. Zajonc and Philippone were bluffing, Tidwell suspected, and this was confirmed immediately by Philippone. He had the money after all, he said in a note, and would be willing to "advance" it to Tidwell for the port fee, an offer Tidwell turned down by refusing to respond.

* * *

As we neared Las Palmas, Sagalevitch warned that the *Keldysh* would anchor outside the harbor and enter only when the port fee had been paid. It was up to us, but the next stop was Kaliningrad. Tidwell decided to try appeasement, and at about ten that night he went to Sagalevitch's cabin with a peace offering. He reminded the Russian of how they had worked together for so long and how he had been willing to lay down $2 million for a voyage to the *I-52* when the Orca people were holding Sagalevitch hostage. Actually Tidwell didn't give a damn about being in the good graces of Anatoly Sagalevitch. It had no bearing on his quest for the *I-52*, which was what mattered. The next time it would not be with the Mirs, which were of limited value as salvage vehicles. But he worried about Anatoly the man. Tidwell knew a little about him personally: his country was in chaos; his career depended on the survival of a bankrupt scientific institute; his personal life was tragic, having lost a wife to cancer.

When Tidwell walked into the cabin, Anatoly was alone. They talked briefly but skirted the issue of the port fee, since Tidwell was depending on Philippone to handle that problem. Tidwell had with him his own underwater camera, a $30,000 Benthos, and he offered it as a gift. Sagalevitch scowled and shook his head. He was still angry and started to speak in Russian but caught himself. His English was faltering, but he knew how to make his point.

"Please leave." He said it so politely that it was devastating. "And please lose my address."

Tidwell made his way down the passageway, stunned. Out on deck the National Geographic film crew had gathered.

"Hey, Paul, what are you up to?"

Tidwell would not recall his exact response, but he knew what was going through his mind. "You want to know what I'm up to? Well, just watch. I'll show you what I'm up to."

The deck railings on the *Keldysh* are about four feet high, and one can see how easy it would be to jump or fall overboard. This had been the scene of an end-of-expedition party the past Friday, at which more than a few had had too much to drink. It was frightening to realize the danger of going over the side.

As he walked to the rail, Tidwell held the camera by the shoulder strap, spun it over his head a few times, and hurled it into the sea. It was a rash act, hastily extemporized without premeditation or conscious rationale. It might have been to pay tribute to Momi for guarding her secrets, but any such explanation would be irrelevant. Whatever happened, whether homeward bound or Christmas in Kaliningrad, the expedition was ending on an uncertain note.

Tidwell now knew there were more ways than one to touch bottom.

8. HIGH TIME TO GET OUT OF BERLIN

The Japanese ambassador to Moscow, Naotake Sato, was uniquely positioned to observe the fall of Berlin, as he did in a dispatch to Tokyo on April 12, 1945. A week earlier Sato had been informed by Soviet Foreign Minister Vyacheslav Molotov that the Soviet Union intended to abrogate the Russo-Japanese Neutrality Treaty.

The Allied forces on the Western Front captured Hanover and Nordhausen to the east on 10 April, and have already approached Berlin within the short distance of 200 kilometers. Their vanguard has now reached the Elbe River, to the south, and they seem to have sufficient strength to enable them to advance from Gotha to the Czechoslovakian border. Then on their right flank they have made a dash from the Frankfurt-au-Mainz-Karlsruhe line toward the east, and are continuing their advance in the direction of

Nuremberg, apparently with the idea of cutting off the region of Bavaria.

Ever since the Allied forces crossed the Rhine and began their general offensive toward the east on 24 March, the rapidity with which they have continued their advance with Berlin as their objective is something that merits admiration. German resistance . . . to this advance is feeble, and the situation is such that we must expect a marked increase in the number of prisoners taken.

On the other hand, on the Eastern Front, while the Red Army is at present maintaining an attitude of inactivity on the front facing Berlin, it reduced Konigsberg on the 9th, and thus will be able to send additional reinforcements to the Berlin front from the troops . . . in East Prussia.

Furthermore, the capture of Vienna has practically been completed (11 April) and the Red Army is now . . . bringing pressure to bear upon Germany from the rear.

Sato had proved himself a candid observer and policy critic, in contrast to Mr. Oshima in Berlin, and he stuck to his guns in assessing the position of Japan's Axis partner at this critical juncture. "The German Army, while mustering its main strength and holding its own . . . on the Eastern Front facing the Red Army," he wrote, "has caused a shortage of men on the Western Front and permitted the Allied forces to continue their advance almost as they pleased. . . . That the German Army was led to devote its main strength in the east and bring about a shortage of men in the west has surely been to the advantage of the joint military operations of the Red Army and Anglo-American forces." Well aware that his audience in Japan was a disapproving one, Sato applauded the enemy for what he termed "a combination of ingenious tactical plans."

The Russian army, for its part, "was ever ready to begin its attack on Berlin, thus attracting as many German troops as could be spared and then some, while Anglo-American forces, taking advantage of depleted legions on the western front, were able to break through on the Rhine . . . and continue their eastward advance. They conquered southern Bavaria and reached the Czechoslovakian border, cutting Germany into north and south sections, and they drew within striking distance of Berlin. Coordinating the drive with a simultaneous Russian attack on the eastern front, the Allies will undoubtedly crush the German Army."

With this dire prediction off his chest, Sato cast the scene surrounding Berlin as the result of joint tactics planned at the Crimean Conference of Allied leaders in February, tactics that were now "displaying their maximum effectiveness." He had just one caveat for Roosevelt, Churchill, and Stalin. "Of course, this way of looking at it," Sato wrote, "places high expectation upon the joint operations of England, America, and Russia, while in reality the solidarity of these nations may not be as strong as is presently indicated."

DAYS OF DESPAIR

Evidence of the critical nature of the *U-234* voyage was the presence of Ambassador Oshima at the flotilla commander's reception in honor of Syozi and Tomonaga. The event occurred in mid-March 1945, when the ambassador was reporting to Tokyo on the "danger of Berlin becoming a battlefield" and expecting "that the abandonment of Berlin may take place in another month." By traveling to Kiel, which like Berlin was being reduced to rubble by Allied bombers, Oshima was expressing hope—on behalf of the emperor and the Japanese people—that the *U-234* mission would enable Japan to avoid a similar fate.

A month later, on April 13, Oshima met with Foreign Minister von Ribbentrop—for the last time, as it turned out—and vowed to stand with the leaders of the Third Reich in their hour of crisis. "I do not wish to be treated in the same manner as other diplomats merely by reason of great danger from the ravages of war . . . ," he announced in typically dramatic fashion. But he was informed that evening by the Foreign Ministry's chief of protocol, Alexander von Dornberg, that all diplomats were to leave Berlin at once, Hitler's orders, except for skeleton security crews. Oshima reached von Ribbentrop by telephone, and the foreign minister revealed a plan to relocate the German high command in southern Germany if the situation worsened. (According to Carl Boyd, author of *Hitler's Japanese Confidant*, Oshima immediately advised Tokyo of this emergency plan—and Washington as well, via American Magic.) Oshima had sent his wife to Bad Gastein, a mountain resort in Austria, and on April 14 he was on his way to join her, accompanied by the army and navy attachés, General Komatsu and Admiral Kojima, and most of the embassy staff. The ambassador's retinue, numbering some 130 Japanese nationals residing for the time being at the Hotel Mozart at Bad Gastein, would soon become American prisoners of war (they were apprehended when Major General Maxwell D. Taylor, commander of the 101st Airborne Division, decided to make the Mozart his headquarters), which had been anticipated six months earlier when the evacuation plan was submitted for approval by the central authorities in Tokyo. Small units of embassy personnel, miniature military missions, however, would continue to function under the guidance of German navy and air force commands in northern combat zones. Likewise, an economic unit with the embassy accounting officer, Commander Haruo Ikeda, in charge, would proceed to Rostock and await orders from Admiral Abe based on developments. Finally, it was noted in a message from Kojima on April 18 that Captain Ya-sumori Taniguchi and two others—Professor Samejima, a histo-rian, and a clerk identified as Yoshiro—"will stay with Admiral Abe and remain in Berlin for the present." Kojima noted that Abe and the military missions were equipped with Enigma code ma-chines. Commander Ikeda meanwhile had deposited 100,000 yen and 989,995.85 "agreement marks" in redemption accounts at the Yokohama Specie Bank in Berlin. (A conscientious Abe acted in behalf of the family—a widow and four children—of Tooyoo Mit-sunobu, the attaché in Italy who died in a guerrilla ambush. In a message to Commander Fujimura, recently named attaché in Bern, Abe asked that arrangements be made for the Mitsunobus to enter Switzerland from war-torn Germany.)

Abe had intended to follow the ambassador to Bad Gastein, but he remained in Berlin to attend to unfinished business that was the subject of an urgent order from Tokyo contained in Secretariat Se-rial 244. It directed Abe to renew his effort to convince German leaders of the wisdom—indeed, it was now seen by Tokyo as a req-uisite for the survival of the German navy—of transferring sub-marine operations to Greater East Asia. Abe got right to it, slightly chagrined by the criticism implied in the order from Imperial Navy headquarters by the way it reminded him of the urgency of the matter. Abe was well aware that time was running out, for joint operations in East Asia would not be an option for a defeated Ger-many. And he was dismayed by the hard-line attitude of Foreign Minister von Ribbentrop, expressed just days before over tea with Ambassador Oshima and his naval and military attachés. "Ger-many intends to fight on to the end and will never surrender," von Ribbentrop declared, leaving little room for compromise or retreat. In his report of April 10, 1945, Abe stressed the necessity of joint operations, as he had to the foreign minister. "We emphasized that the sending of submarines to Greater East Asia and the introduction of special German techniques . . . seem important from the standpoints of both Germany and Japan, and requested that this be communicated to Hitler."

Abe met with Admiral Doenitz on April 15, repeating his previous plea and outlining his latest instructions from Tokyo. Regrettably for Abe, the Kriegsmarine commander in chief had not altered his position, but his reasoning was new, or at least different. Fuel was in short supply, said Doenitz, and the amount of diesel oil required to send a U-boat to Asia and back would keep six to ten U-boats operating in the Atlantic for weeks. Abe argued that a shortage of fuel need not be an issue since the U-boats would be sufficiently supplied by the Japanese navy. Doenitz then reiterated his belief that it was a long cruise by submarine to the Far East, during which his boats would consume not only fuel but valuable time as well, for no immediate purpose. Only half joking, he suggested that if the Japanese had fuel to spare, they might consider sharing it with Germany. Then he stated gravely, "I consider the matter closed." Abe reported to Tokyo on April 17 that the meeting had not gone well. "I have received almost the final reply from Admiral Doenitz, which was just as expected. However, I am not giving in, and in what may be my last service in Germany, I shall take all necessary measures and make every effort to get them to dispatch submarines to the Far East, even if it be only one or two. . . . I have often expressed my thanks to Hitler for presenting two submarines (unhappily the *RO-501* was sunk en route). Accordingly I have been thinking that it might be a very good idea to suggest to them discreetly that from the standpoint of joint operations it would be proper for them to present us also with a new high-underwater-speed submarine, but I fear I may be going too far."

After the meeting with Doenitz, Abe decided to accelerate his approach and seek an immediate meeting with Hitler himself. To this end he met on April 16 with Vice Admiral Brueckner, the chairman of the Military Affairs Committee, and stated that he wished to meet with Field Marshal Keitel, chief of the Combined General Staff, and then hoped to present his case to Chancellor Hitler. Abe had expressed impatience, even disgust, at Hitler's refusal to meet with Japanese officials, including the ambassador prior to his departure. In a report to Tokyo on von Ribbentrop's tea party, he called the situation "inexcusable." "At present Hitler is avoiding conferences with foreigners," said Abe, who in his two years in Berlin had not once been permitted to interview the chancellor. Admiral Brueckner seemed willing to lend a sympathetic ear, so Abe explained his step-by-step approach with the German high command, which he hoped would enable him to make his case for joint submarine operations to the führer directly. "The vice admiral replied to the effect that he would immediately make every effort toward interviews with Keitel and Hitler," Abe reported, "since the Japanese proposal is an excellent one."

On Monday evening, April 16, Abe advised Tokyo on how he was doing in a tone that was appropriately dramatic given his predicament. "I previously reported . . . my plan of action to meet the change in the situation, but the day before yesterday Ambassador Oshima and the military and naval attachés moved to the south. It was originally intended that I should accompany them, but I received the important assignment in your Serial 244, and I proposed a conference with Admiral Doenitz. (The question of an interview with Hitler is difficult in the absence of Ambassador Oshima, but I am still proposing a visit in which I should be accompanied by the counselor of the embassy, Kawahara.) In view of this I have decided to remain in Berlin for the present. However, as the way of getting to southern Germany may be cut off in the future . . . I intend ultimately to follow Admiral Doenitz's movements. . . . At the time of my conference with Admiral Doenitz . . . I learned that he intends to stay in northern Germany. . . . Accordingly, I shall eventually join our naval group, which departed the other day. . . ."

On April 17, accompanied by Brueckner, Abe met with two of the most powerful Nazi leaders—General Keitel in the morning and Minister von Ribbentrop in the afternoon—both of whom insisted Germany would never surrender, and the transfer of submarines to Greater East Asia would not be in the interest of defending the homeland. (Keitel and von Ribbentrop would both be convicted of war crimes and sentenced to death by hanging.) The present situation was a critical one, said Keitel, "but no matter what her situation may be, Germany will not lay down her arms nor will she surrender unconditionally. She will fight on to final victory." As for sending naval forces to Asia, he praised the Japanese navy and spoke in favor of comradeship, but the present war situation demanded that Germany use all its strength in defending the homeland, and that was that. Von Ribbentrop had little of substance to add, but he was more adamant than he had been a week earlier, and he left no room whatever for compromise (leading Abe to believe he was losing touch with reality). "We will exhaust all our strength in the effort," von Ribbentrop declared, "and fight on to final victory. Germany will face the enemy with her great determination, and no matter what the situation is, she will not surrender." He then turned to the matter of dispatching German naval forces to East Asia. "I have naturally conveyed Japan's request to the führer. The decision will come from him." It was primarily a military problem, said the foreign minister, "but if I were to offer my opinion, it would be as follows. . . . Germany is determined to fight through to the end. Though you may have heard that we might not gain final victory, Germany by no means has given up hope. The great Russian offensive which began the day before yesterday was expected, and we had made full preparation against it. We are confident of the success of our surprise attacks, by means of which we shall stabilize the central front; then, although some time may be required, it will be possible to drive out the . . . invading American and British armies. The Germans are making an all-out effort, hence we want every ship down to the last one, and . . . I would even have the naval forces now in East Asia return to Germany. Operations in the Baltic and North Seas and in the Atlantic will be strengthened, enemy supply lines will be attacked. We shall try to turn the tide of battle, therefore it would be very difficult to send German naval forces to East Asia at present. Japan's request is undoubtedly based on the following two conditions. The first of these is if the German situation deteriorates, to have them proceed to Japan for fear of their falling into enemy hands. Or in the event the situation were to improve, Germany would have a surplus of ships, some of which could be dispatched to East Asia."

With regard to a meeting with Hitler, von Ribbentrop replied: "I have been making every effort to obtain it for you, but he is extremely busy and has not had an interview with a foreigner in the

last six months or more. Even I have not seen him for a month."
(GI-A, U.S. Navy Intelligence, appended a comment: "The last interview known to have been granted by Hitler to a Japanese diplomat occurred in September 1944 and was the subject of a report
from Oshima to Tokyo dated September 5.")

Abe met again with von Ribbentrop, at his request, on April 19, accompanied by Admiral Brueckner and the embassy counselor,
Shunichiro Kawahara. Von Ribbentrop continued to dwell upon
two conditions, or contingencies, that might call for moving German naval forces to Asia, presumably having discussed them with
Hitler. The first would be a situation in which German forces could
no longer defend the homeland, and they could continue to fight
on the side of the Japanese. Such a scenario had little appeal for
von Ribbentrop, who promptly dismissed it. "Germany is staking
her existence as a nation on the prosecution of the war and will
fight to the very last. Consequently no one believes that this contingency will come to pass. But if it did, and there was a slackening
of determination, this . . . would then be given consideration. I
would want to consult with Admiral Doenitz." As for the second
contingency, in which Germany emerged victorious in Europe,
von Ribbentrop had this to say: "That there will be a favorable turn
in the situation is not merely a wish but a thorough conviction,
and of course Germany would respond to Japan's desires by sending a fleet of submarines to East Asia." They were meeting for the
last time, so Abe would remember von Ribbentrop for this
supremely confident and totally unrealistic statement.

Von Ribbentrop assured Abe that Hitler would be happy to
grant him an interview, "but he desires to wait a while because he

has no time under existing conditions." Abe was dubious, as his days in Berlin were numbered.

Abe departed Berlin on Friday, April 20 (it happened to be Adolf Hitler's fifty-sixth birthday), moving cautiously by automobile up the Elbe toward Hamburg as Germany collapsed in the presence of advancing Allied armies—Russians from the east, Americans from the south, the British from the north. Abe continued to communicate by radio with the Navy Department in Tokyo, but the messages were brief and few in number. Berlin was the center of worldwide attention, so Abe had little to add, except that he had tried for final meetings with Doenitz, Keitel, and von Ribbentrop, but they were busy "supplying themselves for a last-ditch stand." Captain Taniguchi had remained behind "to the last," but he would join Abe before long. Left holding the fort was Counselor Kawahara, who sent a "very urgent" message to Tokyo at ten p.m. on April 21: "The battle is very near, and shells have already begun to fall within the city."

On April 24 Abe arrived at the Baltic port of Flensburg, along with sixteen members of his secret staff, the Bureau of Naval Intelligence—all but Captain Kazuta Oogi, who was in Copenhagen applying for a visa to Sweden, where he was on orders to report as naval attaché. On April 24, also, the German government notified Tokyo of its plan to dispatch large-type submarines to East Asia. The Japanese Bureau of Military Affairs notified Abe on April 28, reaching him in Flensburg with a joint operations plan based on an overoptimistic assessment: "Toward the middle of May six Japanese submarines and at the end of May, or June, four to seven German submarines, stationed in East Asia, will sortie into the

Indian Ocean. . . . We are acting to have information on the number of submarines to be sent to East Asia . . . to be furnished us . . . by the German naval attaché in Japan. We believe it would be all right to have naval personnel in Germany return to Japan in submarines proceeding to the Far East. . . . We wish to thank you for your labor leading up to the completion of negotiations."

Abe would have been delighted to hear that his efforts were not in vain after all, but that was not the case. Officials in Tokyo were listening to mid-level German officials, whose information ran counter to what Abe had been told by Doenitz and von Ribbentrop. Even if there were some truth to the report—and there was not—the decision would have come too late. It was unlikely that any U-boats would actually set sail for East Asia, including one that might have taken Abe and his party to Japan, since the German naval bases at Kiel and Bremerhaven were under heavy attack and could fall to the British any day. (Abe was in daily contact with German navy headquarters, and U.S. Navy Intelligence continued to monitor his dispatches, such as one on April 27 describing the situation as "basically negative.")

Abe paused to take note of Hitler's suicide on April 30, calling it a "death in battle" and stating that the dictator's passing "appears to have made a deep impression on the German people and on the troops." He had spoken with the foreign office in Berlin, and "in the name of the Japanese Navy, expressed our sympathy and also our best wishes to Admiral Doenitz upon his assumption of the office of chief of state." Abe was in an awkward position, as it was clear that Doenitz's role would be to preside over a German defeat. "Admiral Doenitz enjoys the popularity of the people," Abe reported to Tokyo, "and is the most suitable successor to Hitler." Abe had hoped to accompany Doenitz as he headed north, but was being forced to view his moves from a distance. "Admiral Doenitz arrived in Flensburg at midnight 3 May," he reported. "In regard to his future policy, it is difficult to follow the trend of the situation, but as noted in the admiral's radio broadcast, it appears that they are taking advantage of an attitude of peace toward Britain and America, to further their plans with regard to Russia. They are apparently trying to bring the war to a conclusion by recovering insofar as possible the territory lost in the east."

Abe had not given up on joint submarine operations in Greater East Asia, difficult as it was to pursue the matter with Germany in a state of confusion. "Preparations were made for me to confer with Meisel, the chief of the Naval Operations Department, but with the promotion of Admiral Doenitz to chief of state, considerable confusion arose, and the conference was postponed." Still troubled by the premature report of April 28, he offered a comment: "I believe the matter mentioned in Secretariat Serial 291 does not present any issues not determined by the results of our previous negotiations, but I shall hasten the conference mentioned above as much as possible. After again ascertaining German intentions, I shall do my best to negotiate in conformity with the requests of the central authorities."

Abe's next move was the subject of a message to Tokyo on May 3. "The fall of Kiel is imminent, and acting on the good counsel of the German Navy, we shall depart Flensburg tomorrow morning, the fourth, and proceed to Copenhagen by automobile." Abe added that Flensburg had been in danger of a British attack, and "we were prevailed upon by the German Navy to enter Denmark." He took the advice, but at seven that evening the surrender of German troops in Denmark was announced, effective at eight a.m. the next day, May 5, at which time airlifted British troops would begin arriving. "The Navy prepared for our immediate escape by sea," Abe continued. "We boarded a German minesweeper at 0645 on the fifth . . . going ashore at Malmoe, Sweden, at 0930. . . ." Abe's intelligence staff was present and accounted for, including his two deputies, Captain Oogi and Captain Taniguchi. "Swedish authorities have treated us very courteously up until now, even forgoing inspection of our personal possessions in the customs house. . . . After contacting and conferring with the Minister and military and naval attachés, I shall decide on future action."

A DISPUTE LEAST APPROPRIATE

Abe had recently created a predicament in Sweden by losing patience with the naval attaché there and demanding that he be replaced by Captain Oogi. The trouble was rooted in the stubborn attitude of the attaché, Commander Mishina, and the response of an equally inflexible Admiral Abe, who would not abide the questioning of his position by a subordinate. In November 1944, as part of his top secret *Yamabuki* strategy, Abe ordered the temporary assignment of Genzo Syozi and Hideo Tomonaga to neutral countries, as they awaited transportation to Japan. Tomonaga was sent to Bern, where the naval attaché was Lieutenant Commander Fujimura, an Abe loyalist who knew about the uranium bomb project. Not so with Mishina, whose talent was following enemy activities in publications such as *Time,* the American news magazine. He loudly challenged Syozi's posting to Stockholm, beginning with a complaint to Tokyo on November 30, 1944: "Commander Syozi . . . has arrived here from Berlin. However, considered from the standpoint of enhancing the complete efficiency of Japan, it is better that his duties in Berlin should be carried out rather than his duties here. Therefore, since this man's residence orders have fortunately not been sent, we request that you give this matter your special consideration." Mishina begrudgingly backed down on December 22: "While it is a matter of deep regret that my point of view should not have been understood by the Central Authorities, I have no alternative . . . but to withdraw the representation. . . ." And on December 23, Abe responded to Tokyo, with an information copy to Mishina: "As I want Technical Commander Syozi appointed assistant attaché for the present only, please issue orders for his residence in Sweden. I have studied the matter, . . . and my decision is as given. . . ."

On January 23, Abe sent a message to Mishina directly: "In regard to Commander Syozi . . . scheduled to depart for Japan according to Bureau of Military Affairs. . . . Since he performed numerous duties of liaison with the Central Authorities . . . we want to have him sent back here as soon as preparations can be made. Please be very careful to keep this matter secret." That was that, but come March, as a safe haven in Sweden became a critical element of his European exit strategy, Abe decided that Mishina had to be replaced. The admiral stated his position in a dispatch on March 6 to the navy vice minister and the vice chief, Naval General Staff: "As the position occupied by Sweden will become extremely important in the future from the standpoint of intelligence and state policy . . . we have for some time been studying the assignment of naval personnel in preparation for the trend of European affairs. At this time I believe it best to dispatch Captain Oogi immediately for service in that country. I am hastening to request a visa for him, since it is reported that Sweden has decided to forbid the entrance of travelers generally from 6 March. . . . We should like you to arrange right away for the transfer of this officer to the post of attaché to the Swedish legation, retroactive to March 1. Moreover, we would like the present attaché, Commander Mishina, to remain as assistant attaché."

Nothing further had happened by April 2, when, according to Mishina, he received a telephone call from Berlin informing him that Captain Oogi had been appointed naval attaché in Sweden. On April 3, Mishina addressed his concern to the vice chief of the Naval General Staff: "Since we have not yet received any orders from the Central Authorities, and since it is a matter of my own assignment, I should like you to send the orders." Mishina had heard of a plan, if worse came to worst, for Japanese officers assigned to Berlin "to seek refuge here," and he felt entitled to offer some advice. "It is expected . . . that after the German defeat England and America will . . . try to drive the neutral countries into war with Japan. . . . For one thing, it is very probable that they will try to destroy our information bases in Europe. . . . There will be nothing for the various neutral nations to do in order to protect their own interests but follow America's lead. In this regard it seems necessary to be very careful about . . . such countries as Sweden in the near future. Consequently we are avoiding . . . anything that might irritate the enemy, and are doing our best to maintain the information bases in Europe. This may appear to be a very negative policy, but we believe that it will be to the advantage of Japan in the long run. We believe that plans in Berlin . . . should be carefully considered from this standpoint."

Mishina reported on April 14 that he had been notified by the Swedish Foreign Ministry of a policy to refuse altogether an increase in the staff of the Japanese legation. "I conferred with Minister Okamoto about the appointment of Captain Oogi as attaché here," he further advised, "but since the minister has no official message from the Central Authorities, he said that he could not negotiate formally with the Swedish Foreign Minister. Even if he should receive an order to that effect, the Swedish government's persistence in this policy is clear, and if we state our plans boldly, it will either offend Sweden to no purpose or else end by embarrassing us." Mishina was willing to speak boldly to Abe, no doubt encouraged by the support of Okamoto. "It will be extremely difficult to get a visa for Captain Oogi to enter the country," he argued. "I feel that the only way in which it might be done would be to transfer me."

Abe was not about to back down. "Captain Oogi departed from Berlin on April 13," he said in a message to Tokyo on April 15. "He will stop in Copenhagen until he gets his visa, whereupon he will proceed to his post in Sweden." And sounding like someone accustomed to getting his way, Abe added: "I want Commander Mishina appointed assistant attaché."

Minister Okamoto sent an indignant protest to Tokyo on April 16, having learned of the Oogi appointment from the military attaché, Major General Makoto Onodera. "It is my opinion that if there is any shake-up at all affecting the attaché assigned here, either the Navy Ministry will send a report to me through the Foreign Ministry or the Navy will provide me with a formal report. The attitude of the Foreign Ministry of this country is such that it will not permit any increase in personnel. In this shift is the attaché to be transferred to Germany? (Under present circumstances this would be impossible.)" Okamoto insisted it was not his intention to protect Commander Mishina or to prevent Captain Oogi from coming to his post, but if there was a need to make changes in attachés assigned to Sweden, he hoped it could be handled adroitly. "There is a great deal of intrigue going on about this . . . ," he wrote, "and erroneous accounts, slanders, and denials may be conveyed to you. For this reason I am taking the liberty of speaking up. . . . I have heard from confidential sources that in case worse comes to worst in Germany, Vice Admiral Abe has formulated a plan to escape . . . with 10 to 20 of the officials under him, in a personal plane, and to slip into this country. For this reason his assistant, Captain Oogi, has been appointed attaché here. My own guess is they fear this plan, in view of our efforts up until now not to antagonize the Swedes, would receive our opposition. The military attaché, who I do not believe has given me complete information on the matter, is naturally endorsing the move. (The naval attaché is objecting.)"

In reply to Mishina on April 14 regarding Oogi's visa, Abe advised Tokyo on April 17 that Onodera, the military attaché, had obtained from the Swedish foreign office a more hopeful reading of the matter. Germans and Japanese were barred from entering Sweden, but in the case of Oogi and an aide, the orders had been issued prior to the effective date of the ruling. Therefore their visa applications would be considered, though a formal request by the Japanese minister was required. When Onodera so advised Okamoto, he said he would make no formal request until receiving notification from the Central Authorities. Abe addressed the Central Authorities—politely but firmly—in his April 17 dispatch to Tokyo: "Consequently, we should like you to inform this minister right away by a message from the Foreign Ministry on Captain Oogi's appointment as attaché, and instruct him to request that a visa be issued by Sweden right away."

Abe had prevailed for the moment, but he was entering Sweden not as a diplomat but as a combatant seeking refuge. "In view of the present crisis," he wrote on April 17, "I shall not expect any messages from the Central Authorities. . . . I believe it would be desirable to have instructions issued to this minister to take charge of such requests."

Once ashore at Malmoe on the morning of May 5, there would

be no turning back for Abe and his party, as the German mine-sweeper departed immediately.

ABE AGONISTIC

On May 4, as he prepared to leave Germany the next morning, Abe got through by telephone to Admiral Meisel, the chief of naval operations and former chief of staff of the German navy. Following the usual formalities—and unusual ones having to do with Hitler's death and "Germany's splendid fight"—Abe started at the top of his agenda. "I informed Meisel of the matter mentioned in Secretariat Serial 291 and inquired as to Germany's plans, and it was clear that they did not differ from the substance of our previous conference in Berlin. I therefore reiterated our requests and asked the admiral to use his influence. I concluded, however, that further negotiations on this matter should be conducted with Admiral Wenneker in Tokyo, and I shall discontinue conversations with the German Navy." To Abe's question about the future of submarine warfare, Meisel said U-boats would operate from bases in Norway; in fact, orders to that effect had just been issued. But when Abe asked if the government would move to Denmark should northern Germany be lost, he replied that this was as yet undecided. Abe then asked about Germany in the immediate future—would she continue to prosecute the war? Meisel stated that Germany "could not possibly stand up against British and American air superiority, and was no match for the three countries of England, America, and Russia. Consequently they will adopt a policy of coming to terms with England and America."

The treatment accorded him and his party was described by Abe as "generous" in a report from Malmoe on May 7. His greatest concern was whether he would be permitted to retain his command function, "to continue my previous assignment," as he put it, and a tentative reading was positive. "Consequently . . . ," he said in a message to Tokyo, "please consider that my authority and duties as chief naval officer in Europe, per your Serial 913 of last October, remain the same for the present." Naturally, a second great concern was eventually finding a means of transportation to Japan. "The movement of various personnel when the Germans were routed bears a relationship to the question of dispatching German submarines to East Asia," Abe suggested. "To have them return by German submarine was often considered, but unfortunately Germany surrendered suddenly, and we had no time for that. Insofar as possible, we should like you to consider sending them home . . . via Siberia. . . . Please give your opinion."

Abe and Commander Mishina had put aside their differences in favor of mutual benefit to be gained from cooperation. Abe had demonstrated his authority in the set-to with Minister Okamoto, but he was at the mercy of Swedish authorities, with whom the attaché dealt from a position of influence. Further, the political balance in neutral Sweden was shifting to the advantage of the Allies, as Mishina observed in accounts to the Japanese Naval General Staff. "Arrangements to intern German nationals with Nazi sympathies resident in Sweden will probably be made after 7 May," he advised. "It is thought that Sweden may announce the breaking of diplomatic relations with Germany around that date. It also appears likely that Nazi sympathizers among the members of the German legation will be similarly interned. . . . It is clear from the above that Sweden has now become completely the tool of England and America." On May 7 Mishina had more to say about

Nazi sympathizers in Sweden, and he specifically addressed the matter of Japanese military personnel seeking refuge. "Although I am hoping to do something or other, if only for Vice Admiral Abe, and am confidentially making efforts in that direction," he explained, "the present situation here is that Sweden, as previously reported, cannot act according to her own volition. From now on great caution will be necessary with regard to the pressure which will be brought to bear by the United States and Britain. . . . If one may judge from the attitude of the Swedish government, . . . Vice Admiral Abe and his officials will not escape detention. We are endeavoring to mitigate this."

By "mitigate" Mishina had in mind detention with a minimum of restrictions—that is, freedom of movement within a community to which the detainees were assigned. That appears to be what was arranged, as the attaché described it on May 9: "They can reside unrestrictedly at Jonkoping, 280 miles southwest of Stockholm. It is understood that aside from being restricted in the range of their movements, they will live as ordinary persons." Abe and the others moved to Jonkoping on May 14, and he seemed pleased with the arrangement. "All are in fine spirits and in excellent physical condition," he informed Tokyo two days later. "The Swedish government . . . is according us very generous treatment."

Abe said in a dispatch to Tokyo on May 16 from Jonkoping:

> In the belief that the matter of Secretariat Serial 224 would be my last service in Germany, I made efforts to the very end. . . . I emphasized . . . that if by any chance the German submarines should either have to be scuttled or fall into enemy hands, we should very much like them to proceed to

East Asia. And I said any persons on board, meaning foreigners, will receive protection and hospitality in Japan.
Chancellor Hitler and Foreign Minister von Ribbentrop
made it plain that they were fundamentally in agreement
with this, but since I was unable to make this statement clear
to Admiral Doenitz, who was the authority responsible, I
proposed another interview. But as it was very difficult for
Doenitz to have that interview after he became chancellor, I
repeated our request to Admiral Meisel, chief of operations.
Meisel declared that he would seriously consider our request and do everything he could. Since then, contact with
the German Navy has been impossible. . . .

According to broadcasts the German submarines are . . .
not being scuttled but are giving up to the British without resistance. This to me is a disgrace. . . . There is, however, a ray
of hope that some of the German submarines are at large
and may . . . be on their way to East Asia. I cling to this hope.

Abe turned his attention to "the German submarine on which
Kessler, Syozi, and Tomonaga wer^ proceeding to East Asia . . . ,"
the *U-234.* "I am extremely apprehensive. . . ." Imminent news
broadcasts would confirm that Abe's fears were well placed.

Again from Jonkoping, on May 23, Abe appeared to be running
things, as usual: "We are maintaining liaison with the naval and
military attachés in Stockholm and are cooperating with them in
strictest secrecy." He repeated his plea to continue as ranking Japanese naval officer abroad and requested consent to certain arrangements, "limited to this place and for the time being." He wished to
have Captain Taniguchi appointed naval attaché in Sweden, in place

of Commander Mishina and instead of Captain Oogi, whose appointment was still pending. And he claimed justification for assigning two accounting officers, Commander Ikeda and Captain Inaba, other than their presence as detainees. "The prime requisite from the standpoint of handling economic affairs," Abe advised, "is to strengthen and regulate exchange in Sweden. We are in a particularly dangerous position at this time in that Sweden may restrain our activities by controlling our funds as a result of recent persistent demands and pressure by the United States."

Abe may well have been deluded in believing he could control the office of naval attaché in Sweden from Jonkoping. That was Mishina's interpretation, as indicated by his advisory to the Naval General Staff on May 28: "When money is sent payable to Captain Oogi, various difficulties arise in receiving it. Until such time as Captain Oogi can assume his duty, please make the money payable to Commander Mishina."

The ticklish situation in Sweden was the subject of an article in the *New York Times* on June 8:

> Eighteen former members of the Japanese Bureau of Naval Intelligence in Berlin are stranded in Sweden because Moscow has so far not shown any disposition to grant them a transit visa through the Soviet Union. Because of this circumstance local Soviet observers see an indication of tension between Tokyo and Moscow at the moment. . . .

The Japanese are in Sweden not as diplomats but as refugees, and their presence here may eventually raise delicate questions of international law, should their extradition as potential war criminals be demanded by the United States or Great Britain. They fled here from Berlin before the advancing Russian and Anglo-American armies. . . .

The Swedes assigned them to Jonkoping, an inland city in mid-Sweden. The Japanese disliked this, protesting that they were diplomats and that they preferred to live in Stockholm so that they could be near the Japanese legation. The Swedes turned a deaf ear to the protests. . . .

The Japanese Bureau of Naval Intelligence in Berlin conducted espionage concerning movements of naval and merchant tonnage in European waters. Not an Allied ship was supposed to move in Europe without this bureau's knowing about it. Tokyo's efforts to get the members home may be indicative of how little success the Japanese naval spies have had.

Admiral Abe, head of the bureau, and his staff also were in charge of submarine traffic between German or German-occupied ports and Japan. The traffic was at one time considerable, but losses in submarines and crews were so heavy that the traffic dwindled toward the end of the European war.

It was Tokyo's plan . . . that Admiral Abe

and his staff should return to Japan at the last
moment by submarine, but the swiftness of
Field Marshal Sir Bernard L. Montgomery's advance toward Kiel and Bremerhaven foiled this
plan. . . .

9. A DESPERATE STRATEGY THAT BARELY FAILED

The uranium shipment aboard the *U-234* came as no surprise to the Allied Ultra intelligence monitors who had been watching its progress for nearly a year—since June 22, 1944, when Admiral Kojima notified Tokyo that it would be sent to Japan on the return voyage of the *I-52*. That it was aboard the *U-234* would have been deduced from the identity of the dead Japanese officers, Syozi and Tomonaga, and confirmed in the ship's manifest, an English translation of which was dated May 23: ten cases of uranium oxide weighing 560 kilograms. But the existence of the radioactive material became an immediate military secret, to be withheld from reporters on the scene—understandably, since nothing was more sensitive in Washington in May 1945 than the development of a nuclear weapon. But some basic questions would persist for some time to come: What was the composition of the material, the state of its radioactivity? How did the Japanese intend to use it? How was it finally disposed of? Security was relegated to the atomic bomb bureaucracy, the Manhattan Project, whose director, Major General Leslie R. Groves, was also the Chief of Military Intelligence. Groves had approved a policy of underrating nuclear progress by the enemy even to the point of denial when evidence at the scene indicated such progress. In this case the suspicious cargo was routinely noted in the minutes of a meeting of the Manhattan Project's Washington Group on July 2, 1945—described by Major Francis J. Smith, an army intelligence officer, as "approximately 526 kilos of 77.4 percent uranium oxide, . . . now being held in New York City under Major Smith's name." Naval intelligence officers conducting an investigation in Portsmouth were silent on the shipment; however, Wolfgang Hirschfeld, the *U-234* communications officer, remembered a red-letter day as technicians with Geiger counters swarmed all over the steel cargo containers being lifted by crane from the six forward mine shafts of the *U-234*, and deposited on the wharf. Hirschfeld recalled this happening in late July—on or about the twenty-fourth (which challenged Major Smith's account placing the uranium in New York in early July).

HEARING FROM MR. BROOKS

Hirschfeld's book was written in collaboration with Geoffrey Brooks, who had tackled the issue of nuclear development in an earlier book, *Hitler's Nuclear Weapons*. While Hitler may have considered resorting to the radiation bomb for various reasons, Brooks wrote—"as a German reprisal for a British chemical or biological attack, . . . as a riposte for an atomic attack by American aircraft operating from British airfields, or as a means to seize victory at a stroke—the intended target . . . always was the civilian population of the United States." Hitler no doubt felt in 1941 that he was at war with the United States already, so he had little to lose by siding with Japan, but it cannot be discounted, Brooks maintained, that acquiring the radiological weapon for attacks on American population centers, "as an inducement to the United States to adopt strict neutrality in Europe, may well have determined his decision. It is thus clear that by early 1942 Nazi physics had quietly broadened its perspective to accommodate the atomic reactor, while the atom bomb remained Jewish physics."

Brooks added a few fundamental details about the radiation bomb in a World War II context, pointing out that uranium bombs are not atomic bombs—they do not explode. "One of the methods of distributing the radioactive contents of . . . radiation bombs," Brooks explained, "would be to pack them around a conventional explosive, which would scatter them to all points of the compass." If Hitler had been certain, Brooks continued, that the enemy would not succeed in developing a critical reactor by the time that radiation bombs were ready, he would undoubtedly have used them, "but his information at the turn of 1942 suggested that the United States was close to making an achievement in nuclear science. . . ." Furthermore, German atomic scientists had failed to develop a countermeasure to gamma radiation. Fearful of retaliation—Hitler believed correctly that the United States had built a working reactor—Hitler had devised a weapons policy that precluded first-strike use of a radiation bomb.

In early 1945 it was believed in Japan that a German defeat would come by summer at the latest, Brooks wrote, "and Japan's own position was clearly desperate." The Japanese would welcome "any solution by which they might acquit themselves of the conflict with . . . no loss of face." Hitler, meanwhile, was determined to exact revenge for the destruction of Germany's cities. "Undoubtedly he was willing and eager to use the radiation weapon against the Americans but only without directly implicating Germany." And the Japanese, "who had far less compunction than Hitler about the scattering of blight and plague, would have seen a glimmer of hope for their salvation."

Brooks continued his analysis in an appendix to the book by Hirschfeld:

"We know from the declassified archive material that what the Germans sent was a small quantity of uranium oxide ore (U-308) in ten metal cases of 560 kilos total weight. . . . Wolfgang Hirschfeld described these as resembling modern radioisotope shipment containers. From his additional hearsay evidence it would appear that they were emitting gamma radiation when examined at unloading, and radioactive contamination was detected on all six steel cargo tubes which had been located in the forward mineshafts of *U-234* during the voyage. Uranium oxide ore is inert unless it has been subjected to neutron bombardment in a nuclear reactor. If it has been in a reactor core, the isotopes of plutonium are bred in the ore."

Hirschfeld, one of several *U-234* crew members confined aboard an old vessel at the Portsmouth navy yard, was relied on for advice by American officers who were sorting and itemizing the U-boat's cargo. He noticed that some weaponry—the Me 262 jet fighter, in particular—had been unloaded before the end of May, but it was well into July, Hirschfeld insisted, before most of it—the uranium included—was removed. Hirschfeld felt certain about his recollection of when the unloading occurred because it was a memorable event, a break in the routine. He was invited by one of the naval officers, Lieutenant Commander Hatton, to observe the proceeding from the bridge of the *U-234,* and he asked Hatton about four men who were examining the cargo with handheld instruments. "They're testing for radiation with Geiger counters," Hatton explained.

While there was a discernible reluctance on the part of naval interrogators to delve into the uranium shipment, Brooks was mistaken when he asserted that the matter was not raised until after the material was unloaded "on or about 24 July." Referring to the questioning of a *U-234* passenger, Luftwaffe Lieutenant Colonel Kai Nieschling, Brooks wrote: "The only interrogation report released by the U.S. National Archives to date, the 'Nieschling Memorandum,' is dated 27 July, 1945." There is such a document at the National Archives: a Report of Interrogation regarding uranium and other cargo aboard *U-234.* It is based on the interrogation of Nieschling, a Luftwaffe legal officer and military judge (also described as a devout Nazi assigned by the party to keep an eye on General Kessler), who was unable or unwilling to shed light on the half-ton uranium load, and said so immediately: "P/W [prisoner of war] does not know anything in particular about this ore, but only heard that it was valuable and that it was to be exchanged for some other valuable ore that the Germans needed."

As to Brooks's point about when the report was issued, there is a copy dated July 27, an internal document being transmitted from one intelligence office to another, Op-16-Z to Op-16-PT. It is a near duplicate of the original (a line attesting to Nieschling's veracity is omitted) dated May 24, the day of the interview. For lack of corroborating evidence—and considering he was in custody in a foreign land under arduous circumstances—it appears that Hirschfeld was confused about the date of the cargo unloading. A review of the *Portsmouth Herald* for the period in question revealed that on June 22 local newsmen were invited aboard the *U-234* for a stem-to-stern tour, and it was clear from a report by the *Herald*'s Robert G. Kennedy that the uranium had already been removed.

> Besides carrying an important cargo of merchandise, vital papers . . . and Nazi Luftwaffe officers, the submarine had two high-ranking Japanese officials aboard who committed hara-kiri when the German commander surrendered to the American warships. The hara-kiri cabin was the first place visited by the reporters. . . . The small cabin . . . had two sets of upper and lower bunks and is in the bow of the ship under the petty officers' quarters. All traces of the Japanese had been removed by naval intelligence officers and the quarters tidied up by Portsmouth submarine sailors stationed aboard the vessel. The room was dimly lighted and had a dungeonlike atmosphere. There was a small table and chair as well as several small wall lockers. . . .
>
> It was evident that the *234* was not a real fighting ship although it could defend itself against air attacks and against surface vessels with the after tubes. It was designed primarily to carry tons of cargo. . . . There were six

> mine wells forward and six each on the port and starboard sides. These wells were nearly 25 feet deep and approximately 4 feet in diameter. The Nazis devised a watertight cylinder which fitted exactly into the mine well for carrying their valuable cargoes. The cylinders taken from the submarine at Portsmouth were flown to Washington before being opened.

The Portsmouth newspaper piece, while contradicting Hirschfeld, corroborates the minutes of the Manhattan Project meeting on July 2, in which Major Smith reported on the status of the uranium oxide.

Nieschling was fairly cooperative, considering his rights as a prisoner of war, and in his interrogation he revealed that Germany had turned over to Japan the plans for the V-1 rocket and the latest Messerschmitt aircraft. He was elusive when asked about "the meaning behind the ore," suggesting it would be known to his cabin mate aboard the *U-234*, Lieutenant Commander Gerhard Falck of the German navy. "He knows magnetic problems," said Nieschling of Falck, who had been designated the chief technical officer in Japan, reporting to Admiral Wenneker, the German naval attaché in Tokyo. Falck was also well qualified to deal with "naval mine problems and naval building problems," said Nieschling, and his association with the Imperial Navy reached back to 1941, when he was an adviser to Admiral Nomura and Admiral Abe, chief Japanese representatives to the Tripartite Military Commission.

While there appears to be no report on the interrogation of Falck, a search of the National Archives in College Park, Maryland, turned up lengthy transcripts, in German, of interviews on June 18 and July 9, and an eighteen-page first-person career summary. Falck took advantage of a passive approach by his interrogator and carefully chose the topics he would discuss, which did not include the German mission to Tokyo. Nor was the uranium oxide ever mentioned, and if Falck's purpose was to convince his captors of his uneventful career in the German navy, it appears he succeeded. Much of it was spent dealing with the Japanese in joint naval activities of a less-than-extraordinary nature. In a rambling manner he told of routine activities, allowing his listener to be caught off guard when tragedy abruptly interferes. "I was eager to get written contracts after we had agreed by word. A contract was signed for rebuilding fast boats for only 300,000 Reichsmarks. A German specialist for welding was sent to Japan. For rebuilding a U-boat Type IX, one specialist for shipbuilding and engine construction and another for serial production of U-boat motors and light metal pistons were sent to Japan. When all German experts were in Japan, three Japanese specialists were sent to Germany for training. They did not arrive. The Japanese submarine was destroyed by a mine while in Japanese waters. No further specialists were sent from Japan." (The Japanese submarine was probably the *I-34*, which did not hit a mine but was torpedoed by a British submarine as she approached Penang on November 13, 1943. Her code name, Momi, was bestowed upon the soon-to-be-launched *I-52*.)

In July 1941 Admiral Nomura wrote Falck a letter commending him for his service to the Tripartite Commission: "At the departure of the commission that I was the leader of, I would like to thank you on behalf of my comrades and express my sincere thanks for your infinite effort which you did in spite of your many occupations. Thus we could obtain a great impression of the German Navy." Nomura and Falck had weathered the early days of the Axis partnership when Japanese-German relations were tentative, to say the least. The first Japanese navy delegation had made the long trip to Berlin, arriving in March 1941—by boat to Lisbon, Portugal, and by air from there. As it was quite cold in northern Germany, the newcomers went to a naval supply store to purchase warm uniforms, and as they waited in line they heard themselves referred to by a storekeeper—in German, but enough of them understood—as "little yellow monkeys."

The enigmatic Commander Falck was last seen by Hirschfeld on the evening of May 19, when the *U-234* docked at Portsmouth and the ten German passengers were taken by bus to an airstrip and flown to Washington. Of the ten, Falck was the only one Hirschfeld and Brooks were unable to locate after the war. They suggest he may have been granted U.S. citizenship "in exchange for his silence," which presumes U.S. complicity in a cover-up, which seems far-fetched. There is even less evidence to support another theory, in which Hirschfeld casts Falck in the role of a man who knew too much. "His eventual fate after he disappeared . . . on 19 May 1945 remains a mystery."

HOT CARGO CONFIRMED

Brooks then turned his attention to statements made in December 1995 by John Lansdale, the Manhattan Project's security and intelligence chief in 1945. Lieutenant Colonel Lansdale was interviewed by William Broad of the *New York Times* and by two overseas publications, *Mail on Sunday* of London and *Der Spiegel,* a German newsweekly. U.S. military authorities "reacted with panic" when they discovered the *U-234*'s cargo of radioactive uranium, according to the article in *Der Spiegel*. It was an understandable reaction if what was thought to be inert uranium oxide was emitting gamma radiation, since it would have indicated that nuclear weapons development by the Germans was far ahead of U.S. intelligence estimates. When asked what had become of the "hot cargo," Lansdale said it was shipped immediately to the atom bomb factory in Oak Ridge, Tennessee. "The transfer papers went . . . over my desk," said Lansdale, though he told Broad he only recalled that it went into the Manhattan Project's uranium supply. Broad also interviewed Skip Gosling, the chief historian of the Department of Energy, the government agency that absorbed the Manhattan Project, and Gosling agreed with the German magazine report: the *U-234* shipment went into the mix at Oak Ridge, where uranium was treated to increase its concentration of the critical U-235 isotope. But it remained unclear whether the German uranium was put to a specific use, such as the bombing of Hiroshima on August 6, 1945, or Nagasaki three days later. "My guess is that none of it got in," said Gosling, "but I wouldn't bet my farm on it."

At any rate the radioactive state of the uranium oxide unloaded from the *U-234* was convincing evidence that Germany had a working atomic pile.

In the opinion of Geoffrey Brooks it would have been surprising if Nazi scientists had not built a small pilot reactor by 1944. Four years earlier, he reasoned, Paul Harteck, a chemistry professor at Hamburg University, had informed the authorities that such a reactor could be constructed using twenty tons of uranium oxide, layered in a thirty-ton block of dry ice at minus 75 degrees centigrade, and all the necessary materials were available. Meanwhile Baron Manfred von Ardenne, a biologist interested in medical applications of radioisotopes, was at work in a laboratory at his home near Berlin on a project, for which he had retained nuclear physicist Fritz Houtermans. Von Ardenne financed much of the work from his private fortune, and he received additional funding from the German Post Office, which was not so unusual in light of the scientific proclivities of the German minister of posts, Wilhelm Ohnesorge, a member of Hitler's inner circle. A main objective of the von Ardenne project was radioisotope production in a small reactor, which accounted for the research contract with Houtermans.

In the fall of 1942 construction was completed on a network of concrete underground bunkers on the grounds of the baron's estate, but specifically what was achieved there was never fully revealed. Brooks speculates that in this period von Ardenne and Houtermans had ample time to build a low-temperature reactor like the one described by Harteck in 1940, but this was a long reach for the truth. (Better evidence of to what end von Ardenne—and Houtermans as well—might have directed his effort can be deduced from what he is known to have achieved right after the war, when he was retained by the Soviet Union to develop an atomic bomb. Working at a secret facility on the Black Sea, von Ardenne perfected a method of splitting isotopes to create enriched uranium 235, thus contributing in a major way to a successful test of the first Soviet atomic bomb on September 23, 1949.)

As a young idealist in 1935, Houtermans moved to the Soviet Union, but he was suspected of being a Trotskyite by the NKVD and spent nearly two years in a Moscow prison. He was released after Hitler and Stalin signed a nonaggression agreement in 1939, only to be imprisoned by the Gestapo when he returned to Berlin. He was freed with the help of Max von Laue, the winner of the Nobel Prize in Physics in 1914, who landed him a job with von Ardenne, and by August 1941, in the words of Richard Rhodes in *The Making of the Atomic Bomb,* Houtermans "had independently worked out all the basic ideas necessary to the bomb." In a thirty-nine-page report, which Houtermans kept out of the hands of the German War Office, he addressed fast-neutron chain reactions, critical mass, U-235, isotope separation, and 94, the chemical code for plutonium (which would turn out to be the key to an unlimited supply of fissionable material). By withholding as much information as he dared—about plutonium in particular—Houtermans "probably contributed to the neglect of isotope separation in Germany," Rhodes wrote. "After the summer of 1941 the German bomb program depended entirely on uranium and . . . heavy water." (Heavy water is water in which hydrogen atoms have been replaced by deuterium for use as a moderator in a reactor.)

Following the bombing of Hiroshima and Nagasaki in August 1945, certain prominent German physicists—notably Carl von Weizsacker—drew comfort from a comparison of the Allied atomic weapons program with their own endeavor to develop the uranium engine, or reactor, for peaceful purposes. Such invidious logic fails quite obviously upon recognition of the lethal and vastly destructive potential of reactor-enriched U-235.

LANSDALE TO GROVES, MAY 1945

John Lansdale was a Harvard-trained lawyer whose lucrative practice in Cleveland was interrupted for the five years, 1941–46, which he spent as chief of security and intelligence for the top secret Manhattan Project. The head of the project, General Groves, was tortured by a fear of foreign agents—an obsession arguably justified by the Klaus Fuchs affair—and he worried constantly about enemy activity in the nuclear arms race. Lieutenant Colonel Lansdale was in charge of the antisubversive guard, an enforcer who confronted J. Robert Oppenheimer, director of the test center at Los Alamos, New Mexico, over Oppie's alleged Soviet sympathies. (Peter Wyden, in *Day One: Before Hiroshima and After,* writes that Lansdale was viewed by an Oppenheimer assistant as one who "bossed the hated creeps who read all Los Alamos mail and listened to all telephone calls.")

In the period leading up to the surrender on May 7, Lansdale spent weeks in Germany and reported to Groves that there were three groups working on T.A., or Tube Alloys, a British term for chemical metals (T.A. was used by the Manhattan Project staff as a code name for the never-mentioned nuclear program), though he detailed just two of them. The Kaiser Wilhelm Institute, or K.W.I. group, under Werner Heisenberg, had conducted its experiments in Berlin until the end of 1943, but then evacuated the physicists and small experiments to Hechingen, a town in southwest Germany. "They left the actual pile . . . in Berlin," Lansdale wrote in his report, "where experiments were contained . . . ," but it was decided in September 1944 "that they should have a pile of the best design nearer to Hechingen. They then selected and prepared Haigerloch Laboratory, to which they moved their stock of heavy water, one-and-one-half tons, and metal, 1,500 to 1,800 kilograms, in February and March of 1945." But after all that preparation, Lansdale reported, "they conducted only one experiment at Haigerloch, then hid the heavy water and metal. . . ."

The Haigerloch pile was discovered in April by members of Alsos, a U.S. Army unit reporting to Groves (*alsos* is a Greek word for olive groves), whose mission was to document and destroy enemy nuclear development. Lansdale proceeded to describe the pile in layman's language.

It consisted of a circular aluminum steel tank eight feet high and eight feet in diameter, which enclosed a similar tank four feet high and four feet in diameter. Between the two tanks graphite blocks were placed as reflectors, and about one-and-a-half tons of metal in the form of five-centimeter uranium cubes were strung on aluminum wires in the inner tank. Heavy water amounting to about one-and-a-half tons was fed into the inner tank through a vent in the top, and a half-gram of radium was used as a neutron source.

The pile was not self-sustaining, in Lansdale's opinion. "It appears to be definite that although they knew of the existence and some of the properties of 49 [94, plutonium, with the digits transposed as a security precaution], they never produced any."

Turning his attention to Heisenberg's Hechingen laboratory, Lansdale discovered work going on in isotope separation using various methods, all in the early stages. "One was a method called velocity selector, and the apparatus was seized, as was the individual working on it. Another was a diffusion method, and the apparatus and an operator were also seized. And with a third electro-magnetic method using a mass spectrograph, there was no indication of success."

A second group led by Kurt Diebner of the German War Office

was found by Lansdale to be "more or less independent" of Heisenberg.

> They started in Berlin and built their pile at Gottow. When the Russians reached the Oder, they left Gottow and started to reorganize at Stadiim, but apparently never got a pile in operation there. The foundations discovered in Stadiim indicate that the pile was smaller than the Haigerloch pile. This group had about two-and-a-half tons of metal in the form of plates and about one-half ton of heavy water. We do not know where these materials are. They had about three tons of [uranium] oxide in the form of cubes, five centimeters to a side, which we obtained and shipped to Paris. Apparently the Diebner group and the Heisenberg group exchanged reports, and there was a certain amount of cooperation between them.

Lansdale mentioned Otto Hahn, who in 1939 split the uranium atom and discovered the possibility of a chain reaction (for which he was awarded the Nobel Prize in Chemistry in 1944). As head of the K.W.I. Institute for Chemistry, Hahn had cooperated with both Heisenberg and Diebner, but apparently more closely with Heisenberg, in his work on fission products and isotope separation.

In the city of Celle, south of Hamburg, Lansdale encountered "a man named Groth," who was working on a centrifuge method of isotope separation. "Both Groth and his apparatus were seized," wrote Lansdale, who might have consulted his colleague Samuel A. Goudsmit, the scientific director of the Alsos Mission, who had known Wilhelm Groth well at one time. Goudsmit was a Dutch physicist, a Jew with personal reasons to hate the Nazis, and while Groth would become a Nazi, Goudsmit remembered him as a close friend. "Almost twenty years earlier, when I had a Rockefeller Fellowship for study in Germany, he had been my roommate," Goudsmit wrote in a postwar reflection. "We had become . . . intimate friends. He was a great admirer of Thomas Mann, and that kept him from falling into the trap of the Nazi doctrine. . . . But he had done his duty; early in 1939, he and his colleague, Harteck, had written a letter to the German military authorities about the possibilities of a uranium bomb."

The Harteck-Groth letter was written in April 1939 amid sudden signs—such as a ban on uranium exports—of government interest in a high-priority nuclear research program: "We take the liberty," wrote Harteck and Groth, "of calling to your attention the newest development in nuclear physics, which, in our opinion, will probably make it possible to produce an explosive many orders of magnitude more powerful than the conventional ones. . . . That country which first makes use of it has an unsurpassable advantage over the others." The letter reached Diebner, whose reaction would indicate that Lansdale's estimate of the situation, while it may have pleased General Groves, was perfunctory and flawed.

SAM GOUDSMIT'S WAR

When the master racists of the Third Reich spoke scornfully of "Jewish physics," they were referring to Goudsmit—as well as Einstein, Teller, Wigner, Szilard, and others—who came to America and took revenge on the Nazis by joining the war effort. While not a bomb builder, Goudsmit was uniquely qualified, in the opinion of Peter Wyden, to be the chief Alsos investigator in Europe: "He was an outstanding nuclear physicist; he spoke several languages; he seemed to have been friendly with everybody in European science, including Werner Heisenberg, who had been his houseguest at the University of Michigan before the war; and since Goudsmit had not been connected with the bomb project before, he could reveal no technical secrets if he was captured."

Samuel Abraham Goudsmit was born in 1902 in The Hague, Netherlands, where his father was a wholesaler of bathroom fixtures and his mother ran a millinery shop. He received a Ph.D. in physics from the University of Leiden in 1927, the year he emigrated to the United States and joined the faculty at Michigan. (It was here in his early career that Goudsmit and an associate discovered the phenomenon of electron spin, which led to a fundamental change in the mathematical structure of quantum mechanics.) In 1939 he began a six-year stint as a government scientist, first as a staff physicist at MIT's Radiation Laboratory in Cambridge, Massachusetts, and then as a civilian investigator with the War Department's Military Intelligence Service. He reported directly to Groves, as did Lansdale and other Alsos intelligence officers, since the general was opposed to hierarchies.

If Groves was having second thoughts, it was because Goudsmit was showing occasional signs of emotional instability, and this was where Robert Furman came into the picture. Furman had graduated from Princeton in 1937, an ROTC second lieutenant in the field artillery. By the time he was called up, in 1940, Furman had switched to the Army Corps of Engineers and was assigned to construction of Defense Department headquarters in Washington called the Pentagon. The officer in charge, Leslie Groves, was impressed with him and asked that he be assigned to a new hush-hush agency, so in August 1943 Major Furman reported for duty at the Manhattan Project in Washington. (Manhattan Engineering District, it was named originally, in yet another attempt to confuse enemy agents.) A year later, Bob Furman and Sam Goudsmit were in liberated Paris, tracking down German scientists whose names appeared on the watch list. They made a good team—the brilliant but brittle Goudsmit and the often inscrutable Furman, who expressed himself sparsely, careful not to squander his thoughts. (During the year they worked together, in reports and statements by Goudsmit, Furman was known as the "Mysterious Major.") Furman was busy keeping an eye on Goudsmit, and a night in Strasbourg, an historic city on the Rhine in southern France, was one to remember, as he did in an interview years later with Thomas Powers, author of *Heisenberg's War*. Goudsmit "just went off his rocker," said Furman. "He was thrashing around . . . furious with the Germans." For over a year, Goudsmit had heard nothing about the fate of his mother and father in Holland, and he feared the worst.

The trip to Strasbourg, as the Germans retreated from the city, was in response to a tip from the Office of Strategic Services in Paris. (The O.S.S. more often kept such information to itself, but it was presently busy with a scheme to abduct Heisenberg.) Three leading German physicists—including Carl von Weizsacker, a prominent protégé of Heisenberg—were reportedly in residence at Strasbourg University; equally important was a likely opportunity to collect useful documents there.

With Colonel Boris T. Pash, the military commander of Alsos, leading the way, a team of investigators arrived in Strasbourg in mid-November 1944. Pash went off to round up the scientists, as Goudsmit and an American known only as Fred, searched the premises for the nuclear laboratory, finally finding it hidden in a wing of the hospital. (Fred was Frederic A. C. Wardenburg, like Furman a Princeton alumnus, who was on leave as an executive of El du Pont de Nemours.) In retrospect Goudsmit depicted a "moment of truth," in which it became dramatically clear that the German nuclear weapons program was a total failure, a bust. The interrogations of the physicists yielded little, Goudsmit later wrote, so he and Fred turned to papers found in the laboratory and in von Weizsacker's office. "Tired as Fred and I were," Goudsmit writes in his book, *Alsos,* published in 1947, "there was nothing . . . but to get at these papers at once. . . . It was a rough evening. The Germans were shelling the city from across the river; our guns were answering. . . . We had no light but a few candles and a compressed gas lamp. In the center of the room, our soldiers were playing cards. Fred and I sat in a corner on easy chairs and began to scan the German files. We both let out a yell at the same moment, for we had both found papers that suddenly raised the curtain of secrecy. . . . Here, in apparently harmless communications, was hidden a wealth of information available to anyone who understood it."

Goudsmit failed to explain just what there was to yell about; rather, he rambles on about his and Fred's reaction to their discovery of papers that were of value, apparently, for what they did not contain. "No, it was not in code," he continues. "The papers were not even secret. They were just the usual gossip between colleagues, here and there a minor indiscretion, a hint. . . . Obviously such notes would have told nothing to the uninitiated. . . ." There were factual reports here and there, such as one about the moving of Heisenberg's lab from Berlin to Hechingen, including addresses and telephone numbers. "It is true that no priceless information was given . . . ," Goudsmit concedes, "but there was far more than enough to get a view of the whole German uranium project."

It must be said that Goudsmit reached these conclusions when writing his memoir after the war, with the benefit of hindsight. "The evidence at hand proved definitely," he writes, "that Germany had no atomic bomb and was not likely to have one in any reasonable time. There was no need to fear any attack either from an atomic explosion or from radioactive poisons." It was a noteworthy statement in that Goudsmit would deny the threat of a German atomic bomb and then acknowledge the danger of a radiation weapon by dismissing it as well. He did so knowing there were at least three groups of German scientists who had shown an interest in the "uranium problem." In addition to Heisenberg in Hechingen and Harteck in Hamburg, there was Manfred von Ardenne, an able technician and scientist with a private laboratory at his residence near Berlin. Von Ardenne manufactured experimentation instruments—electron microscopes, cyclotrons, million-volt accelerators—and had been working on a secret project for which funding had been provided by the German Post Office. Goudsmit also was aware of a German physicist, Fritz Houtermans, who was on the verge of unlocking the secret of plutonium. While under contract to von Ardenne in 1941, Houtermans had written a remarkable report suggesting that an atomic pile might produce new materials with the explosive properties of uranium. Houtermans speculated that these new elements (known eventually as neptunium and plutonium) could be separated by a relatively simple chemical process.

* * *

Reflecting on Strasbourg later on, Goudsmit told Furman how pleased he was that an atomic weapon would not be needed in the war with Germany and Japan.

"You must understand, Sam," said Furman, "if we have such a weapon, we will use it."

A GERMAN T.A. RECONSIDERED

Back in Washington briefly at the turn of the year, Goudsmit drafted a memo on the T.A. status in Europe, revealing feelings that seemed in sharp contrast to those expressed two years later in a postwar memoir. "There is positive evidence," Goudsmit declared, "that T.A. is under development in Germany." (By T.A., or Tube Alloys, he meant splitting the uranium atom with enormous explosive effect.) "The effort was originally uncoordinated but was combined under a single director, responsible to Goering, at the beginning of 1943." The effort, he wrote, included applications of nuclear physics to biology, metallurgy, and other sciences in addition to T.A., and in the early stages—up to late 1942—these applications were deemed more important than T.A. to the German war effort. The T.A. program was still in an experimental stage as late as August 1944, and until then greater emphasis seems to have been on technical as opposed to theoretical problems. "There are also indications that energy production rather than an explosive is the principal German goal, though the latter has not been overlooked. Hitler has been informed of the T.A. possibilities. . . . His reaction is unknown."

Goudsmit identified what he called "three centers of activity on the T.A. problem in Germany," beginning with the Kaiser Wilhelm Institute for Physics, originally of Berlin, now of Hechingen, where theoreticians under Heisenberg communicated by blackboard computation. Industrial support in the form of large-scale production of metal was provided by Deutsche Gold und Silber Scheideanstalt. Finally, an intensive T.A. research program was being conducted by the German Post Office, mainly due to the efforts of Ohnesorge, the Minister of Post.

There were additional T.A.-related centers that Goudsmit listed, as follows:

Freiburg in Baden, where Paul Harteck and Wilhelm Groth, until recently of Hamburg University, were at work on isotope separation by centrifuge methods.

K.W.I. Heidelberg, where Walther Bothe, the director of the physics laboratory, maintains a complete record of the German T.A. effort.

The Berlin residence of Manfred von Ardenne, a private experimenter cooperating with the Reichspost.

The Institute of Nuclear Measurements.

The nuclear research section of the Bureau of Standards, where the key figure until recently was Fritz Houtermans.

. . . .

An analysis of the Strasbourg material was submitted on February 24, 1945, by Philip Morrison, a Manhattan Project physicist. "There is every reason to believe that Heisenberg is the key figure," Morrison wrote. "What he does is the enemy main line. That he has administrative power is shown by the letter in which von Weizsacker implies that Heisenberg has made a decision to move the work to southern Germany. Moreover, Heisenberg is in firm control of Germany's nuclear destiny. . . ."

German progress was at a point reached in 1942 at the University of Chicago Metallurgical Laboratory, Morrison proposed, and Heisenberg and von Weizsacker were the counterparts of Enrico Fermi and Eugene Wigner. "It is also clear that Hechingen is the site of at least the theoretical and design work on the 49 project. It is there all these men have gone in the summer of 1944."

The "49 project" was about plutonium (using the reverse-digit code to explain German experimentation with P-94). "In all this material there is only one reference to plutonium. . . ." Morrison noted. "That plutonium is formed by the decay of neptunium is known completely to the enemy. . . ."

The evidence is inconclusive, Morrison admitted, "but the general feeling I have from reading all the letters and lecture notes is one of academic activity in many directions but of large-scale activity in none. This statement is without the strong support which the Strasbourg material gives to the equivalent statement about the 49 route, but the whole body of material cannot help but give the reader a distinctly amateur impression. . . ."

Morrison then seized an opportunity to offer a remarkable recommendation that was no doubt seen as blasphemy in some quarters. "The fact that we are considerably ahead of enemy work in this field and . . . are approaching the time of final utilization implies another approach to the whole question of security. It may be . . . coming near the time for us to release by some means positive information on the scale and success of our work. Such information would have a sizeable effect on both the German and the Japanese, especially if it precedes shortly actual use of one or two gadgets. This sort of thing could be carried out on many different levels ranging from the minimum, which I would define as planting true but incomplete and carefully considered information through some of the double agent contacts we have established; an intermediate level, which might take the form of convincing some of the captured physicists of the overwhelming success in the scale of our efforts and seeking to have them communicate this through private channels into Germany; a maximum program which will involve some form of public disclosure to the enemy . . . on the scale of our activities."

Morrison approved of building a bomb for fear of what was not known about enemy intentions, but he opposed the decision to use it without warning and spent the rest of his life—he died in April 2005 at age eighty-nine—campaigning against weapons of devastation.

In late April 1945 Colonel Pash had rounded up some twenty-five German scientists and technicians and assembled them at the Hechingen lab—all but Heisenberg himself, who had gone home to rest. They were cooperative by and large and treated as "guests" by the Alsos "missionaries." "You're under arrest," Sam Goudsmit said to Otto Hahn, but he could take a day at home in Tailfingen getting ready. When John Lansdale arrived to pick him up, Hahn was packed and ready to go. "I have been expecting you," he said.

On Friday morning, April 27, with the end of the war only ten days away, a convoy of U.S. Army jeeps headed for the university city of Heidelberg. An academic setting, Goudsmit believed, would be more comfortable for six of Germany's leading nuclear physicists, who were to be questioned: Carl von Weizsacker, Karl Wirtz, Erich Bagge, Horst Korsching, Otto Hahn, and Max von Laue. But Goudsmit himself seemed troubled—he was vague and distracted,

Bob Furman recalled. As Thomas Powers reconstructed the scene in his book *Heisenberg's War,* "Samuel Goudsmit had no heart to listen to the explanations of Germans at that point: he was possessed by his own agony. He had heard nothing directly from his parents since March 1943; he had been holding his breath since the previous September, when a young scientist in Holland had told him there was no reason to hope."

When Otto Hahn arrived, Goudsmit asked if he might know what had happened to his parents. Furman heard the question, and he heard Hahn say, yes, he did know: Goudsmit's parents had died in a concentration camp. "That was a sad day," said Furman. What he remembered most clearly was the look that came over Goudsmit's face.

On October 29, 1947, Sam Goudsmit complained in the *New York Times* about a review of his book by a former science editor of the *Times.* "Waldemar Kaempffert discusses a recent report by German physicist Werner Heisenberg together with my popular book, *Alsos,*" Goudsmit wrote.

> Both deal with the question why Germany failed in making an atom bomb, but the report and this book emphasize different reasons for this failure. Mr. Kaempffert favors the reasons given by Heisenberg. . . . "Could there be any doubt," he writes, "that had they been blessed with our resources the Germans would eventually have arrived at neptunium and plutonium?" My answer is that his question misses the point. I would turn it around as follows: "Could there be any doubt that the German authorities would have put all resources at the disposal of their scientists, if the

latter had understood the use of plutonium?" Large-scale government and military support came after Allied scientists were able to present a convincing tale of probable success. The use of plutonium was proposed early in 1941; . . . the Germans, who had started their secret work before us, never arrived at more than a vague notion of the existence of plutonium.

Moreover, the German scientists believed that a uranium pile, which they called uranium "engine," would itself be a bomb if the controls were removed. This is not surprising, as the same idea was for a time prevalent among Allied scientists. It is, therefore, true that the German scientists worked primarily on this uranium "engine," but in back of their minds the hope remained that this would lead to the bomb. . . ."

Kaempffert replied on November 4, 1947.

It is not likely that the physicists of the world will accept Dr. Goudsmit's picture of Heisenberg as a sly villain who tried to throw dust into the eyes of the Alsos Mission by contending that the primary purpose of German wartime research in nuclear physics was to develop atomic power. Heisenberg's record as one of the most brilliant physicists of our time speaks for itself. Liars do not win the Nobel Prize.

What possible motive could Heisenberg have in trying to deceive his old friend Dr. Goudsmit? It was no more discreditable for German than for American physicists to engage in research that might lead to an atomic bomb. Heisenberg and his associates ran no risk of being hauled into court. What if secret official reports mention atomic explosives long after the date when Heisenberg says the physicists had turned from bombs to atomic power? Our own official reports are full of hopes and suggestions that never get as far as the laboratory.

Dr. Goudsmit says little in his book and nothing in his letter about uranium 235, which we used in the first bomb that we dropped in Japan. Enormously difficult as the task of separating uranium 235 from 238 was, the incentive to do so should have been as strong with the Germans as it was with us. But the separation of uranium 235 from 238 would have called for the diversion of huge amounts of energy and material for at least two years and the risk of losing the war by curtailing the building of submarines and airplanes and the production of tanks, high explosives, synthetic gasoline and other weapons and munitions.

There is every reason to accept Heisenberg's statement that the attempt to make atomic explosives was abandoned in favor of the easier task of developing atomic power.

HEISENBERG'S LAST HURRAH

In 1995 a nuclear engineer in Great Britain, Philip Henshall, published a thoughtful analysis that began by asking: Did Germany produce a working nuclear reactor and did their top nuclear physicists really understand what was required to build an atomic bomb? He then added an explanatory note: by nuclear weapon he was referring not only to an atomic bomb but also to the by-products of a reactor in the form of radioactive dust. It was this material, Henshall believes, that became the lethal ingredient of a "miracle weapon" that Hitler decided not to use for fear of retaliation, among other reasons. It is the same material that was found aboard the surrendered *U-234* in Portsmouth, New Hampshire, and had been scheduled for shipment to Japan on the submarine *I-52*. Henshall provides a fascinating account of the origins of this dreadful weapon, whose very existence is missing from official histories of World War II, and of the German scientists intimately involved—Werner Heisenberg and Paul Harteck in particular.

Heisenberg was a man of world renown when the war began, who was awarded the Nobel Prize in Physics at age thirty-two in 1933, the year Hitler came to power. A German nationalist but no Nazi, Heisenberg nevertheless took heed of warnings about seeming to associate with the ideas of Albert Einstein and the "Jewish physics." He was made acutely aware of political realities when being considered for a physics chair at the University of Munich in 1939. Part of the process was a series of interviews at SS headquarters in Berlin, which may or may not have accounted for Heisenberg's failing to win the appointment.

Heisenberg was to become, as Henshall phrases it, "the unofficial, self-spokesman" for those engaged in nuclear research for the German army. But even though Otto Hahn and Fritz Strassmann had pointed the way by demonstrating the fission of U-235, a chain reaction was still just a theory. No atomic pile had been constructed, so it had not been possible to confirm that once started, a chain reaction could be controlled. There was general agreement on the concept of a uranium reactor—or engine, as it was called—using heavy water (deuterium oxide) to moderate the speed of neutrons. And its design had been approved: layers of uranium oxide sandwiched between layers of heavy water, layers of heavy carbon between each sandwich, and a neutron reflector of heavy carbon surrounding the whole. "In short, an enormous amount of work to be done," Henshall comments, while noting an attitude of indifference toward nuclear weapons development among German military brass, who were influenced by the success of conventional armed forces. "By the summer of 1941 Germany either controlled or was allied with most of Europe, and any other nations were neutral."

Heisenberg, then, was not out of tune with military and political leaders who heard him lecture in June 1941, including Albert Speer, the minister of armaments and munitions. Speer affirmed the position of the army: any possibility of producing nuclear weapons was beyond the scope of the present conflict.

Harteck called attention to himself as a professor of chemistry at Hamburg University in April 1939 by writing to the War Ministry about the potential for nuclear physics to provide explosives of unimaginable force, and he asserted that the country that possessed such material "would have a dominant position throughout the world." But Harteck did not come to prominence as a disciple of Heisenberg focused only on explosives, the uranium bomb. Rather he had realized the feasibility of a reactor that generated no heat, no explosive power, but would produce irradiated material in the form of radioactive isotopes plus plutonium. (Harteck was among the first to recognize plutonium as a replacement for uranium in an atomic bomb.) This reactor would have to be moderated at a very low temperature, and for this Harteck suggested solid carbon dioxide, dry ice, fifteen tons of which was supplied in May 1940 by the chemical company IG Farben. Uranium oxide was another matter. When he asked Kurt Diebner—who had moved from the War Office to the Kaiser Wilhelm Institute—if 300 kilograms might be available, Diebner referred him to Heisenberg, who had recently received a large amount from the government. Heisenberg was evasive, suggesting that he delay his low-temperature experiment until he was certain he had made the correct preparations. By June Harteck had obtained only 185 kilograms, none of it from Heisenberg, but the defeat of Belgium in May 1940 produced a uranium windfall—over one thousand tons from the Union Minière mines in the Belgian Congo. Hearing of this, Harteck planned a much larger low-temperature experiment requiring twenty tons of uranium oxide and thirty tons of dry ice, which drew criticism from Heisenberg.

Henshall finds it understandable that Harteck would be opposed by theoreticians like Heisenberg, who resented this experimentalist chemist "trying to leapfrog over everyone." Henshall also points out that Harteck was taking on a formidable foe should he defy Heisenberg, whose influence was soon certified when he was named director of the K.W.I. for Physics at Dahlem, a post that included a chair at the University of Berlin. It was a political appointment, part of a government effort to erase a perceived Jewish stigma, and Heisenberg, who replaced Kurt Diebner, was a willing Nazi pawn.

Harteck was not alone in his determination to build a nuclear weapon that was not an atomic bomb, and because the others were few in number they were not hard to identify. In September 1941 a report was issued by the Forschungsanstalt Deutschen Reichspost, the Post Office Research Institute operating in an underground laboratory at the residence of Manfred von Ardenne. The author of the report was Fritz Houtermans, who was willing and able to explain how a chain reaction could be initiated by a liquid carbon moderator in a low-temperature reactor; no heat or power would be generated, but radioactive isotopes would be produced, by-products of the fission process. These conclusions were reached by Houtermans with no advice or assistance from anyone—none from Harteck in particular, which served to corroborate the findings of two independent studies.

Houtermans's report was not classified—it well might have been, given Henshall's understanding of what it contained—and von Ardenne distributed copies to the nuclear community. Heisenberg responded by paying a visit to the laboratory, accompanied by Carl von Weizsacker, on November 28, 1941, followed by Otto Hahn on December 10.

Henshall speculates that the low-temperature reactor established a link between Harteck and the Post Office Research Institute (von Ardenne and Houtermans). Harteck had received a copy of Houtermans's 1941 report, says Henshall, "and it is more than likely that visits were exchanged. There is also no doubt that Heisenberg's assumption of the role of spokesman for all German nuclear research was not accepted by everyone, especially when it seemed that no real headway had been made under his regime." The dissenters were ambitious men, said Henshall, "and may have felt too restrained. . . . Harteck, especially, would have recognized in the Post Office organization . . . an independent outlet for some of his ideas . . . which had been frustrated since 1940, mainly by Heisenberg."

Heisenberg maintained after the war, in 1947, that Harteck had advocated a low-temperature pile for reasons other than creating a weapon. "Such a pile . . . ," he wrote, "could be expected to produce profitable amounts of radioactive elements for tracer research." Harteck was asked about this in an interview in 1967, and he replied that the primary purpose of the dry-ice reactor was "the production of reactor waste for use in radiological bombs which would target the civilian population of enemy cities."

"Early in 1944," Henshall writes, "the stage was set for Harteck to build a low-temperature reactor, moderated and cooled by liquid pentane to minus 160 degrees centigrade. . . . The objective was not to build an atomic bomb, as there was insufficient time for the reactor to produce enough plutonium; nor was there time to develop the plutonium technology. . . . However, there was time for the reactor to produce enough radioactive material, in the form of spent fuel isotopes, to assemble a radioactive package. . . . The reactor would have to have been operating for several months to produce sufficient radioactive material. . . ." To make this happen, the story goes, nuclear researchers and technicians—from Hamburg University, the Post Office, the German army—had gathered in Erfurt, a factory city in eastern Germany, to help Harteck assemble his reactor in the basement of a school. It is only forty-eight miles from Erfurt to the rocket factory at Nordhausen, and from there by rail, traveling only at night, it is a two-day trip to a launching site in France. "Only minutes before launch," Henshall writes, "the radioactive canister is transferred to the rocket."

Hitler and other Nazi leaders had marveled in private for over a year about a deadly weapon, the V-4 rocket, capable of extinguishing all human life within a two-mile radius of the point of impact.

Heisenberg had moved his laboratory to Hechingen, and in the nearby village of Haigerloch he, Carl von Weizsacker, Karl Wirtz, and others spent the early months of 1945 trying to bring their final-design reactor to criticality. The experiment was terminated on March 1, having failed due to an insufficient amount of fissionable material to sustain a chain reaction. "It is difficult to believe," Henshall comments, "that this was a serious attempt to achieve a critical reaction, as there were several basic flaws in the design of the reactor. . . . If Heisenberg . . . aimed to demonstrate how far behind they were in the practical application of nuclear physics, they could not have arranged a better example."

The situation, therefore, was the reverse of 1941, as German conventional forces failed to halt the advancing enemy armies soon to reach German territory, and by mid-1944 victory depended entirely on the so-called miracle weapons. But a nuclear strategy that depended on the V-2 rocket was also bound to fail. First, there was a considerable safety problem, especially during rocket liftoff, when an accident might cause thousands of deaths and contaminate a vast area of Germany and France for years. And there was a numbers problem. If Henshall is right about Harteck's low-temperature reactor being the only one of its kind, it would take months to produce a single radioactive package. Most of all, Hitler feared retaliation by the United States and Great Britain, so he decided to let Japan do the dirty work.

ARIIZUMI'S LAST BATTLE

Paraphrasing Philip Henshall on Hitler's motive: If this unique cargo of radioactive material—Henshall was convinced of its radioactivity by the lead containers used for shipping it—could be transported to Japan in time, there might be one last chance to restrain the United States and halt the war, at least in Europe. And if there was to be a retaliatory strike by the United States, Hitler reasoned, it would be aimed at Japan. The idea had originated with Heinrich Himmler, head of the secret police, and shipment of the material by U-boat was approved in December 1944. (Henshall's scenario fails to account for the role of the *I-52* before she was sunk in June 1944, probably because he was unaware of it.)

Apparently unconcerned about the human toll of a nuclear strategy, the Japanese military regime seized an opportunity to use ships and planes that had been designed for targets beyond the range of land-based or carrier-based aircraft—the Panama Canal, for example. The ships were the first of a huge class of I-400 submarines—the *I-400* and *I-401*—which were capable of transporting three single-engine airplanes over a surface range of thirty thousand miles. They had been commissioned in January 1945 and would be joined by two large patrol submarines, the *I-13* and *I-14*, each carrying two aircraft. So a total of ten M6A1 two-seaters—Aichi Seiran (Mountain Haze), they were called—would be deployed with the First Submarine Division of the Sixth Fleet, Tatsunoke Ariizumi commanding.

During a training period in the Inland Sea the *I-401* was slightly damaged by a U.S. mine and returned to Kure for repairs on April 12. By then the mission was at a critical point, as the movements of the division were coordinated with the departure March 26 of the *U-234* from the German base at Kiel. Based on earlier voyages to Europe of Japanese submarines (only one, the *I-8* in 1943, completed the round trip, and she took sixty-four days to sail from France to Penang, Malaya), the German boat was expected to arrive in late June. On April 14 the *I-400* left for Luta on the Kwantung Peninsula of Manchuria, returning to Kure on April 27, all for the stated purpose of refueling, which Henshall finds difficult to believe. And on May 27 the *I-13* and the *I-14* sailed from Kure to the Nanao Bay naval base on Japan's west coast, detouring en route to the Korean port of Pusan to replenish fuel supplies.

The four First Division submarines were docked at Kure on April 6, the day the seventy-three-thousand-ton *Yamato*—the largest battleship afloat and the pride of the Imperial Navy— sailed for Okinawa in a hopeless effort to prevent an American landing on the Japanese island seven hundred miles away. The following day, as the *Yamato* headed south at twenty-two knots, she came under a sustained attack by aircraft from the U.S. carrier *Lexington*, and her topsides were torn to pieces before she finally went down. The loss of life was horrendous—2,488 officers and men—in what Philip Henshall believes was a massive kamikaze mission—a shocking revelation, if true, under circumstances even more so. Since it was taken for granted the *Yamato* would not return, she was dispatched with only enough fuel to reach Okinawa. "There was fuel remaining at Kure, certainly, to have brought *Yamato* back, but the mission it was being saved for"—presumably the dirty bomb attack on the continental

United States—"was so important to Japan that the battleship could be sacrificed."

On or about June 1 elements of the First Submarine Division and the 631st Naval Flying Corps, the attack force, assembled at Nanao Bay; however, word had come of the *U-234*'s surrender, and the mission was canceled. The submarines received new orders immediately. The *I-13* and *I-14* were dispatched to the Japanese base at Truk to perform reconnaissance missions (on July 18 the *I-13* was sunk by a U.S. hunter-killer group led by the escort carrier *Anzio*). On July 23 and 24 the *I-400* and *I-401* left the Onimato naval base on Honshu Island with orders to attack the U.S. Fleet at Ulithi Atoll, one thousand miles west of Truk. But before they were within striking distance of Ulithi, the war ended, and they were ordered to return to port.

Aboard the *I-401* as she entered Tokyo Bay, Captain Ariizumi, the division commander, died of a self-inflicted gunshot wound. He apparently expected to be tried as a war criminal for atrocities while the commanding officer of the *I-8* in 1944. (Ariizumi allegedly had tortured and murdered survivors of ships he had sunk and then submerged with some still on deck.)

Had the *U-234* reached Japan with the radioactive package, the attack force would have transported a radiological bomb to a point three hundred miles off the California coast. An Aichi Seiran, catapult-launched from a submarine, would then have delivered the bomb, causing havoc in one of two target cities, San Francisco and Los Angeles, with devastating effect. "Not with a bang but a whimper," as T. S. Eliot wrote. (The scheme does not sound far-fetched considering an O.S.S. report of ten balloons and four bombs, believed to be of Japanese origin, found in areas of the United States, Canada, Alaska, and Hawaii between November 4, 1944, and January 29, 1945.)

10. A WORLD WITHOUT WAR, AMEN

With the German surrender there remained in Europe just three neutral nations—Portugal, Sweden, and Switzerland (denying reality, the Japanese foreign ministry had not removed Moscow from the list). So the assigning of a naval attaché to the legation in Bern was a significant step and a credit to the officer, Lieutenant Commander Yoshiro Fujimura, a legendary figure before coming to Berlin, where he was in charge of the *Yamabuki* long-range submarine program. A heavy-armament expert, Fujimura was a great believer in big ships, and when he learned of the sinking of the *Yamato* soon after arriving in Bern, he became convinced that for Japan defeat was inevitable. He would come to find out that the minister to Switzerland, Shunichi Kase, and the military attaché, Lieutenant General Seigo Okamoto, secretly agreed.

Fujimura was a loyal follower of Katsuo Abe, a stalwart of the admiral's intelligence apparatus. They were not in direct or regular contact in these turbulent times, but upon learning that Abe was "stranded" in Sweden, Fujimura tried to arrange his escape, advising Tokyo on June 7 that "absolute secrecy must be maintained by some such device as the use of a Swiss plane under the guise of a mail flight for British and American prisoners in Greater East Asia." The plan was abandoned for logistical reasons without Fujimura knowing that he was communicating by a broken code, and his messages were being monitored by Allied intelligence. On July 7 he got through to Abe at Jonkoping, via Stockholm, with an anxious personal inquiry: "We would like to know how you are getting along. With best wishes for your health." Fujimura had news of Ambassador Oshima and his party of thirty, who had been taken into custody in southern Germany: they were being sent to the United States. (They had been flown to Le Havre and put aboard a troopship, the *West Point*, arriving in New York on July 11.) Fujimura was also able to report to Abe that the family of Tooyoo Mitsunobu, the naval attaché killed in Italy, was safe in southern Germany and soon would be brought to Switzerland.

Fujimura was comfortable in his position and too busy to be bothered by those who wondered, good-naturedly, about the need for a naval attaché in a landlocked country without a navy of its own. It is clear, though, that his duties as a diplomatic aide were secondary to the intelligence assessments he prepared for the central authorities on the European aspect of a lingering war. Most of his analysis was passive and accepting of a given situation. He was, after all, a man alone against regimes—a relatively low-ranking one, at that— and could only present the facts of a matter. "Ever since the collapse of Germany," he reported on May 25, 1945, "Britain and the United States have been throwing their entire strength . . . into the attack on

Japan. . . . They are even bringing pressure against Switzerland concerning our funds." As for predicting an outcome of the war, Fujimura relied on what he termed "a fairly reliable intelligence report" based on a "synthesis of opinions . . . from sources in France and neutral countries." Yet he distanced himself from those sources. "It goes without saying," he noted on June 25, "that we think it nothing more than an enemy delusion seasoned with stratagems, but we submit it for your information."

He broached the subject of the German collapse, originally expected about the middle of June, and how it affected the postwar measures of the United States, which "speeded up its action in the Far East . . . advancing the concentrated attacks which had originally been scheduled for July and August, and starting a great offensive. Losses greater than anticipated were incurred, and in consequence the former estimates of a Japanese surrender three or four months after the collapse of Germany is now being revised. . . .

"Since it will take at least until September to transport the enormous Allied armies, the beginning of the end of the war on the Japanese mainland will come in the middle or latter part of September. In view of the topography of Japan, from two to four months will be required to subjugate it completely. In the meanwhile Japan will be systematically and completely destroyed."

DULLES IN THE MIDDLE (I)

In a report in mid-May on enemy espionage in Bern, Fujimura observed that Dulles, "the United States special presidential envoy, and Stalin's special representative here . . . are engaging in vigorous activity extending over all of Europe." A month later, he revisited the subject of Dulles—Allen W. Dulles of the Office of Strategic Services, chief of the U.S. Diplomatic Mission to

Switzerland—and implied he was being offered an alternative to the "systematic and complete destruction" of Japan. Fujimura's message was sent secretly, or so he thought, to the two most senior officials of the Navy Department, Admiral Mitsumasa Yonai, the navy minister, and Admiral Soemu Toyoda, the chief of staff. (Fujimura was using a navy Type 94 code machine, which he brought with him by submarine to Europe.) He had been contacted by a go-between and felt qualified to express an opinion of Dulles. "This man was the special representative of the late Roosevelt. From his headquarters in the O.S.S. he has continued his activities throughout Europe, Truman having taken him over in the same capacity. . . . He would seem to be invested with a wide range of authority. . . . Their proposal is authoritative, and although we have been investigating for some days as to whether or not it is in full faith . . . it is recognized that this is not a stratagem but is quite trustworthy."

Fujimura was knocking on the right door, so to speak, as the tenant of the flat on Herrengasse in Bern was the famed master spy, O.S.S. agent 110, soon to depart for Wiesbaden as U.S. intelligence chief for occupied Germany. The identification of Dulles as "special presidential envoy" was inaccurate, though no doubt a result of the O.S.S. cover as a diplomatic mission to Europe. In fact, Roosevelt and Dulles were well-acquainted members of prominent American families, and both entered public service upon graduating from Harvard and Princeton respectively—Roosevelt as assistant secretary of the navy in the Wilson administration, Dulles as a State Department intelligence official at the Paris Peace talks in 1919. (Allen Dulles was the grandson of one secretary of state, John W. Foster, 1892–93; the nephew of another, Robert Lansing, 1915–20;

and the younger brother of still another, John Foster Dulles, 1953–59.) Politically the two men had often been at odds, but both observed a wartime custom of bipartisanship, and Dulles was comfortable serving with former secretary of state Henry L. Stimson, a conservative Republican, now the secretary of war.

The intermediary was Fritz Hack, an anti-Nazi German living in Switzerland, who approached the O.S.S. in Bern in April 1945. For months Hack had been meeting informally with a German-born American agent, Gero Gaevernitz, who remembered him well enough from childhood to recognize him in a chance meeting in Zurich two years earlier. Hack had been a student of Gaevernitz's father, a professor of economics at the University of Freiburg. In 1912 Hack traveled to Japan on the Trans-Siberian Railway, and when World War I occurred two years later, with Germany and Japan on opposite sides, he was imprisoned as an enemy alien. Nevertheless, upon his release at the end of the war, Hack decided to stay in Japan as a purchasing agent for the Imperial Navy. In the course of several trips to Europe to buy weapons and machinery, he became a wealthy man.

Hack had been a sponsor of the Anti-Comintern Pact of 1936, and as such he conferred with von Ribbentrop, the German foreign minister, and on one occasion he met with Hitler. He reacted to these men and what they stood for with unconcealed disgust, and for that he was arrested and then released when Japanese friends intervened. For the first two years of World War II Hack was a constant critic of the Germans, and his influence in Japan dwindled accordingly. Then, when the Japanese attacked the U.S. Navy base at Pearl Harbor, he sent a note to Admiral Naokuni Nomura, the naval attaché in Berlin, severely criticizing "this reckless action," but he promised Nomura that when the time was right, he would help make peace with the Americans. Hack by this time was no longer welcome in Tokyo, so he settled in Switzerland, vowing to remain a friend of Japan and to prepare for her defeat.

Gaevernitz had known Dulles since shortly after agent 110 arrived in Bern in November 1942, and they became a Holmes-and-Watson team. A naturalized U.S. citizen of independent means (his mother was of the family of financier Otto Kahn), Gero was demonstrably loyal to his adopted country and to Allen Dulles. He had not laid eyes on Fritz Hack in thirty years, but one day in 1943, at the railroad station in Zurich, he noticed an older gentleman having lunch who bore a striking resemblance to the former student of his father. Gaevernitz asked if he might be Dr. Hack, and the man said yes, so they enjoyed a happy reunion. This encounter was followed by several more in the coming months, and in mid-1944 Gaevernitz introduced Hack to Dulles and was pleased when the meeting went well. The time had come to show his cards, so Gaevernitz offered to present Hack's views on the war to Dulles, who would pass them on to Washington. Gaevernitz added that if this proposition was not agreeable to Hack, it would not be necessary to continue these meetings. In other words you're with us or you're not.

Hack was agreeable, and thereby became a secret source of American intelligence.

Before moving ahead with Hack and Fujimura, Dulles and Gaevernitz needed to finish a pressing piece of business involving the surrender of a million-man German army in northern Italy. On a skiing trip to Davos in early March, Gaevernitz had been notified by a Swiss intelligence source that the Italian theater commander, a high-ranking SS officer named Karl Wolff, was planning to slip across the Swiss border from his headquarters in Italy, in the hope of meeting with U.S. authorities. The meeting took place at a borrowed estate on Lake Maggiore—just Dulles and Gaevernitz confronting Wolff, while Dulles's wife, Clover, whipped up lunch, and two American generals observed from a nearby hilltop. Wolff conceded that the war was lost, Hitler's refusal to accept reality notwithstanding, and he was determined not to permit the wholesale destruction of northern Italy. "It's easy to start a war but difficult to stop one," Dulles remarked, according to biographer Peter Grose, author of *Gentleman Spy*.

Weeks went by without further word from Wolff, and Dulles learned to his chagrin that the "Bern incident" had reached the level of Roosevelt-Churchill talks. He and Gaevernitz were headed for Paris in April for a meeting with William J. Donovan, the head of O.S.S., when word came that Roosevelt was dead. There was a letter from Wolff when Dulles returned to Bern, but rather than explain the long delay of the surrender, he offered condolences "on the occasion of the passing of the President with whom you were so close." When Wolff finally appeared in Switzerland with a surrender plan, the full German collapse was imminent, and Operation Sunrise, as Grose nicely puts it, had fallen into the "twilight of insignificance." Nevertheless, headlines in the Swiss press served to perpetuate the image of Dulles as a man of esteemed prowess.

Gaevernitz considered it very important that Fujimura had access to a Type 94 code machine, and it would not be surprising, given the degree of Ultra security, that he too was unaware of the code having been broken. (Those who did know, perhaps including Dulles, might have used the intercepted messages to confirm that Fujimura was acting in good faith in dealings with the O.S.S. via Hack.) And there was a development to report in a "secret" dispatch to the Navy Department in Tokyo, for on May 3 Hack was notified by Gaevernitz that peace negotiations with Fujimura had been authorized by the State Department in Washington. This inspired Fujimura to bombard Yonai and Toyoda with eighteen dispatches over a six-week period in May and June, but the few responses that came were vague and hardly encouraging. Fujimura became desperate and considered flying to Japan to present his case for peace negotiations, though he was prevented from doing so by the ban on flights. Hearing of his frustration, Dulles counseled Fujimura via Hack. He opposed a trip to Japan, fearing Fujimura would not return, and he suggested sending a fully authorized Japanese representative to Bern for negotiations, intimating that it was not a job for a lieutenant commander. And the Japanese must also realize, Dulles emphasized, that Washington would only agree to terms that met the specifications of an unconditional surrender.

As Hack explained to Gaevernitz, maintaining the monarchy was of crucial importance to the Japanese, and any discussion that might precipitate the removal of the emperor was just unthinkable. Neither he nor Dulles was in a position to make such assurances, said Gaevernitz, and that was that. On June 20 the peace initiative came to an abrupt end when Fujimura was ordered by Yonai to suspend his activities and turn the matter over to Minister Kase. The admiral offered little explanation—an order is an order. "All of the documents have been turned over to the Foreign Office," said Yonai, "and you should take appropriate steps in close cooperation with the Minister there in Switzerland."

FUJIMURA ABANDONED

He would obey the order, of course, but Fujimura's defiant reply to Tokyo verged on insubordination.

> Your misgiving . . . that there may be a good deal of stratagem in the other party's proposal is a most natural one, and we too are being most vigilant. . . . The other party on or about 20 May, that is before the proposal was made to us, sent a detailed report on the state of affairs to his home government . . . and thereupon asked for instructions in regard to the advisability of trying to contact the Japanese naval officials in Switzerland. . . . The other party received a reply from the Washington government about 10 June to the effect that in principle they approved; no objections . . . Dulles returned to Washington for the period 15 June to 25 June . . . probably for various preliminary arrangements. He returned on the 26th . . . and the other party [Fritz Hack] had encouraging news, tempered with seriousness. He frankly recognized the danger of Russia becoming involved and had hopes for an early end to the war. Nothing suggestive of stratagem was detected. It would seem that the enemy, with the Okinawa battle fresh in mind, is prepared for a long drawn-out war with Japan. On one hand, the . . . violent and incessant air attacks will prove to be the decisive key to the war situation just as they were in Germany, and with the occupation of Okinawa the enemy has become completely self-confident. On the other hand, he intends to adjust his relations with Russia in East Asia and settle down to the war with Japan. . . .
>
> Dulles and his staff acquired self-confidence in concluding

the surrender of northern Italy and are ambitious of becoming contributors to peace by an early end to the war with Japan. . . .

When heard from again on July 17, Fujimura was deeply pessimistic. "If things progress in their present fashion," he wrote, "Japan will ultimately be torn asunder. . . . The populace will likely be reduced by half as a result of the difficult struggle. . . ."

Gaevernitz was in an ideal position to assess the failure of the Fujimura initiative—not too close, yet not too far removed. Foreign Minister Shigenori Togo, Gaevernitz learned, suspected that Fujimura was a victim of army-navy rivalry, and he advised Yonai to give the attaché's proposal a more thorough appraisal. But by this time there was mounting opposition to this particular peace plan within the high command of the navy, largely because its sponsor was a lieutenant commander. Admiral Toyoda, the chief of staff, actually feared a rebellion by younger officers opposed to the plan, and would have no part of it. Yonai went along.

TURNING TO MOSCOW

Apparently unaware that in February Stalin had promised at Yalta to declare war on Japan within three months of a German defeat, Foreign Minister Togo on June 1 ordered Ambassador Naotake Sato in Moscow "to miss no opportunity to talk to the Soviet leaders. . . ." It was "a matter of extreme urgency," said Togo, "that Japan should not only prevent Russia from entering the war but should also induce her to adopt a favorable attitude toward Japan." Togo also asked Koki Hirota, a career diplomat and former prime minister, to engage in talks with the Soviet ambassador to Japan, Yakov Malik, aimed at achieving peaceful relations. At the last of these meetings, on June 14, Hirota boldly proposed a Russo-Japanese military alliance. "Japan will increase her naval strength," he assured Malik, "and together with the Russian army would make a force unparalleled in the world." Hirota also stressed an economic advantage for Russia in the form of East Asian commodities, such as rubber, tin, lead, and tungsten, in return for petroleum. Russia had no oil to spare, said Malik, who would soon come to attention in the world as his government's United Nations delegate. Finally Hirota made a bid for peace in the form of continued Russian-Japanese neutrality, to which Malik replied with blunt eloquence: "Since Russia is not a belligerent in the East, His Excellency Mr. Hirota must be well aware that peace there does not depend on Russia."

An approach to the Soviet Union was the preferred option of the army high command: Yoshijiro Umezu, the chief of staff, and Korechika Anami, the war minister, maintained that Moscow favored a strong Japan emerging from the war as a buffer against American influence in Asia. Foreign Minister Togo disagreed, citing the Yalta meeting and stating a suspicion that the Soviets had secretly agreed to join the Allied side. Prime Minister Kantaro Suzuki, though a navy admiral, sided with the generals, so Togo agreed to draft a statement to that effect. It was approved at a meeting of the Big Six (Suzuki, Togo, Anami, Umezu, Yonai, and Toyoda) on May 14: "It should be clearly made known to Russia that she owes her victory over Germany to Japan, since we remained neutral, and that it would be to the advantage of the Soviets to help Japan maintain her international position, since they may have the United States as an enemy in the future."

With no response from Russia for over a month and the "bitter-end" generals pressing their demands, Emperor Hirohito convened a meeting of the Big Six members on June 22 and announced his wish for a new strategy. Instead of preparing the people for defense against an invasion of the homeland, he "now deemed it necessary to consider a move toward peace." Had any thought been given to negotiations? Hirohito wanted to know. Togo said it had, referring to the Hirota-Malik conversations. As to when an envoy would arrive in Moscow, Togo estimated mid-July, and to a question by the emperor about the likelihood of success, Togo cautioned that Japan would be forced to make many concessions. For a start, Togo asked Hirota to renew his talks with Malik, who immediately dismissed a need for further discussion unless Japan could make a concrete offer. Hirota did so, returning a few days later with a promise of independence for Manchuria in return for a new nonaggression treaty and oil. Malik promised to get back to Hirota, though he knew he never would.

As they parted, Malik asked if it was true that Japan and the United States were conducting peace negotiations in Sweden. "Of course not," Hirota replied. "Japan would surely consult the Soviet Union before engaging in any negotiations at all."

A week went by with no response from Ambassador Malik, and Hirohito, losing patience, complained to Suzuki: they were missing an opportunity to explore the Soviet Union's real intentions. Could not the USSR be asked directly to mediate the global conflict? He then proposed sending as his personal emissary to Moscow Prince Fumimaro Konoye, a former premier and a trusted adviser to the throne. Hirohito and Konoye met on July

12, and the emperor began by asking what ought to be done about the war. Konoye answered candidly: "The people are tired of war. They all wish his Majesty would . . . act in their behalf and do something to relieve their plight. . . . It is necessary to end the war as soon as possible." Konoye also said that while he was opposed to Russia as an intermediary, he was willing to take any step to rectify past mistakes.

Awaiting word on this latest approach to the Kremlin, Ambassador Sato expected little to come of it, and his skepticism was justified. After waiting five days Sato received a letter from Alexander Lozovsky, the deputy foreign commissar (Molotov had gone with Stalin to a meeting of Allied leaders at Potsdam, a German city not far from Berlin), saying the emperor's proposal was so vague and Konoye's mission so unclear that his government could not reply definitely. Sato notified Tokyo of the response and added a personal plea for acceptance of any terms, provided the emperor was allowed to remain on the throne. Sato's opinion was not what Togo or Hirohito wanted to hear. "Moreover, since Russia herself insisted upon the unconditional surrender of Germany," Sato wrote, "and spurred the British and Americans on to the opening of the second front . . . it . . . will be extremely difficult to obtain the support of the Soviet Union for any proposal concerning the negotiation of a peace treaty. In the long run, since Japan sincerely desires the termination of the war, I believe that she has indeed no choice but to accept unconditional surrender or terms closely approximating thereto."

MINISTER KASE GATHERS HIS THOUGHTS

On the occasion of the German surrender in May 1945, Minister Kase assessed the situation as it looked from Bern.

When one thinks of the position of our Empire in light of the situation which I describe . . . one cannot but see that the fighting spirit of America has steadily improved, that her supply capacity in personnel, ships, airplanes, tanks, and so on has expanded, and that her striking power, in spite of the many losses she has suffered in the past three years and a half, has grown steadily greater. Add to this the naval and air power of Great Britain, and our position is not an easy one, all the more so since we do not know when the Soviet Union may move against us from the north. . . . Reflecting on the situation in which we find ourselves, I feel very keenly that we must give up all the consolations of self-intoxication and keep foremost in our minds the necessity of seeing the truth as it really is.

Kase addressed the cause of Germany's downfall—"in terms perhaps too simple," he admitted. It was "the difference in war potential. . . . In particular, Germany's great inferiority in air and naval forces was decisive. The death blows came from the systematic bombing of Germany's industrial cities and the destruction of her vital communications routes. . . . Furthermore, Germany showed an extreme inferiority in manpower reserves. . . ."

Turning to the situation of his own government, Kase presented an articulate analysis. "There are those who insist earnestly that the future policy of the Empire must be to continue the fight. They reason that if we make of the homeland a second Iwo Jima and continue steadfastly to the bitter end to inflict heavy losses on the British and Americans, trying at the same time to improve our relations with the Soviet Union, then even Britain and America may at last change their attitude, and the way may be open for a basic change in the situation." Kase condemned such a strategy as one that would lead to disaster. "If the situation which the Empire faces is indeed as I have described it, then if we merely fight on strongly to the end, we shall . . . be doing nothing but following in the path which Germany has taken."

What was needed, said Kase, was "a plan for effecting some sort of break in diplomatic terms," and for retaining "as much of a foothold as possible." He then proposed two courses of action to achieve these ends: (1) by directing efforts only at the American and British enemy; and (2) by talking to the Russians.

Kase elaborated with regard to (1):

Anglo-American influence will tend from now on to come into conflict with Soviet influence in East Asia. In particular, the situation will become increasingly delicate as it revolves around Soviet-Chinese relations. Moreover, while the British and Americans think they are sure of final victory in the Pacific war, it is clear that they do not think of making great sacrifices of life in gaining this victory. . . . In all probability, the British and Americans would be happy to end the Pacific war, victoriously, before the Soviet Union comes in against Japan. It would appear therefore that the course open to us would be to arrive at some resolution and make a peace proposal directly to England and the United States. . . . In the event of our taking such a step, however—if we were not to bring the Russians into the matter directly, and if the terms of our resolution were more or less satisfactory to the British and Americans—there is a strong possibility that we would be offering a temptation to the Russians indirectly and might stimulate them to fire the first shot in order to make sure of having a voice in the disposition of the East Asia problem.

With regard to (2), Kase had this to say:

The view may still persist that we should try by means of our policy towards the Soviet Union to bring about an estrangement between the Anglo-Americans and the Russians, but no matter how profitable a proposal we might present to the Russians, it is not to be thought under present circumstances that the Soviet Union could thus achieve an influence equaling that of the British and the Americans. In any case, it is doubtful that they would place much value on a proposal to negotiate on what they regard as a fish on the dressing table, so they are not going to sacrifice their relations with the British and Americans for anything we can offer. Accordingly, any such plan . . . is out of the question in the present situation.

Any discussion with the Russians will become meaningful only when we truly make up our minds to take in hand the whole situation in the East Asia war and come to the Russians asking for their help in restoring peace, bringing with us a proposal for a general peace and offering to the Russians themselves a considerable reward. This policy would also be a sound one in terms of our future relations with the Soviet Union. . . .

Kase shifted his attention to ending the war with the Anglo-Americans. "The enemy will surely demand an unconditional surrender," he noted realistically, "and it cannot be denied that a failure may have most serious results both at home and abroad." He therefore urged an aggressive approach.

Success or failure will depend on the terms which the Empire can make up its mind to offer. And there are differences of opinion even in enemy talk of unconditional surrender. As the situation is now, if we just stand by and let things take their course, we have no prospect of finding it any easier to manage the situation in the future. I think . . . that the great necessity is to do something at once.

There are those who will say that we are in the midst of the fight now, and that rather than bow the knee to the enemy we should fight on and offer inspiration to our posterity. But I reply that our heroic blood which has been shed on Tarawa, Makin, Saipan, and elsewhere, and spread over the face of the Pacific, is already a sufficient inspiration.

It is not for me to talk of what should be the terms of the Empire's great decision, but it will surely be no simple thing to save us from our great national peril. . . . But a distinction must be made between the Empire, which is to be eternal, and the responsibility of the present generation. To bear a temporary shame and avoid the worst—the destruction of the foundation upon which our national strength could be rebuilt—would be surely the proper way to concern ourselves with the memory of our many hundreds of thousands of fallen heroes.

DULLES IN THE MIDDLE (II)

Eloquent and deeply concerned, Kase was not in a position to defy his government and act in keeping with his inclination toward a negotiated peace. But there were those in the legation who spoke for him, including Lieutenant General Seigo Okamoto, the army attaché, who had come to see the tragic fallacy of *Ketsu-Go*, a suicidal defense of the homeland. Okamoto, with Kase's blessing, had joined forces with two Japanese bankers, Tsuyoshi Yoshimura and Kojiro Kitamura, in an effort to promote a peaceful alternative. "Y and K," as they were known to U.S. intelligence monitors, were officials of the Bank of International Settlements in Basel (until the German surrender Kitamura managed the Berlin office of the Yokohama Specie Bank), and as such they could confide in Per Jacobsson, a B.I.S. director and respected economist. As a citizen of neutral Sweden, "PJ" was in a position to influence international political issues when so inclined. In this case he called his friend Allen Dulles, who later recalled in some detail what then transpired:

> It was . . . understandable . . . that when my old friend Per Jacobsson, knowing the background history of the surrender in North Italy, was approached by his Japanese friends . . . on a somewhat similar errand, he should think of me as a possible intermediary. Then in conversations which we had in Basel and in Bern, in Frankfurt and Wiesbaden, he unfolded his story. The Japanese knew the war was shortly coming to a close. They wanted to surrender, but the term "unconditional surrender" somewhat disturbed them. They wanted to keep their Emperor and the constitution, fearing that otherwise a military surrender would only mean the collapse of all order and or all discipline within the war devastated islands of Japan.
>
> I was then an official of the American diplomatic mission in Switzerland and was working for General William Donovan, who was the head of the Office of Strategic Services. My business was intelligence, and obviously, in those days with the military victory all but sealed, the crucial intelligence "fact" we wanted to know was how to get the enemy's unconditional

surrender and, at the same time, preserve sufficient order to insure that the surrender terms could be carried out.

I took Per Jacobsson's message to my friend Jack Mc-Cloy, Assistant Secretary of War, who was then in Europe on behalf of the Secretary of War, Harry L. Stimson. McCloy arranged for me to go to Potsdam, where the Allied leaders were then meeting to decide the grave issues they faced as the war came to an end. I recall that I made the Potsdam trip on the 20th of July 1945, just one year after the abortive attempt of the German resistance to eliminate Hitler. I had worked under Stimson when, more than ten years before, he had been Secretary of State. I knew him well and he listened with care as I unfolded the story as Per Jacobsson had received it from the Japanese. From other sources I knew, also, that the whole question of a Japanese surrender, and the treatment to be accorded the Emperor, were among the important issues before the Potsdam Conference. I knew that Joe Grew, in the State Department and our able Ambassador to Japan during the pre–Pearl Harbor days, had already presented his own views. I had an alternative hearing on the part of Stimson. But I did not get an answer, nor did I expect one. This was a matter which even Stimson, with all his authority, could not decide alone. Then I did not know that four days earlier, on July 16, we had successfully tested the atomic bomb at Alamogordo, and that in about two weeks (on August 6) the bomb was to fall on Hiroshima. One wonders whether, if the Japanese negotiators had come a little earlier and had been more clearly authorized to speak for their Government, that explosion would have taken place.

In any event, Per Jacobsson performed his task, recognizing the full gravity of the world situation and believing in the sincerity of the particular Japanese negotiators with whom he was dealing. At least their message reached authoritative American quarters in a timely and, I believe, effective manner.

Dulles had it nearly right, though the weapon detonated in New Mexico on July 16 was a plutonium bomb, and the success of this test confirmed that one like it, known as Fat Man, would be used in the annihilation of Nagasaki, scheduled for August 9. Also on July 16, in San Francisco, a package containing components of a uranium bomb, named "Little Boy," was being loaded aboard the cruiser *Indianapolis* in the custody of Major Robert Furman, the Manhattan Project security officer. The package would never leave Furman's sight over the ten-day run to Tinian Island in the Marianas, where it would be readied for the historic drop on Hiroshima on August 6. (Furman remained at Tinian and went on to Japan when hostilities ceased; the *Indianapolis*, meanwhile, was crossing the Philippine Sea on a course for Leyte when on the night of July 29 she was torpedoed and sunk by Japanese submarine *I-58*.)

WAR WITH AN END

The Potsdam Conference got under way on July 17, attended by President Truman, Roosevelt's successor; Prime Minister Churchill, about to be replaced due to an election defeat; and Stalin, the Soviet premier. Its purpose was to agree on a plan for the occupation of Germany, but the war with Japan was the sole subject of a declaration issued on July 26, which would be described by historian Herbert P. Bix as "an ultimatum aimed at hastening Japan's surrender." Truman had taken Churchill's advice, according to Bix, and issued the provisions of a peace agreement in advance of hearing from the Japanese. Thus the government in Tokyo was being informed that if it fulfilled certain obligations to be imposed after it had accepted the terms of unconditional surrender of all its armed forces and provided adequate assurance of good faith, Japan would be allowed to retain its peaceful industries and resume participation in world trade. The alternative would be "the prompt and utter destruction" of Japan. Absent from the document was a provision for "a constitutional monarchy under the present dynasty," which had been advocated by Joseph C. Grew, the former ambassador to Japan. "Consequently the status of the emperor was not guaranteed," Bix writes.

The reaction to the Potsdam Declaration was predictably negative at a meeting in Basel on the morning of July 28 attended by Jacobsson, or PJ, and the two Japanese bankers, Yoshimura and Kitamura, Y and K. Y had been haranguing PJ for much of the morning, calling the document clumsy and accusing its authors of having failed to understand the Japanese character. Also referring to it as an antidemocratic "proclamation," Y insisted the document had been issued by the Americans and British—and the Chinese—on a "take it or leave it" basis. "Some room for bargaining should have been left," Y said, and the unconditional surrender stipulation should have been put at the end, where it might be more easily modified. Including China in the matter of Japanese surrender, Y added, was humiliating to Japan.

An O.S.S. report dated July 29 echoed PJ's response to Y: "The U.S. was bound to consult and act with China and Great Britain. The Chinese and British are now tied in with this definitive statement. This was the natural way for them to declare their policy jointly. This gives the Japanese a set of written conditions to which they cling in the postwar negotiations." PJ then quoted a respected

Swiss journalist on the declaration: "Harsh though it may sound, [it] is nevertheless capable of becoming a basis for understanding." Y said to PJ he would use those points when he and K had lunch that day at the Japanese legation. But he still hoped PJ would explain to Dulles that the Potsdam Declaration had caused the Japanese to be more fearful than ever. Would the emperor be tried as a war criminal? Would their nation be destroyed?

PJ reported on July 29 that he and Y met again the evening before, following Y's trip to Bern for a meeting with K and Minister Kase. Y had believed initially that the Potsdam Declaration was a classic American blunder. When presented with the points PJ had emphasized to K that morning, however, he became persuaded that the declaration was a skillfully worded document after all. It had also come to his attention that the emperor was not mentioned by name in the declaration—a subtle but psychologically significant gesture. The Japanese were appeased, and it would not be necessary for PJ to complain to Dulles on their behalf. (End of story, for Allen Dulles and the war with Japan. It would be left to his brother, John Foster Dulles—as ambassador at large in 1951—to negotiate the peace treaty.)

It was noted in the report on the activities of Jacobsson and the Japanese bankers that Y had recently received a visit from Fujimura, who had been kept in the dark on the latest dealings with Dulles and the O.S.S. It may have been in retaliation for his having dealt exclusively with the admirals in Tokyo, or because he was a presumptuous lieutenant commander—for whatever reason he was forced to make the best of his role as a perceptive war commentator. "The intervention of Russia," Fujimura wrote on August

11—the Soviet Union had declared war on August 8 and mounted an attack on Japanese forces in Manchuria—"has created a situation differing from that when there was only a China of slight influence, and it will obviously have a great influence on the attitude of the United States and Britain toward Japan." (Prince Takamatsu, a brother of the emperor, was attached to the Navy Department, so it is possible that Fujimura's reports were reaching Hirohito himself.)

Navy Minister Yonai, the sole member of the war cabinet to retain his position, seemed to have a clear understanding of how Japan had reached this moment in history. As Bix writes: "Unable to decide to end the war unless the future of the throne and the all-important prerogatives of its occupant were absolutely guaranteed, the Suzuki cabinet and the Supreme War Leadership Council never framed a peace maneuver from the viewpoint of saving the Japanese people from further destruction. They waited, instead, until their foreign enemies had created a situation that gave them a face-saving excuse to surrender. . . . This is why Yonai could say on August 12: 'I think the term is perhaps inappropriate, but the atomic bombs and the Soviet entry into the war are, in a sense, heaven-sent blessings.' "

"USUAL MOVES" OF THE DEFEATED

Soon after the war ended, a history professor at Stanford, Robert J. C. Butow, did a detailed study of the failed peace feelers, and he published his findings in a 1954 book, *Japan's Decision to Surrender*. In the spring and summer of 1945, Butow writes, the Japanese government was "too involved in trying to find a way out of its difficulties through the Soviet Union to heed the warnings or exploit the efforts of either Fujimura or Okamoto." The United States, at the same time, was too occupied with Soviet intentions "to pay more than cursory attention" to peace overtures in Bern and Basel. There was also a feeling in Washington that it was not up to the Allies to plead with the Japanese to lay down their arms "or in other ways to cajole the children of the land of the gods into acting sensibly."

The bottom line of the U.S. position was that peace overtures by the army and navy attachés in Bern were not offers to capitulate, and this was the point of a lengthy and adamant statement issued on July 10 by Acting Secretary of State Joseph C. Grew, who served as ambassador to Japan from 1932 to 1941:

> We have received no peace offer from the Japanese Government, either through official or unofficial channels. Conversations relating to peace have been reported to the Department from various parts of the world, but in no case has an approach been made to this Government, directly or indirectly, by a person who could establish his authority to speak for the Japanese Government, and in no case has an offer to surrender been made. In no case has this Government been presented with a statement purporting to define the basis upon which the Japanese Government would be prepared to conclude peace. . . .
>
> The nature of the purported "peace feelers" must be clear to everyone. They are the usual moves in the conduct of psychological warfare by a defeated enemy. No thinking American, recalling Pearl Harbor, Wake, Manila, Japanese ruthless aggression elsewhere, will give them credence.

Japanese militarism must and will be crushed. . . . The policy of this Government has been, is, and will continue to be unconditional surrender. . . .

General Okamoto committed suicide on August 15, the day after the Japanese surrender. His friend for twenty years, Fritz Hack, had mentioned to Gero Gaevernitz just two weeks earlier that Okamoto commanded "a considerable prestige amongst Japanese diplomats in Switzerland," and had "a certain influence in Tokyo" as a contemporary of high-ranking army officers. "Okamoto is intelligent and serious minded," said Hack, "although at the time of Pearl Harbor he firmly believed in a German victory in Europe."

In a report on the death of Okamoto, O.S.S. officer Paul Blum added a final touch: "The general . . . collected all the letters from Y and other people in the matter in one bundle, which he said should be left for historians."

When he returned to Japan Fujimura visited Admiral Yonai and eventually wrote about the encounter in a published memoir. Yonai was apologetic and seemed tormented still by the failure of what he termed the peace preparations. "I have no excuses," he said wistfully. As for Fujimura, he made the mistake when glory beckoned of bypassing Minister Kase. But as Kojiro Kitamura explained to Fritz Hack, you could not depend on Kase for real cooperation because Kase was "too scared to take any initiative."

Fujimura died in 1995, the year that Paul Tidwell, searching the mid-Atlantic, located the long-lost Japanese submarine *I-52*.

IN DEFENSE OF FORGETTING

Right after VJ Day, August 14, the ubiquitous Robert Furman led a contingent of scientists, interpreters, and security personnel on a tour of Japan—the Atomic Bomb Mission, it was simply called, as the need for disguise had ended. (Out of habit, Furman had deceptively named it Group Three, but he was overruled.) It was the Asian version of Alsos, a monthlong interrogation of physicists at the learning centers of Kyoto and Osaka and the Rikken in Tokyo, the laboratory of Yoshio Nishina, an acclaimed nuclear theoretician. No evidence of atomic bomb experimentation was found, but a companion investigation of geological exploration turned up "a lot of activity on the part of the Rikken's outposts to gather uranium-bearing ores," reported Robert Nininger, like Furman a Manhattan Project intelligence officer. The scientist assigned to the mission was Philip Morrison, and he advised caution in coming to a conclusion about the Japanese program. "Even now it is not theoretically impossible to make a fine bomb with only three tons of uranium as raw material," he said in a report on September 20, "an easily concealed amount, obtainable with some effort in any country." But Furman chose to discount Morrison's counsel and did not mince words in his report of September 30: "The [Japanese] government and the military gave no priority to research in the field of nuclear physics and had no program to produce a bomb."

Asked in 1997 if he had any second thoughts about his evaluation, Furman answered with characteristic certainty and elaborated a bit. "When we went to Japan I had a list of eight Japanese scientists who had been trained in Germany. Nishina may have been one of them, I don't know. It's hard to remember Japanese names, and I didn't keep the list. I wrote my report while still in Japan and brought no notes with me when I left. No, there were not a lot of questions after that."

Furman was out of there—he was looking forward to a productive career as a home developer in booming Montgomery County, Maryland, and he wanted to forget the war. Who in the world would fault him for that?

ENDNOTE

In August 1997 at the National Archives in College Park, Maryland, Paul Tidwell and Richard Billings engaged in an unusual study of World War II relics. Billings filed this report.

Most of the time materials at the Archives are read and multicopied, excerpted on a laptop computer, or quoted into a handheld audio recorder. Seldom, if ever, have they been examined for radioactivity, but there's a first time for everything. We had heard that cargo from the *U-234*, following her surrender in the mid-Atlantic in 1945—and eventual sinking off Massachusetts by target-practicing U.S. Navy warplanes—was stored at the Archives, and we wanted to know if the documents and packages had been contaminated by the U-235 isotope aboard the German submarine. It had been fifty-two years since the stuff we would be testing was unloaded from the *U-234* and shipped to Washington, but we had been encouraged by a story about Marie Curie, the winner of the Nobel Prize in Chemistry in 1911 for isolating metallic radium. It seems that her cookbooks were still radioactive fifty years after her death in 1934.

It helps to understand that the National Archives is an institution of rules upon rules—no garments with large pockets, no notebooks or pens (pencils are supplied), no moistening fingers with lips to facilitate page turning, and so on. On this particular day, Calvin Jefferson was on duty, which was bad luck because he had recently caught me dipping into a can of Tacky Finger. Taking account of the size of the boxes we had signed out, Jefferson assigned us to a glass-enclosed room reserved for special projects. We welcomed the privacy but knew full well that Jefferson was monitoring our every move with the help of ceiling and wall cameras.

We had positioned Tidwell's Toyota Land Cruiser in the parking lot and turned it into a makeshift laboratory equipped with a Radiological Survey Meter and a video camera. Tidwell had on a pair of clean white cotton gloves, which when tested initially by the meter got an expected zero reading. As he went through the *U-234* records and small pieces of equipment, he rubbed them gently with gloved hands, being careful not to let the gloves come in contact with furniture or the storage boxes, which had been supplied by the National Archives and had not been aboard the U-boat.

I spent the time clipping small pieces of paper used to wrap the documents and pocketing them—a foolish move, I realized later, which might have aborted the project had Jefferson chosen to make an issue of it.

We packed the materials into the boxes and rolled them by cart to the turn-in station. No, we were finished and did not wish to put them on reserve. We left the building after a security guard waved us through, and when we reached the Land Rover, we were both finding it difficult to control our excitement. We took a reading of the gloves and wrapping paper, and there was a definite reading on the meter dial—a perceptible jump by the needle, a positive reading of U-235 contamination.

"Look at that!" I heard Tidwell say.

"Damn, you got it," was all I could muster.

After leaving the National Archives we dropped in on Bob Furman, the Manhattan Project intelligence officer, then living in Bethesda, Maryland, not far from College Park. We told Furman of our "experiment," and he was interested but not surprised. Alsos teams had found some U-235 in Germany, he explained, much of it in Heisenberg's laboratory at Hechingen. Furman had actually lifted a container of the uranium isotope and had found it very heavy.

BIBLIOGRAPHY

BOOKS

Ballard, Robert D. *Explorations: My Quest for Adventure and Discovery Under the Sea.* New York: Hyperion, 1995.

Ballard, Robert D. *The Eternal Darkness: A Personal History of Deep-Sea Exploration.* Princeton, New Jersey: Princeton University Press, 2000.

Bamford, James. *The Puzzle Palace: Inside the National Security Agency.* New York: Penguin Books, 1982.

Behr, Edward. *The Last Emperor.* New York: Bantam Books, 1987.

Bergamini, David. *Japan's Imperial Conspiracy.* New York: William Morrow, 1971.

Bix, Herbert P. *Hirohito and the Making of Modern Japan.* New York: HarperCollins, 2000.

Blair, Clay. *Hitler's U-Boat War: The Hunted, 1942–1945.* New York: Random House, 1998.

Boyd, Carl, and Akihiko Yoshida. *The Japanese Submarine Force and World War II*. Annapolis, Maryland: Naval Institute Press, 1995.

Boyd, Carl. *Hitler's Japanese Confidant: General Oshima Hiroshi and Magic Intelligence, 1941–1945*. Lawrence, Kansas: University Press of Kansas, 1993.

Brackman, Arnold C. *The Other Nuremberg: The Untold Story of the Tokyo War Crimes Trials*. New York: William Morrow, 1987.

Broad, William J. *The Universe Below: Discovering the Secrets of the Deep Sea*. New York: Simon & Schuster, 1997.

Brooks, Geoffrey. *Hitler's Nuclear Weapons: The Development and Attempted Development of Radiological Armaments by Nazi Germany*. London: Leo Cooper, 1992.

Brown, Anthony Cave. *"C": The Secret Life of Sir Stewart Menzies*. New York: Macmillan, 1987.

Buderi, Robert. *The Invention That Changed the World: How a Small Group of Radar Pioneers Won the Second World War and Launched a Technological Revolution*. New York: Simon & Schuster, 1996.

Butow, Robert J. C. *Japan's Decision to Surrender*. Stanford, California: Stanford University Press, 1954.

Carpenter, Dorr, and Norman Polmar. *Submarines of the Imperial Japanese Navy*. Annapolis, Maryland: Naval Institute Press, 1986.

Clark, Ronald. *The Man Who Broke Purple: The Life of Colonel William Friedman*. Boston: Little, Brown, 1977.

Dower, John W. *Embracing Defeat: Japan in the Wake of World War II*. New York: W. W. Norton, 1999.

Dull, Paul S. *A Battle History of the Imperial Japanese Navy, 1941–1945*. Annapolis, Maryland: United States Naval Institute, 1978.

Goudsmit, Samuel A. *Alsos*. Los Angeles/San Francisco: Tomash Publishers, 1947.

Haynes, John Earl, and Harvey Klehr. *Venona: Decoding Soviet Espionage in America*. New Haven, Connecticut: Yale University Press, 1999.

Henshall, Philip. *Vengeance: Hitler's Nuclear Weapon*. United Kingdom: Alan Sutton Publishing Ltd., 1995.

Hicks, Brian, and Schuyler Kropf. *Raising the Hunley*. New York: Ballantine Books, 2002.

Hirschfeld, Wolfgang, as told to Geoffrey Brooks. *Hirschfeld: The Story of a U-Boat NCO*. Annapolis, Maryland: Naval Institute Press, 1996.

Holmes, W. J. *Undersea Victory: The Influence of Submarine Operations on the War in the Pacific*. Garden City, New York: Doubleday, 1966.

Holmes, W. J. *Double-Edged Secrets: U.S. Naval Intelligence Operations in the Pacific During World War II*. Annapolis, Maryland: Naval Institute Press, 1979.

Jones, R. V. *Most Secret War*. London: Hamish Hamilton, 1978.

Kahn, David. *The Codebreakers: The Story of Secret Writing*. New York: Macmillan, 1967.

Kurzman, Dan. *Blood and Water: Sabotaging Hitler's Bomb*. New York: Henry Holt, 1997.

Layton, Edwin T., with Roger Pineau. *"And I Was There": Pearl Harbor and Midway—Breaking the Secrets*. New York: William Morrow, 1985.

Lewin, Ronald. *Ultra Goes to War*. New York: McGraw-Hill, 1978.

Lewin, Ronald. *The American Magic: Codes, Ciphers, and the Defeat of Japan*. New York: Farrar, Straus & Giroux, 1982.

Matthews, Tony. *Shadows Dancing: Japanese Espionage Against the West, 1939–1945*. New York: St. Martin's Press, 1993.

Morison, Samuel Eliot. *The Atlantic Battle Won*. Boston: Little, Brown, 1956.

Morison, Samuel Eliot. *The Two-Ocean War: A Short History of the United States Navy in the Second World War*. Boston: Little, Brown, 1963.

Mosley, Leonard. *Hirohito, Emperor of Japan*. Englewood Cliffs, New Jersey: Prentice-Hall, 1966.

Orita, Zenji, with Joseph D. Harrington. *I-Boat Captain: How Japan's Submarines Almost Defeated the U.S. Navy in the Pacific*. Canoga Park, California: Major Books, 1976.

Padfield, Peter. *Dönitz: The Last Führer*. London: Victor Gollancz, 1984.

Pash, Boris T. *The Alsos Mission*. New York: Award House, 1969.

Powers, Thomas. *Heisenberg's War: The Secret History of the German Bomb*. New York: Alfred A. Knopf, 1993.

Prados, John. *Combined Fleet Decoded: The Secret History of American Intelligence and the Japanese Navy in World War II*. New York: Random House, 1995.

Rhodes, Richard. *The Making of the Atomic Bomb*. New York: Simon & Schuster, 1988.

Seagrave, Sterling. *The Marcos Dynasty*. New York: Harper & Row, 1988.

Seagrave, Sterling, and Peggy Seagrave. *The Yamato Dynasty*. New York: Broadway Books, 1999.

Schratz, Paul R. *Submarine Commander: A Story of World War II and Korea*. Lexington, Kentucky: University Press of Kentucky, 1988.

Toland, John. *The Rising Sun*. New York: Random House, 1970.

Ugaki, Matome. *Fading Victory*. Pittsburgh, Pennsylvania: University of Pittsburgh Press, 1991.

Varner, Roy, and Wayne Collier. *A Matter of Risk: The Incredible*

Inside Story of the CIA's Hughes Glomar Explorer Mission to Raise a Russian Submarine. New York: Random House, 1978.

Weintraub, Stanley. *The Last Great Victory: The End of World War II.* New York: Dutton, 1995.

Wheeler, Keith. *War Under the Pacific.* Alexandria, Virginia: Time-Life Books, 1980.

Wigner, Eugene P. *Recollections, as Told to Andrew Szanton.* New York and London: Plenum Press, 1992.

Wilcox, Robert K. *Japan's Secret War.* New York: William Morrow, 1985.

Winton, John. *Ultra at Sea: How Breaking the Nazi Code Affected Allied Naval Strategy During World War II.* New York: William Morrow, 1988.

Wyden, Peter. *Day One: Before Hiroshima and After.* New York: Simon & Schuster, 1984.

Y'Blood, William T. *Hunter-Killer: U.S. Navy Escort Carriers in Gallant Battle Against the Nazi U-Boat Menace.* New York: Bantam Books, 1983.

NATIONAL ARCHIVES AND RECORDS ADMINISTRATION RECORDS GROUP 457— NATIONAL SECURITY AGENCY

SRH 1—Background, Signal Security Service
SRH 2-398—Studies on Cryptology
SRS—Magic Far East Summaries
SRS—German Navy Reports
SRA—Japanese Army Attaché
SR—Japanese Army Messages
SRO—Japanese Place Names
SRDG—German Diplomatic Messages

SRDJ—Japanese Diplomatic Messages

SRF—Japanese Air Force Messages

SRNA—Japanese Naval Attaché Messages

SRN—Japanese Naval Messages

SRNS—Japanese Naval Radio Intelligence

SRNM—Japanese Naval Communications

SRGL—Berlin-Tokyo Radio Messages

SRR—Japanese Army Water Transport

SRGN—German Navy/U-Boat Messages

SRMN—U.S. Navy Cryptology Records

SRMA—U.S. Army Cryptology Records

SRMD—U.S. Joint Service Intelligence Reports

SRMF—U.S. Air Force Intelligence Reports

SRS—"Sunset" Daily Intelligence Reports

THE ISSUE OF A JAPANESE ATOMIC BOMB

ARTICLES

Arakatsu, Bunsaku. "Japan Believes Russia Has It." *New York Times*, October 15, 1945.

Browne, Malcolm W. "Japanese Data Show Tokyo Tried to Make World War II A-Bomb." *New York Times*, January 7, 1978.

Dower, J. W. "Silence, Society and the Japanese Atomic Bomb Project During World War II." *Bulletin of Concerned Asian Scholars*, April–June 1978.

Parrott, Lindsay. "Five Cyclotrons Wrecked in Japan." *New York Times*, November 24, 1945.

Shapley, Deborah. "Nuclear Weapons History: Japan's Wartime Bomb Projects Revealed." *Science*, January 13, 1978.

DOCUMENTS

"Atomic Bomb Mission, Japan—Final Report, Scientific and Mineralogical Investigation," a 160-plus-page report filed by Major R. R. Furman, under Brigadier Generals Farrell and Newman for the War Department (Manhattan Project) on Japanese work on the atomic bomb. Its last pages were written in October 1945. National Archives, Suitland, Md., Report Group 331, file box 7409. Includes a four-page summary report, "Atomic Bomb Mission, Investigation into Japanese Activity to Develop Atomic Power," which can be obtained from National Archives Modern Military Branch, Washington, D.C., Record Group 243 (USSBS), Sec. 2, 3f(14). New information follows summary, dated September 30, 1945.

"Investigation of Nuclear Research in Japan," four-page section of the Foreign Intelligence Supplement No. 1 to Manhattan District History, Book 1: General. Volume 14: Intelligence and Security (Record Group 374), obtained from National Archives Manhattan Project section.

The Konan project. Main documents unearthed at Suitland include: the Snell story, from RB 331, box 7419, "Magazine and News Articles" file, Bid Sheets 564353, 564354, 564355, from the Military Intelligence Division I.D. files, R.G. 319, Box 3635; Bid Sheet and Military Intelligence Section report 403527, R.G. 319, Box 91; Headquarters, United States Army Forces in Korea, Intelligence Summaries 12 (21 May 46), 14 (22 June 46), 39 (30 June 47), and 42 (1–15 August 47), all from R.G. 19, Box 739.

Alsos List of Scientific Intelligence Targets, Japan and Japanese Occupied Areas, 27 April 1945. Forty pages, obtained from Navy and Old Army Section of National Archives, Washington, R.G. 38 (ONI).

"Uranium from Germany to Japan." Among most pertinent sources, intercepted communications on file at the National Military Branch, National Archives: SRA 01576, Tokyo to Berlin, 7 July 1943; Tokyo to Berlin, 24 August 1943; Berlin to Tokyo, 1 September 1943 (SRA 04221); Berlin to Tokyo, 20 November 1943 (SRA 05501); and Tokyo to Berlin, 15 November 1943 (SRA 06420).

OSS Report (R.G. 226, National Archives), XL 20426, re *U-234* passengers.

INDEX